Just Cause

Freedom, Identity, and Rights

Drucilla Cornell

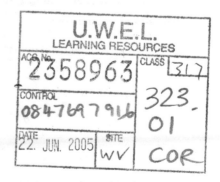
ROWMAN & LITTLEFIELD PUBLISHERS, INC.
Lanham • Boulder • New York • Oxford

ROWMAN & LITTLEFIELD PUBLISHERS, INC.

Published in the United States of America
by Rowman & Littlefield Publishers, Inc.
4720 Boston Way, Lanham, Maryland 20706
http://www.rowmanlittlefield.com

12 Hid's Copse Road
Cumnor Hill, Oxford OX2 9JJ, England

British Library Cataloguing in Publication Information Available

Library of Congress Cataloging-in-Publication Data

Just cause: freedom, identity, and rights / [edited by] Drucilla Cornell.
     p.   cm.
   Includes bibliographical references and index.
    ISBN 0-8476-9790-8 (cl. : alk. paper)—ISBN 0-8476-9791-6 (pbk. : alk. paper)
     1. Civil rights.   2. Liberty.   3. Identity (Psychology)   I. Cornell, Drucilla.

JC571 .F655 2000
323'.01—dc21

                                                        00-025932

Printed in the United States of America

∞™ The paper used in this publication meets the minimum requirements of
American National Standard for Information Sciences—Permanence of Paper
for Printed Library Materials, ANSI/NISO Z39.48-1992.

To Edith Potter (1920-1999)
In memory of all you gave me.

Contents

Preface

I want to begin by thanking Judge Richard Posner for generously agreeing to publish his exchange with me about just-cause statutes. I also want to thank William Bratton who co-authored the original piece on Spanish Language Rights in the Cornell Law Review, which has been re-written for this volume as "Spanish Language Rights: Identification, Freedom, and the Imaginary Domain." Collaborating with Bill was a wonderful experience. He systematically led me through the rich literature on economics and discrimination. His own original approach to law and economics is one of the sources of inspiration for our original essay. Although that essay was too long to be included here, Bill's own careful critical and editorial comments on my section of the essay are still included in the rewritten version. Bill's rigor and demand for clarity certainly pushed me to explain my own concept of language rights in as straightforward a way as possible. His intellectual influence on my life, however, goes far beyond this one collaboration. He is a beloved colleague and friend for over ten years now. His intellectual impact reflected in many of the other essays in this volume as well.

In the course of working through the law and economics literature, Bill and I reread my brother Brad Cornell's work together. We both agreed that my brother's insights into why Gary Becker's original model of discrimination had not realized its own predictions—that the market would ultimately clear irrational discrimination—were invaluable for our argument. Brad also gave us critical comments on the paper and again, his insight has been incorporated in the version that appears here.

My long-term partner, Greg DeFreitas, also an economist, commented on almost every single essay included in this volume. I have gained enormously from his remarks and editorial suggestions. For over 30 years now, he has insisted that I do not let the pull of the ideal take me completely out of engagement with material reality.

My daughter Sarita Cornell is a Latina and bilingual. As has been the case with so much of my writing since I became her mother, the demands of her freedom undoubtedly compel me to return to many of the issues surrounding language rights, transnational literacy, and multiculturalism. Indeed the very idea of the ethics of identification, finds its roots in my engagement with her and what it means for a Latina to have a mother who is a white Anglo. I thank her for the constant ethical challenge that her presence in my life presents.

I also wish to thank Sara Murphy, my collaborator on "Antiracism, Multi-culturalism and Ethics of Identification" for her generosity in allowing her essay be republished in my book. Sara has read each of these essays included in this volume in the innumerable drafts in which I gave them to her. I am one of these people who re-writes constantly, and over ten years now in a number of books, Sara has taken the time to read draft after draft after draft. Sara is an elegant literary stylist and my hope is that some of her talent has rubbed off on me in the course of writing with her.

I also want to thank Evelyn Alsultany, Michelle Zamora, and Constanza Morales-Mair who were research and editorial assistants on this project. As feminists of color, they have become important interlocutors and critics of how, despite my best efforts, I still sometimes forget how much I am influenced by my own position in society as a white Anglo woman with the privileges that go with that identification. They have been crucial in all processes of the publication of this manuscript: research, editing and critical commentary. I thank them not only for all their help, but also for the sheer pleasure of working with them.

One of the joys of working on this collection was that I was able to once again work with Maureen Macgrogan, who was my editor at Routledge for many years. Maureen is a wonderful friend as well as an editor. Her interest in my work and her belief in it has always been a crucial source of encouragement. Working with her is not only to work with an editor but with an insightful social theorist herself. Maureen was one of the lucky ones who worked with Hannah Arendt at the New School for Social Research. Often she has brought Arendt to my attention, particularly in my more recent interpretations of Kant.

bell hooks gave me critical comments on a number of essays in this volume. Her friendship and her spiritual optimism are an important source of sustenance in my life.

I thank my entire extended family, but particularly Irana Molitoris and Uncle Larry Brassell for the constant love and attention they give to my daughter. Writing demands that you sometimes shut out the world. Mothering demands that you never let your child out of your mind. The compromise that has to be made between those two demands can only be met if you are lucky enough to have such wonderful and loving caretakers. My partner

Greg Defreitas has more than met his 50% in the child-care process. My debt to them can truly never be paid.

I unfortunately have to live with a chronic and serious lung disease which requires constant medical supervision. In the best of all possible worlds I would not have lung disease. In this world I have, however, the best of all possible lung doctors, Dr. Michael Matarese. He is one of those rare doctors devoted to treating the patient and always with dignity left intact. During the nine years I have been in his care I have actually gotten better, which goes against the course of my illness. I know I owe this to his vigilance. He also provides me with an inspiration to prolong my life because I have to live long enough to turn him into a social democrat.

This book is dedicated to Edith Potter, 1920-1999. Edith was my German teacher at Scripts College. I went off to college filled with idealistic enthusiasm and rebellious energy. Edith managed to shape those two qualities much to my benefit in that first year and over the course of my life.

For the next thirty years, she remained a beloved friend and mentor. She not only read all my books, but carried on a correspondence with me; sometimes cheering me on, and at other times reigning me in, or trying to change my direction when she thought that was what I needed. Her love and commitment to me made her one of the most important older women in my life. Her death left a hole in it that can never be filled. She taught me more than I will probably ever be able to fully acknowledge, as much by her ethical example as in her actual role in my life as a teacher. It is in love and mourning that I offer her this book.

Introduction

In all of these essays, I defend the philosophical and ethical significance of ideals in legal, moral, and political philosophy. By ideals, I mean the way in which individuals and movements make vivid the challenges to their oppression and their aspirations to a transformed society. We all know the great ideals associated with the democratic revolutions in the West, beginning with the French Revolution: the ideals of equality, freedom, and democracy. By now, the critiques of feminists, critical race theorists, and postcolonial thinkers of how these ideals were modeled on the white, middle-class, heterosexual male as the paradigm of humanity have been widely circulated.

These essays defend ideals in the broad sense that social movements need to imagine and represent the conditions of a changed world for which they are fighting. They also attend closely to the validity of the critiques of how ideals have been articulated in much liberal political theory. To defend ideals at the millennium is a risky undertaking precisely because of the convincing nature of the critiques. But it is also a necessary undertaking in the face of the paralysis and cynicism that has followed in the wake of the proclaimed victory of liberal capitalism in the defeat of its last purported challenger, socialism.

History has supposedly truly come to an end now. Or so the ideologues of advanced capitalism insist again and again. Of course, there are lessons to be learned from the attempts to institutionalize socialism at the levels of state, government, and economic organization. But the lessons are not that history has ended or can end, and that capitalism has won. One lesson for me is that the we/them mentality implied in the proclamation of the final victory is itself part of the imperialist heritage that is now being challenged throughout the world. In the United States, the fierce debates over multiculturalism implicate the increasing challenge to dominant Eurocentric models of modernization. What roles ideals such as freedom, equality, and justice can continue to play has to be reexamined in the light of the dramatic political events that have shaken our world. These essays are a first step in that

1

reexamination. They focus on what these changes mean for feminism within the northern democracies.[1]

These essays were also inspired by a more personal history, which influenced how I address questions of law, politics, ethics, and morality. I identified myself as a left Hegelian with strong socialist commitments from the time I was a teenager and saw the working class as the linchpin of this struggle. As a result, I became a full-time union organizer. The crisis of Marxism and the apparent victory of capitalist ideology provoked me to return to the relationship between social transformation and the role that ideals played in my own experiences as a union organizer and a factory worker. The lesson here was simple. Ideals matter to people. They are willing to fight to change the world because of the power of their appeal.

It has become a commonplace among some political theorists to condemn the articulations of legal political ideals as fundamentally incompatible with a Marxian analysis of the ideological role such ideals play in late capitalism. Again and again in these essays, I return to the argument that this condemnation is a mistake. While these ideals—such as rights and others encompassed in the politico-economic category of the person—have been and continue to be put to use to sustain local and global hegemonies of capitalism, this does not mean that it is advisable or even possible to jettison the ideals themselves. The defense of ideals is not, I argue, incompatible with the tradition of materialist critique—nor is it even necessarily excluded by an engagement with the work of genealogy. In several of these essays, I address how treating these three modalities as mutually exclusive has caused confusion and crippled analysis in works of feminist theory and in debates over multiculturalism.

These essays also reflect a complex relationship to law, which is inseparable from my union activism. On the one hand, my involvement in the struggle to build truly democratic unions has led me to be suspicious of an over-reliance on law in feminist politics. For instance, I advocate self-organization of sex workers as the best response to the pornography industry.[2] On the other hand, exhaustion and demoralization result from having to fight the same battle over and over again. I still hold to the position that it is a significant loss to workers in this country that we no longer have anything like an effective right to unionize or to strike. Yet even without decent labor laws, there has been a revival of militant organizing campaigns.

My insistence on the need for a concept of right, however, is never simply justified on political grounds, but is also morally and ethically inspired by the need to set some parameters for political struggle on the basis of respect for persons. During my years as an engaged union organizer and as an activist in leftist organizations, I saw the dignity of individuals trampled on time and time again in the name of some overarching political goal of the movement. These experiences led me to conclude that Lenin simply had it wrong: The end does not justify the means. This century has taught us about the dangers of totalitarianism. Even political movements with the most democratic intentions need to have ethical parameters imposed upon them by law when they achieve state power. Our dignity as persons should not be open to debate. The right to abortion, for example, is one that must be respected as fundamental to the legal recognition of women as free and equal persons.[3] Thus, I defend a Kantian moment in political philosophy so as to provide a conception of right that respects the individuation and plurality of persons.[4]

Often in today's political debates, we address questions, such as hate speech, as if they can simply be addressed by whether we should regulate them at all. My own response, including in the case of hate speech, is that we have to be clear on the political values we are trying to protect as well as the ethical, moral, and symbolic parameters that are established by a concept of right. Therefore, as will be evident in the essays, it is not simply a question for me whether one chooses to regulate or deregulate a particular political issue. It is more important to justify *how* one should do so.

It is a common place saying in leftist circles that law takes certain issues off the political agenda. The conclusion is that this is a bad thing because it is antidemocratic. But this is not really the case because law is always political. Any concept of right, as I argue in these essays, involves a question of political morality. But law is political in the most basic sense of that word. For example, most judges in our legal system are elected. The decision to establish an independent federal judiciary, as we have done in the United States, is itself a political question, particularly when we remove judges on the federal bench from the realm of electoral politics. Further, since law always involves questions of interpretation, and since certain questions of legal interpretation are inseparable from norms of political morality and involve hotly contested political issues, those interpretations also generate political dispute. A good example of how politics still affects legal interpretations—even when the judges are removed from the direct political pressure of electoral politics—is the ever greater legal restrictions placed on the right to abortion in a series of legal decisions that followed *Roe v. Wade* (the case that initially gave women the right to abortion).[5]

One of the goals of these essays is to seek to cut a middle position between the idealization of politics as an alternative to law, and the idealization of law as an alternative to politics. In like manner, these essays also defend the moral and ethical parameters that circumscribe politics in the name of the persons who are both the participants in political life and the beneficiaries of any package of political, civic, and social rights. They also challenge the communitarian critique of rights as necessarily individualistic. "Rights talk" has long been critiqued for its individualist anthropology, but my defense of rights as crucial to the protection of persons completely rejects such an anthropology. It relies instead on a specific appeal to psychoanalysis as a guide to understanding how human beings are shaped. Indeed, because we are socially and symbolically constructed creatures, whose corporal existence immerses us in a world of physicality and desire, even our most primordial sense of self can be so easily crushed by forces in the world around us. It was Hegel who long ago reminded us that persons are in part constituted by rights and that rights are never simply expressive of already autonomous individuals.[6]

Another major theme that runs through these essays is the question of representation. I understand representation in two senses. First, representations are imaginative acts in which we envision the world. Second, struggles for representation are democratic practices that challenge constrictive political procedures and the institutionalized status of hierarchies that prevent some groups and individuals from participation in both self-organization and in the activities we associate with traditional electoral politics in a modern democracy. These two understandings of representation are intertwined but not identical. Part of the goal of these essays is to more graphically draw out the political and ethical significance of that intertwining for feminist politics. These essays strongly reject the position that "postmodernism"[7] has shown us that a politics of the people is beyond representation in either sense of the word.[8]

I use the example of my consciousness-raising group, which called itself *Las Greñudas*, literally, "the unkempt," to illustrate how an aesthetic act of naming ourselves also informed the kind of politics we wanted to engage in—a politics that was informed by the explicit appropriation of the "bad-girl," "the wild women." I was the only white woman among our group of Latinas and African American women. Many of us were not Spanish speakers. We represented ourselves as *Las Greñudas* not to indicate our alikeness as women, but to challenge the hierarchies and privileges that could potentially disrupt our solidarity. As our group well understood, it was not just difference that could separate us but also class and racial privilege. We represented ourselves as those who would not try to pass or to accommodate ourselves to images of the "good girl," images we saw as already whitened in the popular imaginary.

Questions of representation involve aesthetic, ethical, and political dimensions. Once we understand this interplay among all three, we can come to examine the so-called equality/difference debate within feminism from a new standpoint. In "Diverging Differences," I rearticulate the relationship between representation in both of its senses. Equality, as I have defended it through the ideal of the imaginary domain, which in turn protects the moral and psychic space in which we have the chance to represent our own sexuate being, enhances new possibilities for the aesthetic and ethical affirmation of feminine sexual difference. It also protects, as matter of right, the space for other new forms of representation of sexual difference. All persons are granted this right of self-representation.

These essays also address another dimension of the debates on representation in contemporary feminist and political theory. This dimension has to do with the rejection of theories of representation, particularly as developed by Immanuel Kant and as ensnared with the "philosophy of consciousness."[9] To remind the reader here, the Kantian notion of autonomy is the representation of the free will as the sole causal source of moral agency. The moral subject, in other words, forms itself through its consciousness of its own self-representation as a moral being. It is not enough to do the right thing; we must represent ourselves as doing the right thing for the right reasons. This strong Kantian understanding of the integral tie between the autonomous subject and self-representation is not at all what I mean by the phrase.[10] Yes, self-representation still implies that what we think of as the self, or what I refer to as the person, grows out of representations including the representation that there is someone "there" that is representing that subject and her world. But my understanding of the subject and the person comes out of psychoanalysis, which exposes that even the rudimentary structures of psychic life are formed in a symbolic field. Thus, it denies the possibility of autonomy of the free will in Kant's sense. Indeed, it can be best understood as preserving Kant's insight by turning it on its head. We need the right to self-representation precisely because we cannot be autonomous in Kant's understanding of the autonomy of free will. We come into this world as already represented as a man or a woman, as Black, white, Latino, or Anglo. We cannot escape having already been represented by the social and symbolic worlds around us. We can see this obviously in the commonsense example of the first words out of a doctor's mouth when a baby is born are, "*It's* a girl." From that "it" to the development of an individuated person is a long path to hoe. The struggle over the meaning of representations of ourselves is part of how we grapple with our basic identifications so as to individuate ourselves into those beings that we popularly call "selves."[11] I have used a similar argument based on my understanding of the two meanings of the word "representation" to argue against English-Only statutes and for the rights of Latinos/Latinas in the U.S. to speak Spanish, unless there is a pressing business necessity against allowing them to do so in a particular work-related situation.[12]

Feminism has recently been disparaged as heightening the war between the sexes. The movement is portrayed as ruthless, humorless women fighting for their share of the pie—just one more interest group. The feminism I defend, however, shows how the interests of women who demand that we focus on our corporal and sexuate beings—since these have been so often used to deny us freedom and equality—can lead us to articulate universal legal ideals that enhance freedom for all of us. As was sung long ago in the union song, "Bread and Roses," "the rising of the women means the rising of the race." Feminism regrettably restrains its ethical and political reach when it limits itself to the demand for gender equality in the world as it is. The danger of a limited focus on gender equality is that it particularizes the political meaning of women's struggle for sexual freedom. As I have argued, we cannot demand sexual freedom without demanding it for all sexuate beings. The need for sexuate beings to represent who they are sexually, both to themselves and others, is not a need or an interest of women only.

Traditional liberal philosophers have openly and proudly defended ideals in their work. Indeed, political philosophy can be understood as it "presents an ideal for collective life, and it tries to show people how one by one they should want to live under it."[13] Of course, not all brands of political philosophy have unabashedly defended their projects as the articulation of the ideal of collective life. It was perhaps John Rawls who, at least within the Anglo-American world, broke through the dominance of utilitarianism in the field of political philosophy so as to make the defense of ideals central to its undertaking. Rawls, as is well known, was deeply influenced by the writings of Immanuel Kant. For many years now, my contention has been that when liberal political philosophy proceeds primarily through its defense of the ideals of collective life, it borrows heavily from the tradition of German idealism— a tradition that only bit by bit has come to be acceptable in mainstream political science departments.

My debate with Judge Posner engages the sophisticated version of postmodern utilitarianism that he defends as the jurisprudential basis of the movement known as law and economics. Many significant thinkers, Posner among them, disagree with the Kantian-inspired conception of political philosophy as a reasonable defense of ideals of collective life. But Posner not only represents a form of utilitarianism; he also partakes of a larger skepticism about the role of the ideal in political philosophy and more specifically in actual political life. Posner's skepticism, however, is rooted in his commitment to the empiricist underpinnings of the law-and-economics movement.[14] Skepticism about idealism, understood in the philosophical sense of elaborations of ideals for collective life, has not only come under attack in jurisprudence from thinkers in law and economics. Idealism has also purportedly been effectively challenged by such thinkers as Heidegger, Derrida, and Lacan. Indeed, psychoanalysis is often seen as one of the great debunkers of idealism, because it reminds us that what are consciously configured as ideals may well only be sublimated desires associated with the worst moralistic drive for control over others. The connection between moralism and German idealism was wrathfully brought to life by Frederick Nietzsche, who saw idealists as pitifully succumbing to a slave mentality.

Many of the essays in this collection learn from the warnings and searing critiques that have been made of German idealism by thinkers loosely labeled postmodern. I do not accept what has popularly come to be called metanarratives as the basis for envisioning progress toward a better future. Instead, the question of the role of the ideal and the question of representation are brought together in a reconceptualization of the role of the aesthetic as crucial to both the critique and the elaboration of new configurations of ideals in law and political philosophy.

I do not limit the aesthetic to the traditional domain with which it has been associated—that is, art objects. The aesthetic points us to the affective aspects of life that so inspired Kant's most brilliant insights into the difficulties of the critical project itself.[15] We not only seek to understand the world, we also experience it through our deepest feelings. Feminism carries within it the demand to reconcile the strands of romantic and critical idealism that have often been torn apart precisely because feminism forces us to grapple with the affective aspects of human life. Again, the union song, "Bread and Roses," has it right. "Hearts starve as well as bodies. Give us bread and give us roses." In the long run, feminism is about significant cultural change. Such change has an aesthetic dimension in the sense that it demands not just new forms of knowledge about how we become men and women but also new ways of imagining who we are as sexuate and emotional creatures. Feminism demands the enlarged mentality that allows the imagination to run free. Our political challenge to our current social order desires nothing less than new ways of seeing the world that would allow us to perceive new forms of such supposedly unshakable aspects of life such as sexuality and kinship. Theories of justice that ignore the heart can never deliver on the roses.

As part of this imaginative effort, we need to reenvision the connection among language, citizenship, and lineage. These three institutional structures, which are often thought to go hand-in-hand, have not in my own life turned out to be in any simple relationship to each other; my daughter speaks a language to which I have little access, she is a citizen of a country to which I do not belong as well as a citizen of the United States, and our family tie is not based in blood. The challenge I make to English-Only statutes is only the beginning of the reconsideration we all need to make about the relationships among family, citizenship, and language. We are called to reexamine these basic concepts, in light of not only globalization, but also of the challenge to Eurocentrism which is inseparable in many cases from the demand of migrant peoples to the northern democracies to be allowed official dual citizenship. My daughter was brought into my life through an "international adoption." In order to imagine a place for her freedom, I was forced to reexamine many of my own basic assumptions about family, race, ethnicity, and language and many of the basic assumptions within political philosophy. My commitment to her freedom demands that I engage in a collective process with my daughter toward a transnational literacy. I am only too well aware that these essays are but the beginning of a lifelong process of educating myself so as to expand my own moral imagination.

Part I

REPRESENTATION AND THE IDEAL IN LAW AND POLITICS

1

Las Greñudas: Recollections on Consciousness-Raising

The second wave of feminism, as it has come to be known, started out as an experiment in radical democracy. We called that experiment "consciousness-raising," which was the method of group formation characterizing the movement. All those who came into feminist consciousness-raising groups were to be given a voice and heard with seriousness. It may sound strange to put it that way, as if such a group could give to women what they did not have—a voice. But that was exactly the point. Together, we could find a way to learn both to speak among ourselves and to address a broader public by providing ourselves with the support we could not find alone. Voices were not just something we had, a natural attribute of our human being, but also something we helped each other develop as we struggled to articulate who we were and who we sought to become in the movement we were creating. Since everyone's voice was to count as equally important in the group and in the formation of the group's political agenda, these "spaces" were as often about contest and profound disagreement as they were about agreement.[1] By letting women speak and represent themselves—initially, these spaces tended to be women-only spaces—the process of change was already taking place no matter how deeply women initially disagreed on questions such as what it meant to be oppressed as a woman, how race and class played out in that oppression, and what kind of change we ultimately had to make in order to truly challenge patriarchy. By patriarchy, I mean the state-enforced and culturally supported norm of heterosexual monogamy as the only appropriate organization of family life. This imposed family structure, as I have argued elsewhere,[2] inevitably reinforces rigid gender identities through the psychic laws that are purportedly necessary for the perpetuation of these families and the achievement of so-called normal ma-

ture sexual differentiation.[3] In the course of democratic struggle among ourselves, we were already achieving an ethical and political purpose, which following Marilyn Friedman, I will call "demoralizing the genders," even if some
consciousness-raising groups never engaged in more traditional activism. The
phrase is clearly ironic, and I will return to the misunderstanding of that irony
shortly. By "demoralizing" the genders, Friedman means that we seek to de-
naturalize the narrow moral symbolism and mythologies through which masculinity and femininity are defined and that in turn creates a moral division of
labor, codes of how men and women are supposed to behave, and what kinds
of moral characters are appropriate for them to develop.[4] Consciousness-raising groups ethically challenged the moral norms of femininity just by insisting
that public contest over the meaning of our "sex" should take place. This leads
to another aspect of radical democracy that was to be practiced.

Our "sex," under the patriarchal moral code, was what was to be kept in
secret as part of the sexual shame associated with femininity. The frank discussion in these groups about everything from getting breasts, to having pe-
riods, to living with pregnancy, to exploring our bodies, was clearly an effort
to release ourselves from shame. Our groups were radical in the content of
what was made appropriate for public discussion and group engagement.
We had a slogan for this: "The personal is political." Moralism about what
was appropriate to say about our "sex" would have gotten in the way of this
symbolic and representational practice.

My own consciousness-raising group, made up of Latinas and African
American women with the exception of myself, spent hours discussing the
specificity of how we were *femmed* differently because race and class were
integral to the mapping of femininity on to femaleness. Our consciousness-
raising group was formed in 1974, largely due to Muriel, an African American woman, after she and I were fired for union organizing at our jobs as
phone operators at Columbia University.[5] Muriel was the impetus behind the
formation of the group. One Latina used the example of her mother's insis-
tent warnings to her of the dangers in Anglo society of appearing
"greñuda"—uncombed. Greñuda, in Spanish, implies that a properly
femmed Latina must whiten herself through ladylike hairstyling, a particular
mode of braiding that would show that her hair was not "nappy." But
greñuda is not literally about hairstyling. It is a metaphor about how a Latina
is not supposed to appear or behave if she is appropriately ladylike. For our
group member, her *femming* was inseparable from how she was to morally
distinguish herself from all that was "black." After that evening, we called
ourselves "las greñudas" to represent what we were struggling against, even
though we knew that we did not all share her experience and that the
metaphor would mean different things to each one of us in the group. Yet as
a group, the name represented our solidarity in a struggle for what we
proudly called freedom. Later in my life I would understand this kind of rep-

resentational practice as inversion or mimesis, which through its conscious appropriation inverts the moral meaning it was originally meant to carry.[6] We saw ourselves as creating new representations of ourselves as a group without minimizing the differences of race, class, ethnicity, and national backgrounds among us.

We took our commitment to new forms of representation and democratic practice into the political battles that arose out of our coming together as a group. One of our members was a prostitute who had organized a prostitutes' collective. We joined with her and the other collective members to do what was necessary to allow the women to escape from their pimps. Another project was getting men who were parents of children of group members to keep up with their support payments. We would go to the man's workplace and call on his "brothers" and "sisters" to help us address the problem. We had great success, as "brothers" were reminded by their own co-worker of their responsibilities by having food pelted at them in the cafeteria, smoke bombs put in their lockers, and other creative and collective measures used to ensure that the necessary support was delivered. We never considered hiring a lawyer, not because none of the women in the group could afford a lawyer, but because bringing in the state was never an alternative for this group of Latinas and African American women for whom the state, and particularly the police, were not considered sources of protection. The whole idea here was to find a representational practice that would allow women to be taken seriously, to get their needs met, and yet not to bring in the state against men who, although behaving badly, were never identified as the enemy.

Our representation of ourselves as feminists was inseparable from our antiracism and our attempt to dignify the Spanish language. We were not claiming that the name we gave ourselves was an adequate description of some truth about Woman or that in a like manner, captured our essence as women. Indeed, we did not share the same experiences of oppression. As a result, it was crucially important for us to witness not only to our differences but also to the privileges, including the privilege of a potential "passing" that could separate us from one another. As a white Anglo woman, I was called to witness in front of my sisters that I could never share their experiences of oppression as women of color. I was always already represented by the larger society, as a white woman, and could not simply step out of the privileges that were inherent in that representation.

This leads me to a crucial point about representation: representation is inevitable. Representation is what gives us our reality. But we are not passive before these representations, as if the world is simply imposed on us so that we are effectively limited by how we are shaped by the symbolic codes that give us meaning, including the meaning of the moral symbols of conventional, stereotypical, gender hierarchy. We are always both consciously and unconsciously engaged in representing who we are in the very process of

becoming a "presence" to ourselves and to others.[7] The feminism we practiced in our consciousness-raising group, which clearly understood the cen-
trality of rerepresenting ourselves in accordance with our attempt to explode
the limits of how we had to be in the world, did not essentialize the meaning of these representations. They were understood to be just that—representations, an aesthetic mode of knowledge[8] that also allowed us to develop
a politics in accordance with political and ethical aspirations to challenge the
hegemonic meanings of sexual difference.

Nor, then, was the use of "las greñudas" simply strategic, deployed as a
means to an end. The end was integral in the name which we understood to
be both political and ethical: political in that it challenged the behavior appropriate to women in public, ethical in that we challenged how we had
been hemmed in from divergent race, class, and ethnic positions. As the only
white woman in the group, I came to see myself as not only oppressed because I had been *femmed* so as not to have access to certain kinds of pursuits—in my own case being a mathematician—but also privileged, even if I
saw some of the privileges of white femininity as themselves a prison.

Of course, I am not describing what actually went on in all consciousness-
raising groups, but I am arguing that the insistence on radical democracy was
crucial to the practice we both conceived and lived. It is this insistence on
democratic practice which realizes profound respect for the potential richness of the symbolic field of sexual difference. Without this respect, the
power of our experiences is diminished by a feminist moralism that will tell
us now, in the name of feminism, how we are to behave as women, feminists, or both.

Let me be clear about what I mean by feminist moralism. I mean the remoralization of gender in the exact opposite sense of what Marilyn Freidman
means by demoralization.[9] In other words, if in different guises we moralize
gender and reinscribe a moral division of labor by attributing a specific set
of moral behaviors to men or women as a class, we are engaged in remoral-
izing gender. We see this kind of remoralization amongst younger antifeminists who argue for a new chastity.[10] But antifeminists are not the only ones
who engage in this process. Feminists do it, for example, when we argue that
it is only men who are enticed by sexually explicit literature as part of their
rapacious nature. Such statements often pose as descriptions, but I am arguing that they are moral generalizations—not so much about who men actually are, but how masculinity is symbolically encoded.

I am aware, of course, that my story of my own consciousness-raising
group proceeds through recollective imagination. By recollective imagination, I mean that the story I tell proceeds through a narration of the moral of
the story as I imagine its significance for a future ethical orientation for feminism.[11] It may even risk the nostalgia of an "old girl" reminiscing about her
youth on the picket line, but I take that risk because this radical herstory is

often obscured in accounts of the second wave of feminism. The second wave of feminism was not, for many of us, a school in which we "girls" learned to enter and were allowed to gain access to the straight, white, male dominated professions. If, in my imaginative recollection, there is moral of the story of my consciousness-raising group, it is not, however, that we are left with a political demoralizing anti-essentialism.[12] Nothing in the struggle to demoralize gender, in the sense that I mean it, involves us in denying the need for the ethical, political, and aesthetic representations of who we are, and even a legal translation of these into a conception of the right of personality, as long as it is conceived to be consistent with the overall project of our struggle for freedom. Freedom here is understood as our freedom to be otherwise than in the limited restricted personas of masculinity and femininity. There is a confusion, for example, that laws and movements against sexual harassment need to involve themselves in this remoralization.[13] This project of radical democracy is about opening up the space for new moral, ethical, and political representations of feminism itself, as much as it is against the specific kind of moral symbolization of sexual difference integral to gender hierarchy.

Defined as such, this project encompasses feminists who come from a wide variety of philosophical and political traditions.[14] What has come to be called "postmodern feminism" is better understood as this project to demoralize gender.[15] We are reminded of a radical project of democratic representation that always remembers the metaphor of silencing as that which led us to create spaces in which new voices could articulate themselves and be taken seriously in the first place. There is terrible irony, given our herstory, in the moral imposition of silence on some women because they do not fit into the appropriate behavior that some feminists have decreed as that which makes one a "proper" feminist.

2

Diverging Differences: Comment on Felski's "The Doxa of Difference"

In the last ten years, an argument has raged in feminist theory over the relationship between equality and difference, universality and particularity. Feminist thinkers have been frequently divided into two camps. Rita Felski, for instance, has identified me as a feminist who emphasized feminine sexual difference at the expense of equality. I want to challenge Felski's conception of what I mean by sexual difference, especially as it relates to my articulation of a legal ideal of equality. First and foremost, I am indeed a thinker of sexual difference, but not in Felski's sense. What do I mean by sexual difference? I mean that who we are as sexed beings is symbolic, institutional; second, it is a way of being that claims one's own sex outside of the imposed norms of heterosexuality. The first is a point about how to understand gender. The second is a political aspiration that must reform our dreams of how we are to be sexed and to claim our personhood at the same time. I want to begin with my theory of equality, to which Felski briefly refers.

In *The Imaginary Domain* (Cornell 1995), I advocated a new theory of legal equality that would overcome the equality/difference debate that has plagued feminist jurisprudence. My argument was as follows. The basic postulate of political liberalism is that all citizens are to be recognized as free and equal persons. The feminist demand in the great bourgeois revolutions in Western Europe was that women should be included in the moral community of persons constituted by the new democratic governments. As Joan Scott has eloquently described (1996), that basic demand ran afoul of the reality that the person was represented as the white, male, property owner.

Both Rita Felski's essay, *The Doxa of Difference* and this response by Drucilla Cornell were originally published in *Signs* (Chicago) Autumn 1997, 1–21, 41–56, respectively.

17

The demand to be included in that community had to run up against a paradox. Women were demanding inclusion in a normative political community of persons that by definition excluded them. My attempt to resolve the dilemma posed by the conflation of white masculinity with the purportedly universal person has taken the following form. The juridical person of the early bourgeois government was seemingly "neutered," but of course only "seemingly." Since the characteristics of the person were assumed as given by the equality attributed to citizens, the "sexing" of the representative of the person disappeared. But what do we as feminists do to make the "sexing" of the representative of the person appear? Once we have made it appear, what is our political and, more specifically, our legal demand to the state? Are we to demand the actual "desexing" of the idealized person—as if that could be achieved—so that women can be included as equal citizens with the same rights? But then what about the ways in which women are different from men? What about pregnancy and the division of labor in the family? Perhaps we should instead claim the right to our difference and to the protection of our welfare particularly as mothers. In her book *Only Paradoxes to Offer* (1996), Joan Scott discussed in depth the paradoxes generated over a century of French feminism, as generation after generation have struggled with the question of what exactly women's rights were. In *The Imaginary Domain*, I argued that we might start to resolve the dilemma by reclaiming the ideal of the person for feminist purposes.

First, I have argued that once we add "sex"—or what I have named "sexuate being"—as a category of political philosophy, we can no longer legitimately represent the person as "neutered." Similarly, we can no longer think of the person as simply given. Sexed beings have a phenomenological existence that puts demands on them. These demands must be addressed in political philosophy, especially in a theory of legal reform. Yet how do we do this without reinscribing the "state of injury" (Brown 1995) imposed by gender hierarchy as the definition of women? We are obviously not born as the full-blown adults that social-contract theory models. The concept of sexuate being takes us back to the "prior" point in which human beings become individuated enough to be regarded as capable of the moral capacities attributed to the idealized person of political philosophy.

The person, then, is no longer represented as just "there." Instead, the person must be respected as part of a project. This project must be available to each one of us as a sexuate being on an equivalent basis. My argument is that without the equal protection of minimum conditions of individuation, we cannot effectively engage in the project of becoming a person. These minimum conditions of individuation can only arise in a space that I have described as the imaginary domain. The minimum conditions of individuation include (1) bodily integrity and (2) access to symbolic forms sufficient to achieve linguistic skills that in turn permit the differentiation of oneself from others.

I like to think of these as ensconced in the imaginary domain, because bodily integrity is not used in the way that it has traditionally been used in political philosophy. Again, we do not assume bodily integrity as a given. Instead, the integration of one's own body is understood as a process. The imaginary domain is an heuristic device that allows us to represent the sanctuary needed for any of us to pull ourselves together into that being we think of as a self or as a person. Since, in my definition, the person is a project undertaken by a sexuate being, I am using person in a particular way. *Persona* in Latin literally means "shining through." Even though the concept of the mask is the usual association with the word *persona*, I would argue that, in fact, a person is what shines through a mask. For a person to be able to shine through she must imagine herself as whole, even if she knows she can never truly succeed in becoming whole, or conceptually differentiate between the mask and the self. A person, in other words, is an aspiration because it is a project that can never be fulfilled, once and for all. The person as a sexuate being is implicated in an endless process of working through *personae*. As sexed beings, we are inevitably confronted with this project. In this definition, the person is identical neither with the self nor with the traditional philosophical subject.

It should be noted that the appeal to minimum conditions of individuation is universalized. The uniqueness of feminine sexual differences—if one assumes there is such uniqueness—is not taken into account in the elaboration of the conditions themselves. No form of sexuate being can be evaluated as inherently antithetical to personhood, since such a devaluation would run counter to the fundamental premise of a politically liberal society that each one of us is to be regarded as a free and equal person.

Although the imaginary domain functions as an heuristic device to help elaborate the space that must be protected prior to the beginning of any conception of proceduralist justice, it also serves to displace the current notion of legal privacy. The equal protection of the imaginary domain gives to the person, and only to the person, the right to represent her or his sexuate being. The argument is that the recognition of the right of self-representation of our sexuate beings works backwards. As beings entitled as a matter of right to represent their own sexuate being, women, for example, can no longer be identified in law as a naturalized class whose entitlement and duties flow from this status position. Of course, the idea that the concept of right is constitutive of the person takes us back to Hegel (1967).

If we understand that now the demand for inclusion entails protection of the imaginary domain and minimum conditions of individuation, then we can make a claim to parity that does not turn on any comparison with actual men. For example, in the case of the right of abortion, I have argued that women must have the right to abortion with safe facilities, both provided and paid for all the way, through the cutting of the umbilical cord (Cornell 1995, chap. 2). If we allow the state to impose on women any prohibition against their right to represent their sexuate being (in this case to have an abortion) or to make it extremely difficult (that is, to deny medical facilities), then we are treating women as things for a greater good and not as persons.

The theory of equal equality I have advocated pits itself against the use of gender as a legal category precisely because the "single axis" for discrimination has been exclusionary of claims made by women of diverse nationalities (African American, Latina, Asian, and Native American) in the name of the specificity of sexual discrimination and sexual harassment they endured. For example, in *The Imaginary Domain* (1995), I argue that the "braiding cases" that were denied jurisdiction under our own law would easily be included as making a claim of right under my theory of equality. To be granted jurisdiction is to be given standing to sue. The braiding cases involved situations in which African American women were discriminated against or harassed because they chose to braid their hair. As Paulette Caldwell argued (1991), hair braiding is for many black women one representation of the meaning they give to their iden-tification as African American. For Caldwell personally, the braiding of her hair is an extremely important way of expressing her continuing identification with African tradition. As she elaborates in her essay, hair braiding involves a ritual in which grandmothers braided a young girl's hair on the occasion of her first period. Her own grandmother followed this tradition. For Caldwell, hair braid-ing has never been simply an aesthetic exercise, but also a profound moment of identification both with her own ancestresses and with what being African meant to them.

Under formal equality, hair braiding is not an "immutable characteristic," and therefore it does not fall under the traditional understanding of race dis-crimination. Indeed, African American women themselves have been in-comprehensible to the doctrine of discrimination, since there are divergent standards of legal review under our constitutional law for race and gender. In order, then, to figure out what is the proper legal doctrine under which an African American woman is to be judged, determinations have to be made as to whether she is one-half African American, one-half woman, and so on. The absurdity of this dilemma has been pointed to in a series of articles by critical race theorists.[1] Under the theory of equality I advocate, hair braiding is an excellent example of African American women choosing to represent their own sexuate being as it inevitably implicates both national and racial identification. They would easily be given standing as making a claim of right under my theory of equality.

The feminist purpose of this theory of equality is twofold. First, it serves to extensively critique and replace the single-axis model of discrimination that has been so ineffective in recognizing the rights of African American women, as well as other national differences among women that hardly could be articulated within the framework of Title VII and constitutional law. Another classic example of the failure of formal equality to recognize the specificity of the wrongs imposed on women of color are cases of Latinas who have claimed sexual harassment in the form of being demanded by bosses to speak "dirty" Spanish. Again, such cases frequently have been denied categorization as discrimination because they did not involve race or gender as defined in the model of formal equality that dominates current discrimination law.

Not only have the traditional legal theories of equality excluded women of color—I am reluctant to use the term *women of color* because, as I have argued elsewhere, one of the privileges of being white is that your color is erased so that you appear as the neutralized universal—they also have put gays and lesbians outside the reach of discrimination law. Again, by my concept of right, gays and lesbians easily would have access to the protections of discrimination law because, like all other sexuate beings, they would be granted the right to self-representation of their sexuate being. The basic legal conclusion of my theory of equality is that the state cannot impose the monogamous, heterosexual family, because such an imposition violates the right of the person to represent her or his own sexuate being. Thus, it would no longer be a question of "tolerating" gays and lesbians as an acceptable "deviance" from the norm, because any norm of the family would be outlawed by my theory of right. Patriarchy, as it necessarily involves the state imposition of the heterosexual, monogamous family as the good family, would be "outlawed" as a violation of the rights of persons. The second purpose of this theory of legal equality is an attempt to address, once again, the dilemma that Scott leaves us with in *Only Paradoxes to Offer* (1996): How can we both demand inclusion and reinterpret that demand away from reference to both white masculinity and to substantive characteristics that legally and paradoxically define us as victims or as other than persons worthy of entitlement?

The way in which women's "difference" is to be taken into account in my theory of equality is that it is to be defined by us in all of our diversity. The law should take a woman's experience into account by giving her the freedom to define what her experience means. The equal protection of the imaginary domain gives to women the right to differentiate themselves and to express their identifications in all their complexities, including their national and linguistic identifications. This theory is based on sameness, not on commonality or likeness, since it stems from the political recognition of all of us as free persons. The sameness always turns us back to the normative standard of what it means to be included in the moral community as a person as an initial matter. To summarize again, inclusion is now defined to contain the protection of the imaginary domain and the minimum conditions of individuation as what it means to be politically identified as a free person.

Does that mean, as Felski suggests, that all differences deserve respect? My answer to that has been as follows: in any theory of legal reform we are ad-

dressing the relationship of the individual to the state. There are two legally recognizable limits under my theory of equality as to how persons can express
themselves both as sexuate beings and in the other identifications they wish to
take on.The first is the obvious one, the prohibition of any form of outright,
physical violence. But this limit would be enforced by criminal law. The second
is what I call the "degradation prohibition." The degradation prohibition, as I
define it, takes us back to what it means to be in the moral community of citizens as an initial matter. By degradation, I mean graded down, treated as less
than a person who can represent her or his sexuate being. Obviously, if a gay
or lesbian couple is denied access to housing, they are being treated as less than
persons because the scope of their rights is curtailed due to a prohibition
against their sexuality that is enforced by the state.

To emphasize again what I mean by the degradation prohibition and why
it is irreducible to offense, let me give an example of the exact kind of complexity to which Felski refers when she questions how a society can legally
grapple with identifications that seem to be at war with one another. Several
years ago, a conflict arose between the Irish-American Gay, Lesbian and Bisexual Group of Boston (GLIB), which wished to parade openly as a contingent in Boston's St. Patrick's Day Parade, and the parade's organizers, who
opposed their entry as openly gay and lesbian.[2] Ultimately, it was legally resolved by the U.S. Supreme Court, which did not allow GLIB to march in the
parade. The Court ruled that the inclusion of GLIB violated the parade organizers' First Amendment right to exclude groups whose message they disagreed with. The political argument was over the question of what it means
to be Irish. No doubt, for some, being Irish means being white, heterosexual, and Catholic. For others of us, being Irish means rebelling against all
forms of unjust hierarchies. I consider myself to be an Irish woman in the lat-
ter sense. Under my theory of equality, this conflict would not have been resolved in a court of law. What it means to be Irish ultimately must be struggled with by those to whom it is a meaningful identification. This was not a
case of degradation simply because some prominent Irish people were offended by the mere suggestion that gays and lesbians could march openly as
a contingent in the parade. If they were offended, so be it. The contests over
what it means to identify as an Irish person are best left to the streets.

I obviously strongly agree with Felski that some theories of equality are
better than others. Otherwise, I would not have spent so much time trying to
develop one. Better in what sense? First, my argument displaces the equal-
ity/difference dichotomy and synchronizes the values of freedom and equality more effectively than other feminist theories of equality that have been
defended.[3] What I mean by equivalence does turn us back to the theory of
equality I advocate. It does not and cannot stand alone. In that sense I agree
with Charles Taylor (1989) that any theory of rights certainly demands some

normative framework in which better or worse is given meaning and differences themselves are evaluated.

The minimalist ideal of the imaginary domain, however, is also a reminder
of the coercive power of the state that is endlessly deployed in law and the
importance of what we traditionally have thought of as sexual freedom, even
as it must be reconceived by feminists. I have reconceptualized "sexual freedom" in a platform of legal reform as the right of self-representation of our
sexuate being. Its implications are far-reaching, since, as I defend at great
length in my book, *At the Heart of Freedom*,[4] the heterosexual, monogamous
family could no longer be enforced as the normal family because to do so
would violate the equivalent law of persons I advocate.

Second, the egalitarian theory that I advocate extends the reach of equality because it allows for the elaboration of the wrongs done to women of
color that have previously remained unarticulable in the law. Again, I would
return to the example of both the command to speak "dirty" Spanish and the
denial of the right to speak Spanish in workplaces.

Third, my theory of equality is more effective in that it does not connect a
theory of rights to any substantive view of women that would negate their
entitlement as persons. That is the greatest paradox in Catharine MacKinnon's theory (1989). She positions women as nonpersons and therefore renders incoherent both their claim to full inclusion in the moral community and
the critique of their reduction to object status.

I would defend my theory as a better synchronization of the values of freedom and equality than the other theories offered in feminist jurisprudence—
and this defense would be pragmatic in the specific sense that it defends the
value of its position by assuming a framework in which the ideal of the person is already granted as a postulate of practical reason. However, I agree
with Rey Chow (1993) that any egalitarian theory developed in an engagement with the principles of Western constitutional democracy must be very
carefully incorporated in a more worldwide program of human rights.

Before turning to Felski's interpretation of my reading of Lacan, I want to
make a last comment on my theory of equality. The idea of minimum conditions of individuation clearly recognizes the legitimacy of Felski's argument that we are always engaging with a situation from which we differentiate ourselves. That is why throughout *The Imaginary Domain* I use the
word *individuation* and not *the individual* or *autonomy*. I am in complete
agreement with Charles Taylor's description of self-identification that Felski
quotes. Taylor remarks, "Defining myself means finding what is significant in
my difference from others" (1991, 35–36; quoted in Felski 1997, 16). The theory of difference that Felski advocates is Hegelian, which is fine by me. Both
Taylor and I come out of a long engagement with Hegel. The central idea of
the imaginary domain—that is, that one is a person only as individuated and
as protected in the process of individuation—is clearly Hegelian in its inspi-

ration. Lacan was also deeply influenced by Hegel, and therefore it is not surprising that his incorporation of philosophical insight with psychoanalysis attracted me.

My engagement with Lacan was inspired by the need to try to develop an explanation of the hold of patriarchy in Western democracies that at least superficially recognize women as equal citizens. Why is it so difficult for feminism to sustain itself as a movement and transmit its lessons to the next generation so that we can build on what we have achieved in the past rather than be fated to engage in the same battles over and over again? For instance, why can't we win the right of abortion and never have to talk about it again? My engagement with Lacan was also driven by my own desire to find a more adequate analysis of how race is engendered and how the meaning of "color" is perpetuated through unconscious fantasies that become the underpinnings of a symbolic order.

As I argued in *Transformations* when I engaged with the work of the anthropologist Gananath Obeyesekere (1990), my fundamental reason for relying on psychoanalysis is that we need to have an understanding both of how symbolic systems come to hold sway and of how they are governed inevitably by social fantasies. Of course, the very phrase "governed by fantasy" means that they cannot be firmly grounded and therefore are always open to transformation. I recognize that Lacan may seem like an unlikely ally in my argument that the barriers to transformation can never be *absolutely* effective in their erection. My argument in a series of books, starting with *Beyond Accommodation* (Cornell 1991), however, has been that Lacan's own analysis of the unconscious is incompatible with his defense of the phallus as a transcendental signifier. Thus, his claim to the absoluteness of the barrier to the symbolization of feminine sexual difference is deconstructed by his own insight. I argued in *Beyond Accommodation* that phallocentrism, because of its own logic, *cannot homogenize itself.* I strongly disagree with Felski's interpretation of my work as defending phallocentrism's "homogenizing" force. For a true Lacanian, a woman who thinks she "is" beyond accommodation to patriarchical norms, let alone advocates a feminism that seeks to be beyond "accommodation," would be considered delusional—psychotic in the clinical sense. My alliance with Lacan, then, is about what he has right about the unconscious, *not* about his own philosophical defense of the positioning of the phallus as a transcendental signifier.

Let me return to my effort to rethink the eroticization of race. As I argued in "What Takes Place in the Dark," in *Transformations* (Cornell 1993b), the conception of the "inessential woman" (Spelman 1988) lets white women off the hook too easily. In that essay I wanted to demonstrate that the relationship between African American women and white women is a relationship of inequality and has to be addressed as that. As such, then, white women cannot simply neutralize their own whiteness or their position of privilege in their relationships with African American women. Felski seems not to note this persistent, if not relentless, argument on my part, that it is this inequality and privilege that has prevented solidarity among women of different nationalities, cultures, and linguistic traditions. To show the economy of the asymmetrical positioning of African American and white women, as in part engendered by the eroticization of meanings of color, I have turned to Lacan's understanding of linguistics, and particularly his linguistic analysis of the unconscious.

Lacan, following Saussure but also Hegel, argues that meaning and systems of representation only come to gain significance through the articulation of differential relations between signs and the elements of the signs themselves. It is the differential relationship between letters and words that supports the congelation of meaning we think of as a form of life. Meaning, in other words, is an established set of differential relationships. The "arising" of meaning out of differential relationships also allows for the gaps that open up the space for the possibility of transformation. Lacan's statement, that the signifier is privileged over the signified, means that there is no ontologically distinct order, for example, of race and gender, that can be separated from signifiers. The differential relation between the elements of the signs and the signs themselves means that each term needs another term to be understood, and that that term needs another, and so on. This on and on, or horizontal, process, in which meaning continually tries to create new meanings, is what Lacan refers to as metonymy. Metonymy relies on the endless re-creation of the context that results in the intrajuxtaposition of one term to another through contiguity. For Lacan, contiguity is itself a linguistic relation and is not based on any real relation between objects. Objects connected by metaphoric transference are also clearly in a linguistic relation. Because for Lacan metaphor operates vertically, however, the transferential relationship is often erased in the congelation of meaning in which the substitution implied by the transference is taken for reality. The term that has been substituted easily falls below the bar of consciousness, thus continually producing the material of the unconscious. The substitution process is identified by Lacan with the principle of condensation. In other words, metaphor, through the potential erasure implicit in substitution, can make the replaced signifier disappear into the unconscious. The unconscious has no ontological status. The unconscious "is" only the signifiers that have disappeared because the process of condensation has erased the past in which they were pushed under.

I use a "real life" example to try to make what I know seem to be abstract arguments become vivid as a different way of analyzing race and gender. This story goes back twenty years or so to the time when I was a full-time union organizer. The solidarity between the workers broke down because one of the white women on the organizing committee developed a sexual relationship with an African American man who was a partner of one of the African American women, who was also a leading activist in the factory. The African American women on the committee asked me to give the white woman notice that if she continued to behave in this manner—flagrantly having sex with this man in the parking lot—there would be consequences for her. There had already been consequences for the union drive. Ultimately, there was a serious scuffle between this white woman, who would not desist in her sexual activity with the African American man, and several African American women. The scuffle took place in the parking lot before all of our eyes. To see to it that I would not intervene and thus get hurt, I was escorted to my car and guarded by two women until the incident had played out. The white woman left her job the next day. She was a member of a Marxist-Leninist organization to which I also belonged and justified her action in part because it expressed her adherence to "third world leadership." Obviously, the African American women did not regard her action as a righteous political statement. She was a student at Stanford, and for her, the job and the success of the union drive was not a crucial matter of survival. But it was for the other women.

Those of us who remained after her departure worked to put our union drive back together. For me, it demanded a confrontation with the way in which my own sexual imago had been colored as white. The demand on the part of the African American women was the recognition of the eroticization of privilege. The "white girl" is fantasized—obviously only by some black men—as the one who is desirable precisely because she is the woman of the Man. Femininity is modeled on this whitened desirable object, which, of course, has little to do with actual "white girls" but instead depicts how they exist in the imaginary of our culture. But this imaginary in which this "desired female" is represented is only too real. In *The Bluest Eye*, Toni Morrison portrays the rage at "white" dolls as hardly being child's play. The white "doll" is the other by which the black female child is judged as not desirable in her blackness: "I destroyed white baby dolls. But the dismembering of dolls was not the true horror. The truly horrifying thing was the transference of the same impulses to little white girls. The indifference with which I could have axed them was shaken only by my desire to do so. To discover what eluded me: the secret of the magic they weaved on others. What made people look at them and say 'Awwwww,' but not for me?" (Morrison 1970, 22).

Our organizing committee read *The Bluest Eye* together, and for me it was a moment of revelation of the "white-skin privilege" inherent in who is marked as a desirable object, a "doll." Of course, as feminists, none of us would easily admit to embracing the desirability of the doll, the one who gets the "Awwwww." Who wants to be a "doll"? And yet on some unconscious plane, what white heterosexual woman has not sought safety and protection behind that "Awwwww"? In order for the solidarity to be remembered, those of us on our committee who were white had to confront the racialization of prettiness, color, and value. Since that time, I have never been able to "see" myself as other than white.

The demand on us was to understand the differential eroticized articulations through which "white" and "black" are given meaning. The relationship between African American and white women exists as an asymmetrical relationship in which what is held in common can be recognized only by struggling with and against the asymmetrical positioning of white and black women. To understand white and black in this, the Lacanian manner helps us understand how the condensation of meaning creates a fundamental asymmetry that is inseparable from the way in which racial inequality is not only symbolized but also justified on a day-to-day basis. It would make it a mockery to assume that the experience of black and white women would be the same. But an understanding of this asymmetrical relationship would also deny that color can be reduced to a set of positive characteristics separate from the chain of signifiers in which it is given meaning. In other words, there are not just "white" and "black" women who are just there and can be reduced to their whiteness and blackness as if color could signify separately from the matrix of desire in which it is given meaning. What it means to be "white," in other words, can be grasped only in a relationship of privilege, not of difference, within the asymmetrical articulation of white and black womanhood. Lacan's insight into the linguistic "nature" of the unconscious can elaborate a different understanding of the asymmetrical positioning of African American and white women, particularly as this coloration plays out in the way we are rendered visible and eroticized.

As a lifetime activist, I have been one of the "multitudes of women" engaged in cultural activity—"the artists, the revolutionaries, the mothers, the teachers"—and therefore have argued strongly against the idea that we are, again to quote Felski, "really nothing more than the passive vehicles of phallocentrism" (1997, 6). Here I believe that Felski collapses my position with that of Catharine MacKinnon, whom I critique (Cornell 1991). Unlike MacKinnon, I have insisted that part of the desirability of a psychoanalytic feminism is that it separates the masculine and the feminine from actual men and women. Indeed it separates, and necessarily so, patriarchal and phallic institutions from the lives of actual men. The phallic "ideal" is unattainable, as I have argued so many times and in so many places, and does not exist, and yet because it is idealized, it is still sought after in representations of masculinity. But in spite of their phantasmatic underpinnings, the dynamics of castration are only too real. As Frantz Fanon has argued eloquently (1963), the rape of a people's "women" as a public enactment of castration is a mark of imperialist domination. An obvious example within the United States is lynching. In this horrifying ritual, castration is not only symbolized but also played out on the dead body of the hanged African American man, whose penis is stuffed in his mouth. This is metaphor becoming living "theater" in the most horrific sense.

In spite of my critique of Felski's interpretation of my own reading of Lacan, I have come to see it as a legitimate and important question whether or not Lacan and Lacanianism inescapably privilege, and in spite of themselves, ontologize the divide between idealized masculinity and the feminine other.[5] Again, I want to stress idealized masculinity because of Lacan's insight into how and why the cultural organs of patriarchy are in no real sense in the interest of most men. In *Beyond Accommodation,* I use Beckett's *Happy Days* to allegorize the suffering articulated by Beckett, an Irishman, of living with oneself as castrated from the standpoint of an idealized and unreachable masculinity. In my life as a union organizer, I saw only too many times how the gap between an idealized masculinity and the failure to live up to it (when deeply internalized norms of what it meant to be a man collapsed before economic disaster) led to intense psychic suffering and, on certain tragic occasions, to suicide.

In spite of my criticism of Lacan, I have returned continually to him, at least up until *The Imaginary Domain,* not only to explain a linguistic basis of the unconscious and the role of fantasies as a work of culture, but also to explain the continuing bar on the articulation and affirmation of feminine sexual difference. Of course, in a deconstructive reading of Lacan, the bar is not "real," but just because it is not real does not mean that it does not have power or cannot operate.

The utopian aesthetic project which I continue to affirm wholeheartedly is a feminism involved in an endless struggle to rearticulate and reaffirm both the divergent and not-yet-dreamed-of ways of setting forth lives as sexuate beings. This project insists that feminism has an aesthetic dimension, but also that this aesthetic dimension is inseparable from the way in which "qualities" are given to women. The theory of equality gives to women of all nationalities and "races" the right to represent their own meaning of their racial, national, and sexual identification. The symbolic aspect of feminism implicates renaming and reshaping our form of life. A symbolic project is inseparable from any materialist feminism because how the world comes to be materialized is in language (Butler 1993). Within the legal world, an obvious example is the renaming of obsessive behaviors that previously were considered the way of the world—sexual harassment and date rape are two examples. But in the work of artists, cultural workers, mothers, teachers, union organizers, and activists of every sort, there is also this attempt to rename, resymbolize, and reimagine the world.

As I have already argued, I not only recognize but also insist on a feminist analysis that clearly sees that any actual specificity that is given to feminine sexual difference is inherently and necessarily racialized, nationalized, and linguistically conditioned. It is in Morrison's *Sula* that I find best described my own version of utopia, which would start with the turning of the world upside down:

"Oh, they'll love me all right. It will take time, but they'll love me." The sound of her voice was as soft and distant as the look in her eyes. "After all the old women have lain with the teen-agers; when all the young girls have slept with their old drunken uncles; after all the black men fuck all the white ones; when all the white women kiss all the black ones; when the guards have raped all the jailbirds and after all the whores make love to their grannies; after all the faggots get their mothers' trim; when Lindbergh sleeps with Bessie Smith and Norma Shearer makes it with Stepin Fetchit; after all the dogs have fucked all the cats and every weathervane on every barn flies off the roof to mount the hogs . . . then there'll be a little love left over for me. And I know just what it will feel like." (1973, 145–46)

My argument is that the feminine within sexual difference must be affirmed rather than repudiated if there is to be "a little love left over" for a woman "with glory in her heart." I begin with the basic Derridian insight that one cannot simply neutralize dichotomies. For if we repudiate the feminine, we end by reinstating its evaluation as the degraded other that no person would want to be. Of course, what it means not to repudiate the feminine, and to affirm it, can be determined, discussed, and contested only within the specifics of any historical struggle.

The heart of my response to Felski is reflected in the title *Divergent Differences*. If I have a criticism of Felski, it is that she pigeonholes many of the thinkers whom she addresses. I did not recognize my own interpretations of the other thinkers she discussed in her essay.

For example, I read Chandra Mohanty's article "Under Western Eyes: Feminist Scholarship and Colonial Discourse" (1984) differently from Felski. Mohanty brilliantly demonstrates the way in which the representation of "third world women" completely eclipses the national and linguistic specificity of those women. She also effectively argues that this representation is grounded in the projection of these "third world women" as a kind of absolute other. As Mohanty argues throughout her essay, the "third world woman" is identified as the victim, as the one who needs help, as opposed to the "freer" "first world woman." Of course, the words *third* and *first* already imply a hierarchy. This representation erases the specificity of the actual national struggles and also erases the accomplishments, dignity, and history of feminism in other parts of the world as they have developed and made a contribution not only to feminist theory but also to feminist politics throughout history.

To develop my point, I want to take the example of Puerto Rico. Puerto Rico has a unique political history with the United States because of its continual standing as a commonwealth. The political struggle of Puerto Ricans for national and linguistic identity is inseparable from this "unique" relationship with the United States. Indeed, the United States also has been deeply and profoundly influenced in its engagement with the Spanish language and its place in our political culture with Puerto Rico, as it has not with other Hispanic cultures, precisely because of this relationship. Even the category "Hispanic" misrepresents many of the people in South America, because, of course, the Spanish language was brought here and imposed on the native populations at the time of imperialist invasion. If one identified Puerto Rican women as "third world," it would clearly erase their unique struggle within, and against, the United States and for their cultural and linguistic identity. "Third world women" are not just represented outside of their national context, they are also subjected to fantasies of themselves that undermine their historical accomplishments. Of course, this undermining, which translates itself into a view of the people, is inseparable from what I have called the symbolic underpinnings of imperialist domination.

Mohanty's work exemplifies the kind of work we need in order to expand the reach of the field of representation in which women can articulate their national and linguistic differences. Of course, there may be many times in which it will make sense for there to be unions and alliances of South American peoples and indeed of cultures and national identities that we think of as Hispanic. Nothing in Mohanty's work denies the desirability of such alliances—or the generalizations on which they may be based—in a particular political context any more than her article out of hand implies any critique of overarching theories of imperialist domination.

Felski reads a different theoretical ambition into Mohanty's work from the one I find there. Felski, at least to some extent, is addressing straw women. Thus, I do not find it surprising that I did not agree with her interpretations of the work of either Ien Ang or Rosi Braidotti.

I do not have much to write about Madonna. But I do want to remember Eva Perón. Eva Perón was a relentless fighter for the rights of women's suffrage in Argentina. She was determined that under her rule with Perón, women would be given the right to vote. They were. The year she died, twenty-one women were elected and seated for Parliament for the first time. We now have a makeup kit called "Evita." Her political accomplishments are not given credit in either the movie with the "icon" or in the advertisement that tries to convince women that we cannot live without lipstick. The makeup kit is an only-too-vivid reminder of how "third world women" are remembered . . . as . . . sexual objects that can be reduced to the components of a made-up face. Where could Eva Perón be "truly remembered"? Only in the imaginary domain. Certainly not in Hollywood.

REFERENCES

Brown, Wendy. 1995. *States of Inquiry: Essays on Power and Freedom in Late Modernity.* Princeton, N.J.: Princeton University Press.

Butler, Judith. 1993. *Bodies That Matter.* New York: Routledge.

———. 1995. "For a Careful Reading." In *Feminist Contentions: A Philosophical Exchange,* by Seyla Benhabib, Judith Butler, Drucilla Cornell, and Nancy Fraser, 127–43. New York: Routledge.

Caldwell, Paulette. 1991. "A Hair Piece: Perspectives on the Intersection of Race and Gender." *Duke Law Journal* (April): 365–96.

Chow, Rey. 1993. *Writing Diaspora: Tactics of Intervention in Contemporary Cultural Studies.* Bloomington: Indiana University Press.

Cornell, Drucilla. 1991. *Beyond Accommodation: Ethical Feminism, Deconstruction, and the Law.* New York: Routledge.

———. 1993a. "Pragmatism, Recollective Imagination, and Transformative Legal Interpretation." In Cornell, *Transformations: Recollective Imagination and Sexual Difference,* 23–44. New York: Routledge.

———. 1993b. "What Takes Place in the Dark." In Cornell, *Transformations: Recollective Imagination and Sexual Difference,* 170–94. New York: Routledge.

———. 1995. Introduction to Cornell, *The Imaginary Domain: Abortion, Pornography and Sexual Harrassment,* 3–27. New York: Routledge.

———. 1998. *At the Heart of Freedom: Sex, Equality and the Enactment of Personhood.* Princeton, N.J.: Princeton University Press.

Crenshaw, Kimberlé. 1988. "Race, Reform, and Retrenchment: Transformation and Legitimation in Anti-discrimination Law." *Harvard Law Review,* vol. 101 (May).

Fanon, Frantz. 1963. *The Wretched of the Earth.* New York: Grove.

Felski, Rita. "The Doxa of Difference." In *Signs* (Chicago) Autumn 1997, Vol. 23, #1, pp 1–21.

Hegel, Georg W.F. 1967. *The Philosophy of Right,* trans. T. M. Knox. London: Oxford University Press.

MacKinnon, Catharine. 1989. *Toward a Feminist Theory of the State.* Cambridge: Harvard University Press.

Mohanty, Chandra Talpade. 1984. "Under Western Eyes: Feminist Scholarship and Colonial Discourse." *Boundary* 2 13 (1): 333–57.

Morrison, Toni. 1970. *The Bluest Eye.* New York: Penguin.

———. 1973. *Sula.* New York: Knopf.

Obeycsekere, Gananath. 1990. *The Work of Culture: Symbolic Transformation in Psychoanalysis and Anthropology.* Chicago: University of Chicago Press.

Scott, Joan. 1996. *Only Paradoxes to Offer: French Feminists and the Rights of Man.* Cambridge: Harvard University Press.

Spelman, Elizabeth V. 1988. *Inessential Woman: Problems of Exclusion in Feminist Thought.* Boston: Beacon.

Taylor, Charles. 1989. *Sources of the Self: The Making of the Modern Identity.* Cambridge: Harvard University Press.

———. 1991. *The Ethics of Authenticity.* Cambridge: Harvard University Press.

3

Antiracism, Multiculturalism, and the Ethics of Identification

With Sara Murphy

Can multiculturalism be understood only as remedial, a bandage on the wounds of history? In the last several years, this has been the predominant understanding. Associated with the language of "recognition," multiculturalism as a stance and as a series of institutional initiatives has been defended as a compensation for the effects of imperialist domination, of which intractable structural racism is the most evident. Multiculturalism, so the argument goes, responds to the demands of minority cultures for recognition so long denied to them, with devastating effects on both a group and individual level. In perhaps the most prominent example, school curricula on all levels are being rewritten, the "canon" of texts in the human sciences being reevaluated and taken apart, so that minority cultures and those formerly silenced by imperialist policies can be represented to new generations of students. These initiatives are all well and good; they must be pursued, with all the work of scholarship and pedagogical research that this entails.

Frequently, however, the demand for recognition is articulated with the supposition of the authenticity of minority identity. That is, it seems integrally tied to the substantiation of an already formed or pregiven identity. In this essay, we seek to disconnect the claim to "authenticity" of identity from the demand for recognition. Multiculturalism, we argue, must be understood not simply as the acknowledgment of established and literalized identities, but as fundamental to the recognition of the equal dignity of all peoples.

Perhaps the most well-known discussion of recognition and multiculturalism belongs to Charles Taylor. In his essay "The Politics of Recognition," Taylor defends the rights of minority cultures to the equivalent evaluation of their significance to global history.[1] Taylor argues for what he terms "a start-

33

ing hypothesis with which we ought to approach the study of other cultures . . . Indeed, for a sufficiently different culture, the very understanding of what it is to be of worth will be strange and unfamiliar to us" (66–67). The presumption of equal value, for Taylor, is designed to negotiate between "the inauthentic and homogenizing demand for equal worth on the one hand and the self-immurement within ethnocentric standards on the other" (72). Later in this essay, we will return to a more detailed consideration of Taylor's position, but for the moment it is important for us to draw attention to the way in which Taylor grounds his discussion of cultures and values.

For Taylor, the moral imperative to recognition is associated with a conception of authenticity. Deriving his understanding of the concept from Lionel Trilling's *Sincerity and Authenticity*,[2] Taylor notes that in the modern West, authenticity is understood as carrying moral weight precisely insofar as it describes a relation to oneself: "it comes to be something we have to attain if we are to be true and full human beings"(28). Taylor, of course, is not alone in positing something like this authenticity as crucial for a defense of multiculturalism. What we want to suggest here, however, is that while the aspiration to authenticity may indeed be a vital component for some cultural movements and individuals within those movements, it cannot be the linchpin of a demand for recognition.

As Taylor himself points out, and as Trilling did before him, authenticity derives its moral force, whatever that force may be, from the assumption of an already constituted and stable identity. Recall the often-cited locus of such a conception, the opening moments of Rousseau's *Confessions*.[3] Rousseau's famous proclamation here locates morality in authenticity, insofar as authenticity is understood along the lines of being true to one's own feelings (*"I feel my own heart . . . I am made like no one else I have ever seen"*). Whatever else he may be, Rousseau has, he tells us, a stable identity—warts and all. For our contemporary discussions of multiculturalism, however, linking recognition to authenticity such that stability is presumed, implicitly or explicitly, raises some serious questions. Since recognition is understood to be something demanded of the dominant culture, we must be aware that there is the considerable risk that recognition will shade into an adjudication of authenticity. Recognition tied to authenticity implies that it is already-constituted identities that are at stake; in that case, new formations of minority cultures can fall through the cracks. Only the form of the minority culture acknowledged by the dominant culture—institutionally, socially, politically—will receive official status.

To remark, however, that in the contemporary world identities are in flux is not an arch theoretical observation. New nation-states arise and so do new cultural minorities within them. Political alliances create new identifications with demands for new representations of those identifications. In Great Britain, for example, many different minorities today take on the conscious identification as "Black" in order to make visible a common struggle against marginalization and oppression in this "postcolonial" era. This identification is dialogic; that is, it simultaneously works to resignify an identity degraded by the dominant culture at the same time as it does not purport to represent a homogeneous group with a shared history, language, or culture. Multiculturalism comes to seem a rather weak term for the complex relations between unconscious identifications, conscious alliances, and strategic affiliations that shape many people's experiences today.

The current discourse of recognition appears to beg the question: From whom? The notion of recognition, of course, finds its principal articulation in the celebrated "lordship and bondage" parable in the *Phenomenology of Mind*. There, the initial source of recognition at least is the lordship or master. However, this marks a stage in the development of the human spirit toward freedom, a freedom that for Hegel is achieved in the northern democracies. Clearly, minority cultures are not always, or even mostly, addressing their demands for recognition to the majority culture—at least if we are to understand recognition as a comprehension of the minority culture's identity. That freedom that Hegel saw achieved in the Western European democracies has been, after all, often written on the backs of precisely those minority cultures now struggling for their own national identities, cultural voices, and economic sustainability.[4]

Indeed "recognition" understood as a form of tolerance for and even interest in minority cultures can easily mask continued cultural hierarchization associated with Eurocentrism. Gayatri Spivak remarks that "the real demand is that when I speak from [the position of a Third World person] I should be listened to seriously; not with that kind of benevolent imperialism . . . which simply says that because I happen to be Indian or whatever . . . A hundred years ago it was impossible for me to speak, for the precise reason that makes it only too possible for me to speak in certain circles now."[5] What Spivak sees in contemporary intellectual life as a "suspicious reversal" was described in another context by Frantz Fanon as "mummification"; the future orientation of the culture as incarnated by its members is ignored in favor of only apparently respectful attention paid to a stilled and silent image, a synecdoche that is forever split off from the whole living world to which it refers. Fanon saw in this "a determination to objectify, to continue to imprison, to harden"[6] that should resonate only too forcefully with us today, as a commodified "globalism" flies off racks and shelves in the forms of hennaed lamps, sari silk curtains, and satin cheongsams.

Minority cultures do not want the nod of acceptance under the guise of tolerance for what the master sees as their established, stabilized differences. Nor are they necessarily demanding recognition in the sense that they should be received as having a legitimate, legible place in the majority culture. The demand of minority cultures can even be that they remain unreadable.[7] As a demand of right to the state, we think this can best be interpreted through the rubric of freedom and the recognition of equal dignity.

Thus, our argument reconceptualizes ethical and political struggles with our basic identifications so as to undermine any static or essentialist understandings of "identity politics." The demand for freedom must be understood as the affordance of the psychic and moral space necessary for groups and individuals to engage with and recreate their multiple identifications. The practice of literature is one place where we can see this work of re-creation, of what Toni Morrison has termed "rememory," quite vividly. In the poetry of Aimé Césaire, for instance, Africa becomes a place of the imagination; for this poet of the *négritude* movement the continent is no longer just a geographical place, nor is it comprehensible as a homeland to return to or a locus of recoverable identity. Instead, Africa becomes an elaborate and complex trope for imagining a future free of oppression.

At the core of our argument, then, is the insistence that all of us must have the potential to shape our identifications recognized by the state such that we—and not the state—are the source of the meaning they have to us, as individuals and as members of groups. The recognition of this freedom is integral to Taylor's elaboration of a new basis for equal dignity.

However, we also must return to an even more primordial conception of equal dignity. Colonization inevitably involves the identification of the colonized as below the boundary of the human—as beast, an animal, as savage. The colonized are other to humanity; humanity then has been substantiated by the figure of the colonizer and with this figure the most shocking forms of brutality. To challenge this figure would be to challenge the meaning that has been given to humanity.

The idea of humanity *as an idea*, Kant reminds us, is contentless.[8] Humanity, indeed, is just one example of the postulation of free creatures with the capacity of shaping their own moral destiny. Our argument is that the demand for multiculturalism is the freedom to struggle for a different humanity, for the possibility of living otherwise than through the cultural hierarchies imposed by colonialism.

In order to grasp fully the dangers of understanding recognition as a demand for the legitimation of an "authentic" minority culture by the majority, we need to carefully explore the relationships among culture, identity, and representation, which we will do in what follows through readings of Nathan Glazer and Anthony Appiah on multiculturalism. We need to examine what harm multiculturalism is meant to remedy, or whether multiculturalism should be articulated as protection against prior or potential injuries. As should already be evident, we do not defend multiculturalism on that basis. Through a reading of Toni Morrison's novel, *Jazz*, we attempt to show that the relationship between freedom and dignity demands a complex rearticulation of our basic racial, ethnic, and linguistic identifications including the cultural forms in which they are represented.

WHY MULTICULTURALISM NOW?

Nathan Glazer recently declared that "we are all multiculturalists now." For Glazer, the ethical mandate for us all to be multiculturalists stems from the failure of our society to effectively undermine racism. Given that racism seems to be so intractable, the least "we" can do is let racialized minorities affirm their own cultures—indeed, retreat into them as places of safety where they can confirm and develop their own representations of what, for example, it means to be Black. For Glazer, our failure to overcome racist treatment of African Americans has effectively undermined his own earlier dream that all of us citizens of the United States would come to see ourselves as one people who, despite our lived diversity in private life, would share enough of a public culture to agree on what was crucial for the education of our children. Although Glazer is aware that African Americans are not the only group that has been racialized, he believes that their treatment and their reaction to it is an exemplary instance of the political and ethical circumstance that has led many minority groups to insist on multiculturalism in the educational curriculum. Multiculturalism is explicitly understood as a response to the harm of racism. We must integrate into "our" curriculum who "they" tell "us" they are and have been.

But for him, this is an unfortunate if necessary reparative measure, insofar as it is divisive. It is divisive because it is based on the loss of our ability to identify as "Americans"[9] instead of through our differentiated cultural and religious identities. The identification "American," as Glazer understands it, is one that presumes assimilation of the many languages, religions, and cultural identities of its citizens. Glazer both proclaims and mourns the victory of multiculturalism as a compensation for the harm of racism. Would that it all could have gone differently in this country so racism could have been defeated and the good old ideal of assimilation could still be credibly embraced.

ARE CULTURE AND IDENTITY MISTAKENLY CONNECTED?

Glazer assumes that the assertion and acceptance of a minority culture can be the solution to racism. It is this assumption—that culture is a cure for racism—that K. Anthony Appiah rejects. Indeed, he argues that culture cannot be such a cure. We turn now to Appiah because the question he raises about the relationship of culture to racism has to be examined before we can turn to our own alternative justification for multiculturalism other than the one offered by Glazer.

In his recent writing, Appiah has questioned what he sees as the excessive use of the term "culture," arguing that most of the social identities that make up our diverse society do not actually have independent cultures that need to be represented in school curricula.[10] What is ultimately at stake for Appiah is our freedom to create ourselves and free ourselves from tightly scripted identities. We share his concern with freedom, although, as will be seen, we do not agree with him that we must disconnect culture and identity in order to protect it.

Prior to his attempts to disentangle culture and identity in the name of freedom, Appiah argues that what are frequently coded as "cultural identities" are in fact social ones and cannot be understood as independent cultures. Appiah recognizes that ethnic groups rather than racial groups have at least historically defined their distinctive identity through the members' attribution of cultural uniqueness. But, according to Appiah, even this attribution of cultural uniqueness comes post facto; the uniqueness of cultural identity is only truly constituted retroactively, as members seek to maintain their distinctiveness by highlighting cultural attributes as "theirs." A strength of Appiah's insight from our standpoint is that it presents cultural identity as formed through recollective imagination.[11]

We mean by this phrase that even more traditionally conceived assumptions of identity—social as well as cultural—always involve the imagination as they rework the meaning of the past. Although Appiah does not highlight the role of the imagination in the post facto attribution of cultural identities, we believe that his emphasis on their constructed and imaginative nature is integral to his desire to disconnect culture from identity so as to promote freedom. If cultural identity is at least in part the result of imaginative agency, then this can show that the individuals and groups who are attributing the culture to themselves as part of its further development are doing so as an exercise of their freedom. Identities formed through recollective imagination have the potential to be held lightly by the individual because they are already formed through an imaginative effort to envision what they are, how they should remain, or instead be reshaped. Still, Appiah accords some traditional ethnic groups the kind of identity that could potentially recollect itself through common cultural markers. In modern "America" however, most ethnic groups have lost the distinctive identity that makes such a quest for the reinforcement of a common culture either possible or ethically desirable. Most ethnic groups have lost the potential precisely because they have met the ideal of assimilation that Glazer argues has been available to immigrant and minority groups that have not been racialized.

Appiah uses "Hispanics" as an example. According to Appiah, "Hispanic" culture has thinned out as this ethnic group has been effectively assimilated following the traditional immigrant pattern of the third generation losing the Spanish language.[12] Appiah's point here is that the assimilation of minority ethnic groups into American society leaves them little motivation to maintain their cultural distinctiveness even if they remain a recognizable group with a social identity. The idea of social identity is expressive of the diluted and relational reality of the cultural life of these groups once they are assimilated into the larger American society. The traditional view of culture and identity, as at least maintained in the private zone of the family and neighborhood, is gone. For Appiah, ethnic groups have become more like gender identities. Women may be distinct from men, but they do not have a different culture. What these groups are assimilated into is a social and political culture, not a common national culture.

For Appiah this dilution is a good thing, because it keeps us from being engulfed by ethnic identity. Liberal multiculturalism would teach us about the diverse social identities that currently make up the population of the U.S. This program should be consistent with the liberal emphasis on individual freedom. As Appiah explains, "Nevertheless, contemporary multiculturalists are right in thinking that a decent education will teach children about the various social identities around them. First because each child has to negotiate the creation of his or her individual identity, using these collective identities as one but only one of the resources; second, so that all can be prepared to deal with one another respectfully in a common civic life."[13]

To this reasonable form of multiculturalism, Appiah contrasts another sort which is not consistent with individual freedom: "but," he writes, "there is another side of multiculturalism that wants to force children to live within separate spheres defined by the common culture of their race, religion, or ethnicity."[14]

Appiah finds one cause of illiberal multiculturalism in nostalgia for ethnic groups that did share a "pervasive culture."[15] He also argues that there is no common culture that is "American," indeed there could not be and should not be any such culture. One of the good things about the United States is that it does not try to capture its citizens into a common culture thus taking away from them or at least limiting the field of possible identifications within the spread of social diversity. In one sense, then, Appiah is insisting that an American liberal curriculum would naturally be multicultural precisely because so many divergent peoples have come to this country and made their histories, traditions, and languages part of this culture and these have in turn been reshaped by their integration into the United States. In the vaunted homogenization of U.S. society, Appiah sees no loss for ethnic and racial groups who no longer have a culture which marks them as a cultural group distinct from the dominant social and political liberal culture; this is seen instead as the necessary condition for the freeing of the individual. Unlike Glazer, Appiah is also not mourning the decline or lack of a common American culture.

Appiah further argues that there are no racialized cultures, and that more specifically there is no African American culture. For Appiah it is "cultural geneticism"[16] to attribute to the members of any group, simply because of race or nationality, the cultural artifacts that are rightly or wrongly associated with that group. Since for Appiah there is no unique African American culture—in the sense of shared language, values, practices, and meanings—it is necessarily cultural geneticism to argue that African American cultural identity should be taught in the schools as if all African American students could claim Toni Morrison, for example, as of their own culture even if they have not read her.

Appiah's point here is ultimately ethical. He is not just describing what has happened to most ethnic groups in the United States. He is also calling for an understanding of culture as individual cultivation. Culture, for Appiah, is an ideal and, indeed, an ideal of character development. Thus, freedom and cultivation come to be tied together; we can focus on what is truly important in life by educating ourselves so that we are not too tightly scripted by un-examined identifications. This reaching for freedom is the first aspect of what Appiah means by cultivation.

To be encompassed by a single culture is to be sunk in either unwelcome or narrowly circumscribed identifications. To understand cultural identity this way is to make it and freedom oppositional poles. His ideal subject, "the cosmopolitan patriot,"[17] is free to reject or absorb whatever cultural artifacts or experiences come his way due to the coincidence of national and lin-guistic origin. Free to cultivate his subjectivity, Appiah's cosmopolitan ideal is unapologetically grounded in the capacity to refuse any but "recreational" identities that do not tie him down. But the cosmopolitan patriot also has a responsibility to cultivate himself in the sense of immersing himself in the best of what art has to offer us. This responsibility to educate oneself is the second aspect of what Appiah means by cultivation.

As Appiah explains, "no African-American is entitled to greater concern because he is descended from a people who created jazz or produced Toni Morrison. Culture is not the problem and it is not the solution."[18] Illiberal multiculturalism involves us in pandering to the lazy and undermines our commitment to cultivation, a commitment that should be expressed in the education of the young.

MORRISON ON JAZZ, BLACKNESS, AND THE ETHICS OF IDENTIFICATION

But is Appiah right that culture should be disconnected from identity? Be-fore turning to this question, we at least need to consider that Appiah is working with a concept of identity as constituted through both abjection and disavowal. This is why he is so suspicious of heavy-handed identity politics, no matter who practices them. Although Appiah's concern is with the freedom of the person, this concept of identity potentially justifies the devaluation of minority cultures and other more graphic violations of them. We need then, at least to explore, the possibility of other modes of identification—including those that are affirmations of cultural identity. To do so, we now turn to the work of Toni Morrison, with particular attention to her novel, *Jazz*.[19]

Much of Toni Morrison's work is concerned both formally and thematically with the relations between identity, abjection, disavowal, and violence. Morrison's *Jazz* in particular uses a scene of violence, the murder of a young woman and the disfigurement of her corpse, to trace the intricacy of abjection and identification. What her literary work does that discursive treatments cannot do is offer both a vision of the complexity of the social-historical-cultural identifications and a hope that there are other modes of identification that allow us to come to terms with the figures that haunt us.

For Appiah, the fact that one can produce a genealogy of the term "Black"—demonstrating the historical and geographical contingency of the term over at least three centuries of Western cultural and political history—leads him to argue not only that African Americans have in effect no culture, but that Black identity does not really exist.[20] In fact, he raises a question about identification and the kind of status Black identity might have; Morrison raises a similar question, but answers it rather differently. Throughout *Jazz,* she draws attention to the excessively scripted narratives of identity in which the characters are caught. But, contra Appiah, her fiction does not suggest that the constructed quality of identifications (of "blackness," of jazz, of female sexuality) permit them to be dismantled easily and quickly, nor that basic identifications are necessarily imprisoning. In order to understand this more clearly, the complexity of the concept of identification Morrison is using needs to be discussed.

In *Jazz*, Morrison tells the story of a love triangle in 1920s Harlem that ends in violence. Fifty-something Joe Trace cheats on his wife, Violet, with a "yellow-skinned girl," the teenager Dorcas, whom he ultimately kills. Violet breaks in on Dorcas's funeral and cuts the face of the dead girl as she lies in her coffin. Understanding this related pair of incidents is the task of the narrator of the novel and the reader as well. Though the narrator begins the story with a sniff of certainty—"Sth, I know that woman"—what is thrown into question throughout the novel is what the narrator, as well as characters and reader, can and do actually know.

This larger question is posed through the narrator and characters' engagement with jazz. Knowing jazz not only comes to be a way of engaging with otherness, but also and in particular a way of engaging the otherness inhabiting the self. The one thing the narrator knows at the beginning of *Jazz* is that jazz is "Black." The narrator's initial self-certainty comes from an unconscious identification with Dorcas's guardian, Alice Manfred, who has a definite take on "all that jazz" in which Joe, Dorcas, and Violet become entangled. Like the fear-driven Alice, the narrator's stability turns on the naturalized attribution of jazz as Black "race music" that is somehow responsible for sexual and social disorder.

Alice waited this time, in the month of March, for the woman with the knife. The woman people called Violent now because she had tried to kill what lay in the coffin. She had left notes under Alice's door every day beginning in January—a week after the funeral—and Alice Manfred knew the kind of Negro that couple was: the kind she trained Dorcas away from. The embarrassing kind. The husband shot; the wife stabbed. Nothing. Nothing her niece did or tried could equal the violence done to her. And where there was violence wasn't there also vice? Gambling. Cursing. A terrible and nasty closeness. Red dresses. Yellow shoes. And, of course, race music to urge them on.[21]

This "race music," according to Alice Manfred and the narrator who identifies with her, is responsible for the mess Dorcas got herself into. But it is also responsible or at least in some way directly associated with Black people acting out in the streets. "Alice thought the lowdown music (and in Illinois it was worse than here) had something to do with the silent Black women and men marching down Fifth Avenue to advertise their anger over two hundred dead in east St. Louis, two of whom were her sister and brother-in-law, killed in the riots. So many whites killed the papers would not print the number."[22] Alice Manfred identifies jazz as the problem and seeks to protect her niece Dorcas against it. But this music cannot be contained. It keeps breaking in and breaking out. While her aunt "worries about how to keep the heart ignorant of the hips and the head in charge of both," Dorcas is listening for the clarinet, the piano, the voice of the blues singer. Authorities have told Alice Manfred what to make of this music, that it is not as troubling as she is making it out to be, but she is not reassured:

> She knew from sermons and editorials that it wasn't real music—just colored folks stuff; harmful, certainly; embarrassing, of course; but not real not serious. Yet Alice Manfred swore she heard a complicated anger in it; something hostile that disguised itself as flourish and roaring seduction. But the part she hated most was its appetite. Its longing was its appetite. Its longing for the bash, the slit; a kind of careless hunger for a fight or a red ruby stickpin for a tie—either would do. It faked happiness, faked welcome, but it did not make her feel generous, this juke joint, barrel hooch, tonk house music. It made her hold her in the pocket of her apron to keep from smashing it through the glass pane to snatch the world in her fist and squeeze the life out of it for doing what it did and did and did to her and everybody else she knew or knew about. Better to close the windows and the shutters, sweat in the summer heat of a silent Clifton place apartment than to risk a broken window or a yelping that might not know where or how to stop.[23]

What does Alice Manfred hear in this music? What is it that needs so desperately to be shut out, so shut out that she must box herself into a steaming, airless apartment alone in order not to hear it?

The answer is not simple, for what Morrison is attempting to represent is not that jazz itself is a threat to Alice Manfred's person. Rather, Morrison's aim in this novel is to articulate the conditions under which jazz is audible. The music that Alice Manfred hears is bound to representations of "her and everyone she knew about"; a series of images of African American life as angry, appetite driven, sexualized in the extreme. Jazz is mediated for Alice through news reports from the white press, through "authorities" proclaiming it unimportant, a lesser musical form. Thus, it is for Morrison a trope not only for Black culture in twenties Harlem, but also for the way in which that culture comes to be mediated to its own constituents, of which Alice Manfred, in all her repression, in all her rage, is one possible representative.

By no accident, then, is Alice Manfred the guardian of young Dorcas, the niece whom she raises under the iron fist of repression and who breaks free to head out into Prohibition-era speakeasies and jazz clubs. The "under the sash" culture of Prohibition Harlem functions as a figure for the conditions under which African American culture can be represented—and in the figure of Alice, we might say can represent itself to itself—in this novel. Dorcas, dressing up and sneaking out at night with her friend Felice, is emblematic of all those things that Alice comes to hear in the music; she is the girl of the "flourish and the roaring seduction" under which is rage, the rage that Alice can't bear to recognize inhabiting her, too. Everywhere in this novel there are avatars of wild women, armed women, sexualized women, violent women who cut and bite. In her airless apartment, Alice Manfred tries to shut them all out.

There is a feminine persona that comes with this "colored" music; the call of all that wildness that echoes in the music is the stuff of disavowal out of which the narrator draws the character of Alice Manfred. At the center of the narrator's discourse is the ultimate representation of this feminine persona, "Wild," Joe Trace's purported deserting mother. Wild is the mother who may or may not be his; Joe never finds out with certainty. Wild functions in this narrative allegorically as both the site and figure of abjection: A feral woman who lives in a cave near the West Virginia town where Joe grows up, Wild gains her name when she tries to bite a man who has helped her through childbirth. As a quasi-mythological point of origin, Wild represents both the feminine personae in their different manifestations across the narrative as well as the impossibility of knowing what is beyond those personae. Like Alice Manfred's idea of jazz, Wild can only be figured insofar as she is outside the conventional frameworks of identification provided by the structures of law and order.

By breaking into the funeral and slashing Dorcas's face, Violet too exceeds these frameworks of identification; the narrator begins to describe the slashing Violet as "that Violet," while some of the characters refer to her, post-stabbing, as "Violent." What is at stake in this central event of the narrative, this bizarre scene of excess, the defacement of a corpse by a Violet who is no longer her regular self? What does "that Violet" see in the dead face of her husband's teenaged lover, the inanimate "cream at the top of the milkpail face," framed by hair that probably never needed straightening? This whitened girl is what has shut Violet out of her own world of sense. Dorcas has to be marked as other, as the one the narrator cannot identify with. In her attempt to draw out "that Violet" who picks up the knife and cuts Dorcas, the narrator has to confront the ultimate figure of the "savage" woman, the woman known only as "Wild." Her risk of identification with this most blackened of all women, Wild, shakes up her story and allows her to begin again, through a re-evaluation of the imposed identifications that had blocked her relationship to the characters as other than kinds of "colored" people.

The paradigmatic Black character in this novel is the racialized and sexualized figure of "Wild," the possible illegitimate mother of Joe Trace who lives in a cave in the West Virginia countryside. Toward the end of the novel, the narrator returns to Wild, only now the figure of the feral woman is no longer envisioned as alien and fear-inspiring. Describing Wild's home, a silent cave full of traces of a life lived and a history marked by her complicated engagements with the world around her, the narrator asserts:

> I'd love to close myself in the peace left by the woman who lived there and scared everybody. Unseen because she knows better than to be seen. After all, who would see her a playful woman who lived in a rock. Who could without fright? Of her looking eyes looking back? I wouldn't mind why should I? She has seen me and is not afraid of me. She hugs me. Understands me. Has given me her hand. I am touched by her. Released in secret. Now I know.[24]

No longer afraid of her "eyes looking back," the narrator asserts a kind of knowledge—but interestingly enough, it is not in terms that replicate exactly the opening of the narrative. The scoffing "I know that woman" of the first page has been replaced by a different kind of knowing at the end. Yet if this is one way of articulating an identification as Black, as female, it is certainly not one that follows from a tightly scripted identity. In fact, this knowing with which *Jazz* ends is one that breaks out of the tightly scripted stories of identity that are everywhere put into play in the novel.

Jazz is a daring novel, because it proceeds through the narrator's own acknowledgment of her disavowal of jazz in the elaboration of her original identification with Alice Manfred, a point of view which has already condemned the characters to play out a limited script. Morrison is seeking to make identification explicit as an operative force in narrative, since it necessarily designates and delineates it as a character. She is using identification in at least two senses. First, by making explicit the narrator's transformation of perspective, Morrison is emphasizing the ethical force of identification in narrative fiction: Precisely insofar as the characters are culturally marked out so that they can be knowable, they become unknowable/racialized stereotypes. In *Jazz*, then, the very conception of character as clearly designated, continuous, and unified is thrown into question; the time-honored conventions of realist representation are shown to be precisely that, conventions.

Second, Morrison is engaged in working through the identification of jazz as a Black cultural form and this identification as it in turn sets the cultural parameters in which the authorial perspective can be articulated. In Appiah's terms, the narrator's victory in her storytelling is to reach the viewpoint where her characters are not so tightly scripted by what kind of "colored" people they are as disclosed through their relationship to jazz. For instance, the character of Dorcas is represented in terms of a variety of "scripts"—the light-skinned seductress, the wayward teenager, the disobedient daughter, the "jazzy" one. But at the end, it is revealed that she, like everyone else in the narrative, exceeds the identifications others use to name her. We learn that she in effect let herself bleed to death the night of the shooting for reasons that are never clear. Dorcas, who seemed barely more than a plot device, turns out to have been unfathomable. The narrator manages to unbind her characters from the networks in which racial stereotypes are constituted and suggest what it means to individuate them.

That the musical form, jazz, is itself both subject to imposed identifications and constantly exceeding them is the deep background against which the novel works. This background is that jazz is "Black" in two senses: first, it is a cultural form created by African American people; and second, as associated with African American culture it has been "blackened," becoming a metonymic reminder of a whole series of fears and fantasies to the dominant culture. Anyone who hears the music is going to be engaging with their own identifications or dis-identifications with the complex meaning and unconscious fantasy with which jazz has been imbued. White readers, African American readers—all readers—must engage with this process if they are to read the novel. Since the narrator is involved in a series of disavowals and identifications, the reader is obligated to engage explicitly with them as well.

The secret is that no one knows in advance what it means to be released from the identifications that lock us in to telling pre-scripted stories of the sexually voracious teenager, the shooting husband, and the knifing woman, particularly when all readers will know in advance that the characters are all identified as Black and scripted by a Black woman writer. Novel reading, Morrison's tale reminds us, is a practice closely bound to identifications through character; *Jazz* pushes its reader to acknowledge those identifications that bind character to reader with the aim of both releasing the grip of that process and encouraging a recognition of the process itself as it does so.

This is hardly a novel that engages in what have come to be called identity politics. The narrator does not come simply to attribute positive value to jazz and blackness. There is no simple inversion of Alice Manfred's early terror of jazz music where "just hearing it was like violating the law."[25] The point is not to whitewash Black women with knives or to tame jazz. The ethical injunction of *Jazz*, if it can and should be read that way, is the one we as readers share with the narrator. We are called to confront our own racialized identifications in part as an engagement with the response to jazz as Black music. But we can only begin to undertake an ethics of identification, which is what the narrator undertakes, if we start with the recognition that jazz is Black and that the narrator was at least right about one thing when she spoke through the voice of Alice Manfred: This is a music meant to be taken seriously.

As Morrison has explained again and again, fidelity to Black cultural difference drives her work. But this fidelity to cultural difference seems to take the form elaborated by Homi Bhabha.

> The very possibility of cultural contestation, the ability to shift the ground of knowledges or to engage in the 'war of position' marks the establishment of new forms of meaning, and strategies of identification. Designations of cultural difference interpolate forms of identity which, because of their continual implication in other symbolic systems are always incomplete or open to cultural translation.[26]

What it means for jazz to be received culturally as Black—the very complexity of that meaning—is what allows Morrison to represent Black cultural difference as distinct from the scary forms that her narrator initially gives it, forms that have already reflected its shaping by white authority. When Appiah asserts that there is no African American culture, he is returning us to his ideal of culture as cultivation, as a quasi-Arnoldian repository of "the best that has been known and thought." Morrison is using a broader concept of culture, which makes central the ethics and politics necessarily involved in the development and perpetuation of a cultural identity. Rather than a just mode of acculturation or an array of objects and texts that acculturate subjects in their consumption, for Morrison "culture" signifies the day-to-day practices of people living among each other in specific communities and institutions and how these practices are experienced.

We'll recall that Anthony Appiah has insisted that culture is not the problem and not the solution to racism in contemporary U.S. life. But under this broader definition of culture, the elaboration of culture difference and the new strategies and positions it makes possible for identification can be understood as part both of the problem and of the solution to racism in two senses. First, racism proceeds in part through the devaluation of the culture of those who are racialized. Jazz itself in some of its initial reception by white listeners showed how racial fantasies loaded down the meaning that was given to that music.[27] In *Playing in the Dark*, Morrison describes exposure to the music of Louis Armstrong as the event that drives the autobiographical heroine of Marie Cardinal's novel *Words To Say It* into therapy.[28] Morrison queries: "Would an Edith Piaf concert or a Dvorak composition have had the same effect? Certainly either could have. I was interested, as I had been for a long time, in the way Black people ignite critical moments of discovery or change or emphasis in literature not written by them."[29] Morrison is clearly addressing the need to render blackness and the actual art of African Americans visible in its conscious engagement and structural involvement with American literature. This insistence on representation is itself a demand for antiracist correctives. The first antiracist corrective consists of what Morrison describes as the "contemplation of this Black presence which is central to any understanding of our national literature," which "should not be permitted to hover at the margins of the literary imagination."[30] The second corrective is the development of a theory of literature, and pedagogical approaches coherent with it, for school curricula that would truly value African American literature in its cultural difference. Such a theory would grapple with African American literature "based on its culture, its history, and the artistic strategies the works employ to negotiate the world it inhabits."[31]

Of course, the advocacy of this program of basic antiracist correctives turns on a central disagreement with Appiah. Morrison not only believes that there is an African American culture; she explicitly identifies her work as part of it. What does it mean for Morrison to identify herself as a Black writer? By analyzing the opening lines of several of her novels Morrison seeks to demonstrate what constitutes the art of a Black writer:

> The points I have tried to illustrate are that my choices of language (speakerly, aural, colloquial), my reliance for full comprehension on codes embedded in black culture, my effort to effect immediate coconspiracy and intimacy (without any distancing, explanatory framework) as well as my (failed) attempt to shape a silence while breaking it are attempts (many unsatisfactory) to transfigure the complexity and wealth of Afro-American culture into a language worthy of that culture.[32]

For Morrison, African American culture is expressed in her struggle to be faithful to its richness and complexity. The meaning of a people's culture is constantly being recreated by those who engage it—listen to jazz—and by those artists who identify with it and represent it as what makes up the constitutive basis of their art.

But culture and identity also are connected in another way. Culture is not only presented as artifacts but also as the presentation of personae. In *Jazz*, this re-identification with the Black feminine persona, represented by Wild, opens up a different script for the characters because it opens up the narrator to a different story. The articulation and representation of cultural personae both in art and in life are some of the ways we open up possibilities that allow us to free ourselves from the tight scripts we associate with devaluation of ways of being for the human beings that are identified both by themselves and others as belonging to racialized and marginalized groups. Appiah believes that in order to free oneself from too tightly scripted identities one must proceed through the disassociation of identity and culture. We would argue that it is only through the representation of culturally available personae, which through this reformulation then shift their meaning, that we struggle toward freedom.

In Morrison's work, the ethics involved in identification are classic in at least two senses: first, how one comes to know oneself is part of a normative quest for self-knowledge; and second, how one can and should identify with that which the dominant culture has abjected is part of the struggle to end the social structures of oppression that mark us all in a thoroughly racialized society. Both Joe and Violet Trace come to understand their attachment to each other differently by coming to terms with lost love objects and the fantasies of those objects—fantasies of loss itself. This constitutes an ethics, both as a practice of self-responsibility and as an encounter with how we come to articulate who we are through our identifications, which take us beyond ourselves as individuals precisely because we can never be completely in control of the social and symbolic meanings of racial and ethnic categories.

There is a sense in which we, as joint authors, can be called to identify as white and Anglo, as well as many other identifications, because these categories continue not only to represent privilege but also to enforce it. To deny that we are part of the privileged group, then, is not only false; it is, more importantly to us, unethical. The fluidity of categories of race and ethnic identity in no way takes away from the social reality that ethically demands that we confront the meanings of our own identifications. To identify as white and Anglo is a "salutary estrangement,"[33] an effort to see how we are seen and the privileges that inhere in being recognized as part of the dominant race, ethnic, and language group. This is not a so-called politically correct gesture toward guilt, but rather an effort to struggle against the rationalizations that are inherent in the denial that privilege brings with it. No one is above race, ethnicity, and linguistic background. No one is simply human.

To argue that you can reshape an identity and that none of us are entirely captured by our identifications indicates the freedom that we have associated with the work of cultural politics—but it does not mean that we are free to be anything we want to be, because these categories take on symbolic lives of their own with material consequences. Certain identifications clearly mark out a group that is devalued. Discrimination is a reality and, indeed, had the effect of fixing racial and ethnic categories. Racialization and socially enforced grouping of individuals into an identity are inseparable, as Appiah continually reminds us. The fight against racism and discrimination cannot proceed by denial of categories that have made race so determinative of a person's fate. For some identifications, their meaning is politically and ethically capable of re-articulation. For others, for example in the case of whiteness, which paradoxically presents itself so as to erase its particularity, the move is not simply towards re-representing whiteness and European heritage, but by particularizing it. By making whiteness appear as an identification, whiteness not only becomes visible, it becomes separable from the ideal of humanity that it has come to stand in for in Eurocentrism.

Disavowal that we are all shaped by our identifications has led to the assumption that we are free to choose between identity politics or some other form of politics that resists the appeal to identity. For us, the ethics of identification demands that the person recognize both the political and the ethical significance of the ways in which she articulates her identity as well as the socially enforced meanings that create it. If, for instance, we simply said that being white and Anglo had no meaning to us, we would be denying the hierarchies that inform our social and political world. What is not noted cannot be changed; thus by recognizing that, like it or not, we are white and Anglo because we are inevitably shaped by how we are seen, we are ethically respecting the need to call attention to the hierarchies as a first step in calling for their change.

The political contest over the meaning of identifications, including how ethnicities and national identities can be reformed so as to respect the differences among the members who take on that identity as their own, takes place within a specific context of both imperialism and racism. This is why, for us, it is more appropriate to think in terms of a struggle over the meanings of identifications rather than in terms of playful relations to our self-representations. To describe oneself as white and Anglo is an ethical and political decision, but one that is necessary precisely because of the inegalitarian structures of a racist society. In this sense, we are not in any way advocating that the political insistence upon such identification either reduces us to it as a descriptive matter or captures either one of us in all her complexity. Our point is that our freedom to reform our identifications takes place within parameters that we must also be ethically called upon to recognize as we try to articulate who we are.

TWO REPRESENTATIONS OF CULTURAL IDENTITY

When blacks discovered that they had shaped or become a culturally formed race, and that it had specific and revered difference, suddenly they were told there is no such thing as race, biological or cultural, that matters and that genuinely intellectual exchange cannot accommodate it. In trying to understand the relationship between race and culture, I am tempted to throw my hands up. It always seemed to me that the people who invented the hierarchy of "race" when it was convenient for them ought not to be the ones to explain it away, now that it does not suit their purposes. But there is culture and both gender and race inform and are informed by it. Afro-American culture exists, and though it is clear (and becoming clearer) how it has responded to Western culture, the instances where and means by which it has shaped Western culture are poorly recognized or understood.[34]

Morrison's wry comment draws attention to the limits of current models of thinking about race, culture, and identity. We have suggested that those models are represented on the one hand through the cosmopolitanism argued for by Anthony Appiah and on the other through the mournful accession to multiculturalism discussed by Nathan Glazer. In the current landscape, we find either an injunction to postmodern, postnational identities or a conception of identity that insists upon a rigidly referential relation between individual and cultural. In both cases, the complexity of identifications as they take form and shift in the histories of individuals and cultures is foreclosed. As a musical form then, jazz with its codes of improvisation that constantly rework the relations of individual to group and group to cultural legacies—the rhythms and structures of ancient African musics—is an apt trope, a beginning point for a rethinking of the relations between culture and identity.

But if we do rethink it this way, what we come to is not a proclamation on what identities are or should be. Instead, we come to questions about the conditions under which identifications can be developed, constituted, and represented. The language of recognition that has shaped so much of current debate has much to offer in this regard, due to Charles Taylor's rightly influential article. However, we would want to shift the object of that recognition from legitimation of the value of pre-given cultural identities to identities that demand for equal dignity on the part of cultural minorities. When the demand is made as a matter of right, we would argue that we should usually turn to the equal dignity of persons, but that does not mean that such a demand should not include group differentiation rights when that is the best articulation of the right at stake.[35] What is at stake here is the acceptance of what Taylor calls "deep diversity," a diversity that will inevitably result if the state publicly recognizes the freedom of minorities to reconstitute themselves, including the reconstitution of the significance of their cultural difference.

Taylor himself seems to favor this emphasis on dignity, although he gives it a particular meaning. For him, equal dignity turns on the potential to shape an identity. Recall that Taylor can be legitimately read as if the struggle for recognition is in effect a struggle for the expression of authentic identity.[36] While Taylor does sometimes write in that language, since for him the injury to human beings is at least related to the authenticity of group identity being undermined by the degradation imposed upon the minority group by the majority culture or group, his central argument need not be connected to any idea of an underlying authentic identity that minority groups are seeking to have recognized. He ultimately rests his argument on an appeal to our shared dignity as persons, understood to be free in a particular way, rather than on an appeal to the recognition of an authentic identity.

For Taylor, and in this we agree with him, this Kantian-inspired idea of dignity turns us back to a potential that human beings have to shape and form an identity. So far in this essay, we have tried to articulate the complexity of what this freedom might mean as it allows us to shape an ethics of identification in our thoroughly racialized culture. It is not simply the capacity to form an identity that is the basis of our dignity, but also our capacity to make ethical sense out of these identities. We would even dare to interpret Frantz Fanon's humanism as a highly specific appeal to dignity. The dignity of the colonized is rooted in the recollective imagination that allows for a people to shape themselves into a movement through which the struggle for a freedom can be articulated. The truth of an identity is found not by testing the authenticity of its claim to existence but by participating in the ethics and politics it makes possible. As Fanon puts it, "universality resides in this decision to recognize and accept the reciprocal relativism of different cultures, once the colonial status is irreversibly excluded".[37] Universality turns then on the recognition of the equal dignity that includes the colonized as part of humanity with "culture." The animalization of the colonized is inseparable, as Fanon constantly reminds us, from the presumption that the colonized are without culture, which is why they purportedly need to be cultivated by the so-called "civilized" white man. This presumption, of course, can only be made true by the violent shattering of the people's culture. For the colonizer, as Fanon states, "The enslavement, in the strictest sense, of the native population is the prime necessity. For this its systems of reference have to be broken. Expropriation, spoilation, raids, objective murder, are matched by the sacking of cultural patterns, or at least condition such sacking. The social panorama is destructured; values are flaunted, crushed, emptied."[38] It is not then, as Appiah would have that culture is a cure for racism. The point is somewhat more complex than that. Crucial to the brutal oppression of the colonized is the attempt to crush their culture as part of excluding them from the reach of humanity. It's affirmation, then, is part of the resistance against this exclusion. "Reciprocal relativism of different cultures" is impossible without some version of cultural assertion, because it is part of the insistence on equal dignity, an insistence that rejects the universalization of European culture as "culture."

If we are to recognize, on the basis of equal dignity, the right of persons to shape their identifications into an identity they claim as their own, then we cannot seek to take back with one hand what we give with the other. We can't with any moral consistency ask that those who identify with a minority group to value their identification so as to be consistent with certain goals or visions of the larger hegemonic society; whether such consistency is articulated as postmodern cosmopolitanism or as a form of identity politics, it ultimately reproduces ethnic and cultural identities as instrumentalized, deployable to meet a wider notion of the good.

The cultural critic, Stuart Hall illustrates this point when he discusses the ways in which some Black artists in England have defined their project as one of cultural discovery rather than the articulation of a fully developed political positionality. He acknowledges that there have been at least two broadly understood moments in this process, one addressing the politics of representation and another the relations of representation. Taking up "cultural identity" in terms of the politics of representation, Hall writes the following:

> one shared culture, a sort of collective, one true self hiding inside the many other, more superficial or artificially imposed selves which people with a shared history and ancestry hold in common. Within the terms of this definition, our cultural identities reflect the common historical experiences and shared cultural codes which provide us as one people with stable unchanging and continuous frames of reference and meaning beneath the shifting divisions and vicissitudes of our actual history. This oneness underlying all the other, more superficial differences is the truth, the essence of Caribbeanness.[39]

This understanding of cultural identity is one form of recollective imagination that allows people to emerge and claim their shared reformed history. Such a commitment to articulate what might be shared by marginalized and oppressed groups is often an important part of the struggle for cultural identification and the movements that are formed through them. Crucially, the artists in Hall's example address themselves to their communities. Bringing what Hall here calls the "oneness . . . the essence of Caribbeanness" to representation is in part an act of displacing representations of Caribbean people and culture made and circulated in the dominant culture; works that pit themselves against stereotypes and imposed invisibility are not directed, at least primarily, at the dominant culture, since it is precisely the dominant culture's conscription or occultation of the minority culture that this art seeks to fight. Indeed, one misunderstanding of the claims made by minority cultures for their representation is that they are literalized. One aspect of this literalization is the failure to understand the specific use of literary language to evoke the meaning of identity. As Benita Parry has convincingly argued, the literalization of movements, including that of *négritude,* stems from the failure to grapple with it as in part a literary practice, explicitly influenced by surrealism. In many of his poems, Césaire celebrates the defiance involved in his recollection of himself as a nègre, a recollection of himself which is clearly also an act of the imagination. To quote Parry:

> This concrete coming to consciousness was realized by Césaire as a poet; and because many of the writings of Négritude are open to some or all of the charges made against it as an ideological tendency, any argument that as a literary practice it performed a textual struggle for self-representation in which the indeterminacy of language ruptured fixed configurations, invented a multivalent blackness, and wrenched "Africa" out of its time-bound naming and into new significations, is most readily made by referring to his over-determined and polysemic poetry. Although made possible, as he concedes, by surrealism, this exceeded the influence of European modes and violated its forms in what Arnold calls a "sophisticated hybridization, corrosion and parody" of western traditions.[40]

What minority cultures must do to represent themselves against such con-scription and occultation depends a good deal on the circumstances in which a given cultural group finds itself. For example, Hall points out that *négritude* was a vital political movement for its time and place. Thus, al-though Hall clearly advocates what he terms a "new ethnicities"[41] represen-tation of cultural identity, his insistence on qualifying that advocacy with a discussion of "essentialist" representation demonstrates his ethical caution. Respect must drive the demand for representational space. Otherwise, recognition can only too easily disolve into the "benevolent" tolerance that effectively objictifies the native's culture. This kind of "recognition," as Fanon reminds us, does not take into account the values that are actually borne by the people who bring it to life. The "I know them" or "Look at the wonderful artifacts they have produced" stiffens the colonized into the living dead. It also freezes the one who claims this knowledge into a set of rigidi-fied identifications inseparable from racism. As Toni Morrison aptly remarks, "I hate ideological whiteness. I hate it when people come into my presence and become white, either aggressively white or passively so, using this little code saying, 'I like Black people' or 'I know one.' It is humiliating for me and should be for them."[42] The antidote to ideological whiteness is the recogni-tion of the equal dignity, the universality of reciprocal relativism of cultures for which Fanon calls.

This ethical demand can begin to show us a different way of thinking about a problem noted by Taylor, who observes that "the demand for equal recognition extends beyond an acknowledgment of the equal value of all humans potentially and comes to include the equal value of what they have made of that potential."[43] If equal dignity means that people are to be rec-ognized as against the state as the source of the meaning of their own iden-tifications, then the ways in which these identifications are worked out in the course of struggle must be respected. We should recognize that this respect for our equal dignity as persons who inevitably represent themselves through their identifications either consciously or unconsciously is crucial to us all. This must inform how we treat cultural difference, including differ-ence within any particular cultural identity. To argue for equal dignity does not mean cultural and social identities are in some sense "out there," as if there were persons separate from identities; it is because such separation is unthinkable—that the recognition of the equal dignity of each one of us is crucial. A person whose cultural identity is degraded is degraded in her per-son precisely because there are inextricable connections between who she is and her basic identifications.

Thus, the claim for equal dignity need not rely on an individualism in either the philosophical or common sense meaning of the term. We accept Hegel's analysis that human beings are always constituted by the institutional and so-cial relationships that bring them into existence and frame their reality. Free-dom for us is always relational freedom. But it is just because freedom is relational that we need respect for our ability to shape our identifications. As Hall points out in his discussion of *négritude*, the claim for pride in oneself as a Black man or woman is exactly what dignity sometimes demands.

However, exactly what dignity demands in different contexts cannot be theoretically determined in advance, since it is linked with the recognition of our freedom to shape an identity and to make ethical sense of them. Our equal worth as persons cannot be reduced to a pregiven value horizon, particularly—in the sense of what our identifications mean for us—because such a reduction would deny that we, as against the state, should be recognized as the source of the value of our identity. It should be clear that this is a normative judgment about how human beings should be treated; it does not claim that human beings are in truth the only source of the value they give to their identities. Obviously, our evaluations are deeply influenced by our social worlds of institutional structures and culturally hegemonic viewpoints and evaluations that stamp out how identifications are supposed to work. Hegel recognized that it is precisely the fragility of the freedom of social selves that makes legal and political recognition of freedom so crucial; we agree with Hegel. But we can say that the value of our identifications, including those bearing on our cultural identities, must be left to us since to impose some preestablished value on any particular identity would take away from some their right to represent who they are.[44] This is why we cannot advocate a version of postmodern identity in the interests of a presumed greater good that this construction of identity would produce. In contrast to a model of postmodern identity, Hall's conception of "new ethnicities" implicitly recognizes the importance of the respect for dignity within the constitution of new ethnic identities and the inevitable contests over representations of identity that come with such recognition.

Underwriting what Hall understands as the new ethnicities approach is a recognition that even the most vital of representations of the "true" Caribbean identity are to some extent necessarily constructions, "rememorations" of identities that have been disappeared in the sandstorms of the history of imperialism. While Appiah, as we have seen, is concerned that assertions of cultural identity necessarily tie people to the past and limit their capacity to develop new identifications, Hall's analysis of "new ethnicities" makes clear that just such assertions of cultural identity can be understood as the refusal of such limitations. Hall writes, "It seems to me that, in the various practices and discourses of Black cultural production, we are beginning to see constructions of just such a new conception of ethnicity: a new cultural politics which engages rather than suppresses difference and which depends, in part, on the cultural construction of new ethnic identities."[45]

As Hall points out, the very concept of ethnicity is one that will require considerable redefinition, bound up as it has been with conceptions of nationalism, imperialism, and racism. British "ethnicity," or national identity, found its moorings in nineteenth-century discourse precisely through the writing of empire; what is English was defined over against what was French, German, or "uncivilized," belonging to the geographies of imperialist domination. Yet Hall is optimistic:

> I think such a project is not only possible; indeed, this decoupling of ethnicity from the violence of the state is implicit in some of the new forms of cultural practice. . . . We are beginning to think about how to represent a noncoercive and more diverse conception of ethnicity, to set against the embattled hegemonic conception of "Englishness" which under Thatcherism stabilize(d) so much of the dominant political and cultural discourses, and which because it is hegemonic does not represent itself as ethnicity at all.[46]

Hall, like Fanon, sees that the true trauma of the experience of colonization was that it was never just a matter of the simple imposition of Western European modes of governmentality; there is therefore no return to a grounded authentic identity, no simple sense of belonging available. Thus Hall insists:

> cultural identity . . . is a matter of becoming as well as of being. It belongs to the future as much as to the past . . . Far from being eternally fixed in some essential past, (it) is subject to the continuous play of history, culture, and power. Far from being grounded in mere recovery of the past, which is waiting to be found and will secure our sense of our selves in eternity, identities are the names we give to the different ways we are positioned by, and position ourselves within the narratives of the past.[47]

The recuperation and constitution of what Hall calls "new ethnicities" then can best be understood as a practice that must be ongoing and while future-oriented, constantly engaged in working through of the past; the temporality of this process is exactly why we have named it recollective imagination.

AESTHETIC VALUE AND FAIR JUDGMENT

When we turn our attention to new forms of cultural production that participate in the constitution and representation of such ethnicities, we often see the much-vaunted crises over the "canon" and criteria of aesthetic judgment flare. Both U.S. and British culture have seen such crises in this decade; the examples are numerous. But Hall provides us with one, recalling his debate over aesthetic value and recent films with novelist Salman Rushdie. For Hall, the stakes of the debate bore more on the categories of analysis and judgment Rushdie deployed than on the particularities of the novelist's judgment. "(Rushdie) seemed to me to be addressing (the films) as if from the stable, well-established criteria of a Guardian reviewer," Hall explains. The position of upholding hegemonic standards, Hall points out, is not only inadequate as a basis for political criticism; it also necessarily "overlooks precisely the signs of innovation and the constraints under which the filmmakers were operating." To refuse to resolve questions of aesthetic value by the use of "canonical cultural categories," Hall notes, is surely not the same as commending the films in question simply because their directors and writers are Black. "I think," he writes, "that there is another position, one which locates itself inside a continuous struggle and politics around Black representation, but which then is able to open up continuous critical discourse about . . . the forms of representation, the subjects of representation, above all the regimes of representation."[48] While Hall's example is drawn from a debate around film, where issues of access to technologies and distribution render the question of regimes of representation particularly prominent, we think that the larger implications for aesthetic judgment and standards go to other forms of cultural production as well.

What does and can "fair judgment" mean? Charles Taylor has advocated that we adopt a minimalist, aesthetic rationality that would begin with two presuppositions. First, all human cultures should be considered to be of value, including of value to the humanity beyond the reach of that culture. The second presupposition is that it is possible for us to achieve what Taylor terms a "fusion of horizons"[49] of cultures and standards of judgment that would affect the way cultures conceive of themselves, their standards, and the standards of others. This fusion of horizons would create new forms of judgment. But the very idea of a fusion still implies a more static idea of culture than the one that we believe is necessary. A fusion of horizons given the violent oppression of so many different cultures by British imperialism does not adequately grapple with that history nor with the need for rearticulation of the meaning of those cultures in the context of antiracist struggles.

We want to make an addition to Taylor's call for a minimalist rationality. We are not arguing that a fusion of horizons is inconsistent with or inappropriate to the reform of critical judgment. In fact, we agree with his first presupposition as crucial to the development of fair standards of aesthetic judgment. If these standards are to be addressed to emerging cultural identities, they must be consistent with Fanon's understanding of universality which absolutely demands the complete exclusion of the colonized status at least in our efforts to *imagine* what fair judgment might mean. What needs to be added are standards of critical reflection on the regimes of aesthetic judgment themselves. The existence of cultural artifacts, for example, must be reflected upon within the history of imperialism which has provided the cultures of the North with so many of the metaphors through which we have come to understand what constitutes culture.

The ascription of equal value does not undermine entrenched systems of judgment. Simply saying that all cultures are "equal" both homogenizes cultures and, in a sense, elides the issue, since we are able to proceed as if we didn't have to use standards of judgment when we reflected on the conditions under which cultural objects are created and circulated. Still, since human beings are of culture there must be some way to tie together the recognition of equal dignity of persons with fair standards of evaluation of cultures. It is this tie that we understand Taylor's two presuppositions to be making without collapsing the recognition of our equal worth into a preconceived judgment that all cultures are in fact equal. The whole point is that such a comparison inevitably demands the articulations of standards by which cultures are to be judged and thus compared.

However, the presumption of equal worth due to the demands of equal dignity does not mean that we actually say that culture X is equal to culture Y; it is instead the critical force which has to be pursued in the name of fairness in education. This is not a simple antiracist corrective but a serious engagement and rearticulation with the way in which judgments are made about who we are as creatures who inevitably develop out of cultures and the systematic inequalities that have been imposed on us by racism and imperialism. A crucial aspect of a multiculturalist program then must proceed at this level of abstraction. Multiculturalism insists upon the rethinking of our standards of judgment as well as the engagement with and introduction of students to the many cultures that make up our contemporary societies.

For example, in a multicultural curriculum designed to meet what we mean by fairness, students should not only be exposed to different languages but also to the history of those languages within our country. Take Spanish: the United States has the fifth-largest Spanish-speaking population in the world, so there are obviously practical reasons why U.S. students should study the Spanish language. But the Spanish language itself—and its suppression—are also an irrevocable part of U.S. cultural and political history. As we all know, large portions of the southwestern United States were originally Mexican territory.[50]

There is one sense in which this kind of multiculturalism is the practice of critical education crucial to what Appiah sees as the modern liberal society. But it is not identical with what he calls liberal multiculturalism, because it insists on the right to representational space in which minority cultures are shaped and reformed by the members of a given community. That is why there is a democratic moment in multiculturalism. Maybe with this notion of the right to representational space, we can begin discerning a new relation between the political and the aesthetic in the sense that struggles to articulate and represent new cultural identities can be understood neither as subjected to the transcendent categories of aesthetics that have most often informed aesthetic judgments over the last two hundred years, nor simply as the effects of a politics drained of the explicit recognition of its own aesthetic dimension. This is what we interpret Hall to mean when he insists there must be "another position" on the judgment of cultural productions: it is impossible to comprehend the cultural works that he refers to outside the framework of struggle. There is no detached position for the traditional aesthetic observer.[51] These practices and discourses cannot continue and fulfill their objectives if they do not remain open to a constant metacommentary and critique on their status as representations. Thus, the inextricability of the struggle for new identities with the conditions under which those identities are represented implies an ethics of identification. And this then demands that the way we see the world and judge it is inseparable from how we judge both who we are and where we stand.

4

Freedom's Conscience

In his masterful work *Women, Gays, and the Constitution*, David Richards proposes a moral interpretation of the nineteenth-century Reconstruction Amendments. This reading is inspired by "abolitionist" feminism, Richards' name for the philosophy developed by men and women who extended their opposition to slavery into a fight against all forms of racism then existing. Beginning with these feminists, Richards develops an original interpretive methodology. This methodology enables Richards to argue that the stance of the abolitionist outsider provides a moral viewpoint from which to criticize the irrationality and unreasonableness of our basic institutions. The moral viewpoint of this recentered outsider also allows an expansive enough legal interpretation of the Reconstruction Amendments to fully protect the fundamental rights of women, lesbians, and gay men.

Women, Gays, and the Constitution presents close readings of the lives and philosophies of the abolitionist feminists. Through this examination, Richards argues that we can learn moral courage from these outsiders who refused to shape their consciences to fit the unjust reality that surrounded them. This unjust reality created "moral slavery," a "structural injustice based on the abridgment of basic human rights to a whole class of persons on illegitimate grounds."[1] Because they challenged the moral slavery that society demanded, nineteenth-century "abolitionist" feminists exemplify the moral courage needed in constitutional battles today. Indeed, Richards links the abolitionist feminists' opposition of moral slavery to contemporary feminists' and gay and lesbian activists' refusal to accept their own irrational subjugation.

Richards' defense of abolitionist feminism is both a powerful critique of the injustice of treating any of us as less-than-equal members of the moral

59

community of persons, and a relentless protest against the rationalizations of a political community that attempts to justify that kind of degradation. A challenge to moral slavery allows us to call for solidarity among those who have been so oppressed. Because solidarity grows out of a common interest in ending all forms of moral servitude and not out of a simplistic identification among subjugated groups, it can transcend many of the heated debates about the *truth* of racial, national, ethnic, and gender identity that have recently paralyzed the movements calling for justice in this country. Richards' book thus delivers a crucial message to activists, committed legal reformers, and constitutional scholars.

Let me now turn to the abolitionist feminists who, by their lives and writings, began the morality tale that, Richards argues, is left to contemporary feminist and gay and lesbian activists to retell and pursue.[2] I can in the short space of this essay only highlight the normative significance that Richards gives to abolitionist feminism. But Richards himself offers an in-depth historical account of both abolitionist and suffragist feminists to bolster his interpretive defense of what is constitutionally at stake in the contemporary demand of feminists, gays, and lesbians for basic rights.

The lives and writings of the Grimke sisters, for Richards, embody the moral power of the abolitionist feminist message. The Grimke sisters, Sarah and Angelica, grew up on a southern slave-owning plantation.[3] Horrified by their firsthand experiences with the brutality of slavery, they became early and eloquent members of the abolitionist movement.[4] Abolitionism was hostile to the entrenched values of the South, which justified slavery as an acceptable moral institution. Indeed, as the abolition movement increased in both size and militancy, many states took legal and illegal measures to suppress it.[5] Abolitionists had their journals censored, their speeches and meetings interrupted by harassment or outright violence, and their lives threatened even when they tried to withdraw into the quiet of their own homes.[6] To be an abolitionist was to risk one's life, just as being a civil rights activist one hundred years later could be life threatening.

But female abolitionists faced a social ostracism uniquely directed at women who dared to violate the traditional southern ideology of the Southern Lady.[7] Richards identifies the integral connection between the corruption of public reason embodied in discursive justifications of slavery and misogyny; the repression or outright denial of the abolitionists' prized rights of conscience and speech; and the unfair exclusion of any human being from the moral community of persons. This integral connection generates the paradox of intolerance: "the greater the tradition's vulnerability to independent reasonable criticism, the more likely it is to generate forms of political irrationalism (including scapegoating of outcast dissenters) in order to secure allegiances."[8]

There are, for Richards, two components to the relationship between the denial of equal respect for persons and the corruption of reason. First, the free public debate that lies at the heart of the democratic community was corrupted by the unreasonable and irrational defense employed to rationalize the exclusion of African Americans from the political community. Richards gives a number of examples to illustrate this process. He notes that suspect scientific ideas about the "natural" inferiority of African Americans were allowed into public debate as irrefutable truth, even by supporters of slavery's abolition.[9]

Throughout most of the Civil War, Abraham Lincoln accepted the proposition that, once African Americans were freed from slavery, they would have to be re-colonized. Lincoln had clearly been swayed by deeply entrenched views of, and fantasies about, African Americans that reflected the hegemonic opinion of his time. In this he was not alone. Many other opponents of slavery simply took it as the "way of the world" that racism in the form of the defense of white superiority was valid even if slavery was not.[10]

Unlike most of their comrades, however, the abolitionist feminists were fierce critics of the colonization movement, attacking the antislavery sentiment that continued to endorse openly racist views toward African Americans. Lydia Maria Child, Richards explains, offered a searing and sophisticated critique of racism. To her, racism was a product of the unjust institution of slavery: "We first crush people to the earth, and then claim the right of trampling on them forever, because they are prostrate."[11]

Through his discussion of the abolitionist feminists, Richards demonstrates that the identity of the American was "whitened" during debates over slavery. Black people were by definition "other" to the American identity—how else could their terrible treatment be justified under the Constitution, which purportedly guaranteed that all men were created equal? To Child, and to the other abolitionists who sided with her, the ideological role of racism was to put unjust institutional racism beyond the reach of public debate by constructing African Americans as less than human.[12] The effectiveness of this ideology in swaying not only President Lincoln but also, the Reconstruction Congress undermines the legitimacy of Congress' interpretations of the Reconstruction Amendments. Such interpretations are revealed as products of a public reason corrupted by the racism stemming from slavery.[13] For Richards, the abolitionist position:

> enforced its own vision of truth against both the standards of reasonable inquiry and the reasonable capacities of both blacks and whites that might challenge the conception. A conception of political unity, subject to reasonable doubt as to its basis and merits, had unreasonably resolved its own doubts, consistent with the paradox of intolerance, in the irrational racist certitudes of group solidarity on the basis of unjust group subjugation.[14]

The second aspect of Richards' analysis of the relationship between the corruption of reason and the denial of equal respect for persons lies in his consideration of equal dignity of persons. Equal dignity of persons was the "cure" for the paradox of intolerance. To recover this dignity, abolitionists returned to Locke's argument that, without toleration, there could be no democracy because there would be no free debate. Free debates need free persons to carry them on. Without that freedom, dissenters would simply be condemned as heretics and their political judgments ridiculed, or worse yet, attacked as treason to the community or nation.[15] In order to reinstate political conditions of toleration, the abolitionists appealed to the social contract, an abstract hypothetical experiment of the imagination that included African Americans as free and equal persons.[16] The need for the abolitionists' appeal to their particular version of the social contract was tied to the critique. Abstract theory had the ability to root out the irrational prejudice that had infected reason. Any appeal to the actual political morality of white Americans would replicate intolerance, because this morality had come to justify itself through a deep acceptance of racism. By appealing to the theory of social contract, abolitionists presented a unique form of the argument that slavery was evil: They explained that slavery, and the intolerance stemming from it, effectively undermined democracy. Intolerance was based on an unjust reduction of some human beings to some "thing" less than a person. Such intolerance contaminated the actual workings of democracy, since certain groups were foreclosed from expressing their views in public.

Richards demonstrates that abstract political theory became the much-needed tool of activists working to dismantle a racist society. Richards' own interpretive method, by taking us back to the abolitionists' searing critique of American democracy, provides us with a unique understanding of the role of theory in political movements for justice and legal reform. Richards demonstrates that the justification of theory cannot be made solely in terms of the philosophical consistency of the theory itself. That is, the full justification of a political theory should include its historical rootedness in a particular national history. Such rootedness must include not only the mainstream conventions that dominate a particular historical period, but also the movements for social justice that, through their internal criticism of the society's institutions, become its conscience.[17] Despite an insistence on historical context, Richards does not find a political theory justified simply on the basis of its historical grounds in the hegemonic institutions and legal principles of a particular national community. A theory's relevance to a people, due to its historical, political, and cultural familiarity, should be considered an important part of what makes it a *reasonable* theory, because relevance is what makes actual people able to respond to it morally.

By drawing attention to the ways in which political theory can enlarge our idea of what is reasonably possible, Richards offers us insight into the contemporary significance of the relationship between history and the ideal of reasonableness. He carves out a position that is sensitive to history without being reducible to historicism. But his understanding of the relationship between theory and practice also speaks to one of the oldest debates on the left: Is theory only for the intellectual elite? Is it kept alive only by professional academics? Richards' appeal to the abolitionists answers both questions in the negative. Theory needs the moral insight of the outsiders, and the dissenters and activists need theory in order to remain true to their vision of a society in which all of us are recognized as free and equal persons.

To illustrate the connection between theory and practice, Richards again presents examples from the lives of a number of abolition feminists. When they found themselves ostracized and with no choice but to flee to the North, the Grimke sisters turned to theory. Exiled both literally and figuratively from the moral community of their time, they sought, in their theorizing, the moral community in which they could be included as women.[18] The sisters knew that for women to claim their full standing as persons—to be able to raise their voices as citizens—they would have to claim for themselves the most basic moral right. That right was to lay claim to their own person with full legal rights of conscience, speech, work, and intimate association. In their struggle to speak out against slavery, both sisters came to recognize that they were, in Richards' sense, moral slaves.[19] Their enforced servitude was inseparable from the idealization of the Southern Lady. Both sisters had the insight to see the psychosexual dynamics that, in the name of chivalry, oppressed both "white" and "Black" women.

Indeed, reading Richards' account of the Grimke sisters' understanding of these psychosexual dynamics deepens the feminist understanding of how race and sexuality were mutually constitutive. The differential articulation of "Black" and "white" through the structures of desirability and accessibility gave color to the fundamental splitting that Jacques Lacan has called the psychical fantasy of Woman.[20] Under this fantasy, Woman is signified through the fundamental divide of the good and the bad: in the case of the pre-Civil War South, the "white" woman keeps her virtue intact if her sexuality is denied, and the licentious, "Black" woman's purported sexuality makes her an object for the taking. African American women could not be raped because they were owned outright. A rape of a white woman, often imagined, or called rape—even though it was a consensual relationship with an African American man—became the justification for the most brutal mob violence against African American men: lynching. Thus, the ideology that justified racism was sexualized and turned on a fantasy of white women that necessarily denied them freedom of personality.

The Grimke sisters saw clearly that white women did not come close to enduring the horrifying day-to-day brutality of slavery. Thus, they did not appeal to the shared *experience* of women in their call for the abolition of both racism and sexism. They instead argued against the colonized *imagination* of those forced into servitude, and those who imposed it, on both African

Americans and white women.[21] By identifying the effects of moral slavery instead of calling on identical experiences of oppression, they could make a powerful argument that African American men and women, and white women, were alike subjected to moral servitude. A possible alliance could be made between African American women and white women if white women had the courage to call for an end of all forms of moral slavery. Richards demonstrates that confronting women's moral servitude involved a challenge to the so-called natural division of labor that relegated women to the private realm, a realm that became a prison if any woman tried to escape it, as the Grimke sisters did. The Grimke sisters understood why the personal had to be political long before the second wave of feminism. Women's moral servitude was based on the patriarchal definition of their "sex" and the roles of the wife and mother that supposedly went with it. To challenge moral servitude meant to challenge patriarchy.

Richards explains that Harriet Jacobs and Ida Wells-Barnett took this insight into the struggle of African American women against miscegenation laws.[22] These laws not only expressed the drive for racial purity promoted by racism, but were also deeply involved in the coloring of the psychical fantasy of Woman. Richards points out that even women like Frances Willard, who fought bravely against slavery, could not accept the truth that Wells-Barnett forced into the public view, that many of the so-called rapes for which African American men were lynched were consensual relationships with white women.[23] Willard's racism, combined with her insistence on women's difference, made it impossible for her to imagine white women as sexual creatures free enough to pursue their love beyond the most ferociously imposed conventions. Richards includes a discussion of Harriet Jacobs' frank account of how her own sexual life, crucial to her personal struggle for freedom, and including sexual relationships with white men, scandalized both men and women in the anti-slavery movement.[24] Both Wells-Barnett and Jacobs argued that women's sexual freedom and their right to intimate association were crucial to the recognition of women as full members of the moral community of persons, supposedly the basis of American democracy.[25]

Discussing their stories in combination, Richards shows that the Grimke sisters, Jacobs, and Wells-Barnett all refused to give any validity to theories of their sexual difference that legitimated their standing as any "thing" less than free and equal persons.[26] However, he also underlines the ways in which the appeal to women's moral difference as well as to the racism that promoted it—since this moral difference was the providence of white women only—became prominent as suffragist feminists turned away from the abolitionist feminists' analysis of women's moral servitude.[27]

To illustrate this movement away from the emancipatory potential of the abolitionist feminists, Richards includes a discussion of Elizabeth Stanton. Stanton began her life in feminism in sympathy with the abolitionist feminists.[28] But as she experienced the defeat of justice that accompanied the brutal resistance to a true reconstruction of this country, she turned her back on her own principles.[29] To win suffrage became the single goal. In fact, Stanton used overtly racist arguments to justify the need to give white women the vote: If they did not have that right, they were being treated as not really white, potentially subjected to out-of-control, Black, freed men.[30] As Richards powerfully argues, by claiming white feminine virtue as the basis of the right to suffrage, suffragist feminism defeated itself even as it won the limited goal it had set as its target.[31]

Richards draws four normative and critical insights from his historical analysis of the moral significance of abolitionist feminism, and from the moral failure of suffragist feminism in accommodating a racist social reality. First, he gives a new twist to the epistemological privileging of the oppressed, long a crucial part of leftist theory. For him, it is not only that the oppressed have to see beyond the ideology of the majority, in this case that of the so-called scientific basis of women and African Americans' moral inferiority. They also have to engage in a kind of hypothetical experiment of the imagination and by so doing remember what was demanded by a fair society which did not exclude so many from the fully human:

> It is, in my judgment, precisely because abolitionist feminism was, during the period under question, so remarkably critical in the way it was of a pervasive political orthodoxy both of race and gender—and so unsuccessfully at war with the dominant political consensus based on this orthodoxy—that it achieved the kind of enduring critical insights of principle that it did. Its very critical distance from and rights-based dissent to the dominant political consensus constitute the keys to its impartiality and thus to its permanent contribution to our normative understanding of a more principled contemporary interpretation of the Reconstruction Amendments in various domains.[32]

Put somewhat differently, in a social world that foreclosed the possibility of their freedom, the abolitionist feminists had to creatively imagine a world beyond moral servitude. This kind of hypothetical experiment of the imagination can still, one hundred years later, provide insight into what women, gays, lesbians, and people of color can demand in the name of justice.

What they share is a condition of moral servitude, not the identical experience of oppression. Under this analysis it is unnecessary to decide who is more oppressed. The wrong done is moral servitude imposed.

The second relevant normative insight that Richards draws from the abolitionists is that abolitionist feminists did not turn to any theory of Woman in order to make their call to freedom. Instead, all such identities reflecting the exclusionary ideology that justified treating women and African Americans as less than persons were challenged. The moral right they demanded was precisely the right to be free from the so-called essential identities that marked them as less worthy than white men to pursue their lives in all aspects, including both sex and work, as they saw fit. As Richards states:

> Their struggle, expressing the demands of moral personality, transforms their own identities as much as that of the larger constitutional culture. . . . The struggle for identity, as we have studied it, must be understood in terms of the distinctive arguments of rights-based justice central to each person's sense of integrity, the sense in which, for example, gay and lesbian identity is literally defined and renegotiated by the self-respecting claims of basic rights and the reasonable criticism thus made against the traditional force of one's unspeakable moral slavery.[33]

The connection Richards makes between the struggle for freedom and the problems of exclusionary identities is a much-needed addition to the now paralyzed debates about the value of "identity politics."

Richards next argues that the abolitionist feminists were right in their insistence on sexual freedom. Indeed, for Richards, suffragist feminism faltered because it fell prey to what he calls the "Wollstonecraft repudiation."[34] Richards names the Wollstonecraft repudiation after the rejection by suffragist feminists of the ideas of Mary Wollstonecraft, a brilliant advocate of women's rights at the time of the French Revolution.[35] Wollstonecraft spurned the conventional limitations on women's sexuality and refused to deny the intense psychic suffering and cruelty she endured as a result of nonconformance to standards of proper female decorum. She openly admitted to affairs and had a baby outside of marriage.[36] The brilliance of her writing was buried under charges of wantonness and insanity.[37] It was easier to call a woman a crazy whore than to recognize that she was right, particularly when she was calling for an end to straight men's sexual privilege.

The Wollstonecraft repudiation, as Richards defines it, is the refusal of women's right to claim their own sexuality as part of a legitimate feminist struggle for legal reform. The repudiation is an attempt at "passing" and, I would argue, is inseparable from the psychical fantasy of Woman. Indeed, the repudiation is of the "bad girls," including the "bad girl" in oneself. The corresponding assertion that one is a "good girl" seeks to prove to the establishment that feminism is acceptable because it does not challenge the entire structure of gender hierarchy. Richards carefully describes how destructive the Wollstonecraft repudiation was to suffragist feminism.[38] In addition, Richards shows that women like Emma Goldman and Victoria Woodhull were condemned by suffragist feminism because they demanded that feminism insist on sexual freedom for everyone.[39] For Woodhull at least, the demand for sexual freedom also meant a challenge to compulsory heterosexuality.

Richards' fourth normative argument concerns gay and lesbian rights. In this powerful section, Richards uses the abolitionists' insight into how the psychical fantasy of Woman corrupts public reason. Richards shows how the gay man is othered as a "bad woman," worse yet than all those "feminist whores" because he could have been a "real" man.[40] Drawing on the insight of the poet Walt Whitman, Richards effectively argues that love between men is rendered the worst possible evil because it challenges the entire construction of gender hierarchy with its rigid meanings of the "straight path" that a man must take if he is to deserve his place in the hierarchy.[41] What man would be willing to be "fucked"? That's the fate of women. It is precisely this conflation of fantasies of woman's "sex" as a penetrable object with the act of sodomy that nineteenth-century sexual radical Edward Carpenter used to explain the strength of the hold of homophobia on the public imagination.

This homophobia reduced love between men to a sexual act rather than respecting this love as a relationship.[42] Drawing on Whitman's and Carpenter's insights, Richards connects abolitionist feminism with the struggle for gay rights.[43] In order to demand their freedom as persons, both movements must challenge the psychical fantasy of Woman. There is a possibility of solidarity between feminism and gay rights' advocates that does not appeal to a simple story of identity and oppression, but instead commonly opposes a symbolic ordering of rigid gender identifications and the appropriate sexualities that reinforce them.[44]

Although Richards has less to say about lesbians than he does about the structure of homophobia endured by gay men, he is relentless in his demands for the rights of both gay men and lesbians. He interprets the constitutional significance of the abolitionists' critique of racism, and their claim for moral right, as the legal demand for a different reading of both the Thirteenth and Fourteenth Amendments.[45] The Thirteenth Amendment condemns moral slavery, defined as the abridgment of the basic rights of conscience, speech, work, and intimate association, based on the illegitimate grounds of the irrational prejudice that, because of race or sex, some people can be treated as less than free and equal persons.[46] The prohibition of moral slavery becomes Richards' "hermeneutic pivot," used to clarify "the proper interpretation of structurally related principles of the Fourteenth Amendment."[47] According to Richards, the two principles of the Fourteenth Amendment that remain of special interpretive concern are "the nationalization of the protection of basic human rights against both the state and national governments" and the "guarantee of equal protection of the laws" so that those rights attend all persons.[48] For Richards, what has been nationalized is exactly the prohibition of moral slavery. Richards also interprets equal protection of the laws through an appeal to the pivotal prohibition of moral slavery. On his interpretation, the guarantee of equal protection of the law demands "that all forms of political power must be reasonably justifiable to all persons in terms of both equal respect for their basic human rights and the pursuit of acceptable public purposes of justice and the common good."[49]

In addition, Richards rejects both of the current interpretations of suspect class analysis—immutability and political powerlessness—that have floundered before the demand that women, gays, and lesbians be recognized as suspect classes.[50] For Richards, suspect class analysis should be "a demanding constitutional suspicion. . . of the enforcement through public law of cultural stereotypes that rest on a history of moral slavery."[51]

Richards shows that once gays and lesbians are treated as a suspect class under constitutional law as he formulates it, the glaring wrong—of all the forms of discrimination gays and lesbians continue to endure in all of those aspects of life that matter most to people—becomes exposed and finally made available for legal correction. Again, following the analysis he attributes to the abolitionists, Richards forcefully argues that the denial of the right to marriage for gays and lesbians tramples any meaningful interpretation of the right to conscience.[52] This intolerance corrupts public reason and debate in a form similar to that imposed by the attempt to silence the abolitionist movement and to legitimate the public's irrational investment in racism. One need only turn to the often irrational debates in Congress over the Defense of Marriage Act to see how right Richards is to draw a connection between homophobia and the corruption of the democratic process.[53] Through his interpretation of the Reconstruction Amendments, Richards offers a convincing argument that gays and lesbians—and I would add all other forms of sexuate being[54]—should be accorded full standing as free and equal persons with all the fundamental rights that attend the recognition of personhood.

Richards' argument sometimes conflates moral and legal rights. This conflation has the potential of undermining the full moral power of Richards' demand for justice for women, gays, and lesbians, as well as making his analysis an easy prey for critiques of "rights" talk. Following Kant, I would argue that the moral right to claim one's person is the basis of all legal rights.[55] Rights accrue to persons. The wrong in moral slavery is that it denies to persons the status of personhood, attributing positive characteristics to them that purportedly render them unworthy of that status. A prohibition of moral slavery means that no one may be denied their freedom to claim their own person, the ability to postulate themselves as an end in themselves. It was Kant's great insight that human freedom cannot be disproved by theoretical reason.[56] As a result, the denial of that freedom is only rarely, very rarely indeed, ever going to be reasonable. Richards' searing critique of contemporary legal principle is moral, in that it appeals to the right in which personality is based. But it is also legal, in that it provides a test for the legitimacy of any legal system that incorporates a system of subjective right: the test of abolishing moral slavery.

The difference between the moral right to personality and legal rights becomes particularly important in any analysis of the politics of second wave feminism, including Richards' careful analysis of the legal victories of that movement. The battles for women's legal rights have often been won at the expense of the moral right to free personality that Richards so brilliantly defends. Legal victories, and the strategies to achieve them, often involve moral compromise with the "real" world. No one was clearer about this than Emma Goldman, who tried to stay on the side of moral right, often by defying the law. Goldman certainly would have been perplexed by her designation by Richards as a rights-based feminist, at least if we mean by a rights-based feminist one who turns toward the existing legal system of the time for the achievement of either freedom or equality. But she could certainly be said to be one who would have approved of Richards' conception of moral right.

In part because he sometimes conflates moral and legal right, Richards tends to idealize the second wave of feminism, particularly as it has been translated into a platform for legal reform. However, a classic example of the Wollstonecraft repudiation within the second wave of feminism has been the failure of many feminists to understand that their fight is integrally related to the struggles of gays and lesbians. Indeed, some feminist lawyers have argued that, for the purposes of Title VII and the Constitution, sex should mean gender even though interpreting sex narrowly means excluding gays and lesbians from the reach of antidiscrimination law. Some feminists have thought that they have to pass into the mainstream in order to achieve certain legal victories, but to some degree that means an acceptance of the confines of compulsory heterosexuality. Whoever a "good girl" is, it is clear that she is not a lesbian and she is not "Black."

It is time that feminists, particularly white feminists in the legal academy, publicly recognize the wrong in this Wollstonecraft repudiation, and insist that all of us as sexuate beings have the equal right to free ourselves from moral servitude. Richards' book is a call to be unflagging in our fight against all forms of moral servitude. As an out gay man long before it was safe to be so, Richards has for over twenty-five years served us well as freedom's conscience.

5

Enlightening the Enlightenment

Many thinkers in political theory and cultural studies have recently advocated for a return to the sound liberal values associated with the ideal of the Enlightenment. The fear is that cultural studies has undermined the basis for any struggles in the name of justice or some other liberal, or for that matter, radical ideal. In its place, we are left with a process of infinite critique and relativization that serves politics only by reminding us of how small and local our goals should be and how limited our dreams must be. Some leftist literary critics, unrepentant former activists of the '60s, have turned against what they see as the extreme criticism of cultural theory in the name of a revival or return to liberalism. But what is to be revived, and how are we to conceptualize that revival through the Enlightenment program, particularly as it is inevitably associated with Kant's political philosophy? To look more closely at what is at stake in this return to the Enlightenment liberalism, I examine John Brenkman's essay, "Extreme Criticism," which exemplifies the political and ethical fear of what "extreme criticism" has wrought.

In his essay, John Brenkman moves with breathtaking speed through a discussion of the conditions of the publicness of aesthetic form; a defense of the nation-state as the necessary institutional form for Hannah Arendt's civic humanism; a critique of cultural studies for its race, class, and gender mantra and its anti-Enlightenment stance; and ultimately to a strong reaffirmation of Enlightenment humanism and the ideal of the person. It would be impossible in a short response to address any of these positions in the depth they deserve. I should say up front that I am not in disagreement with Brenkman's affirmation of the ideal of the person and the continuing relevance of Kantianism to political and cultural theory. Indeed, in a number of books, I have argued that Kantianism is indispensable for an articulation of both legal and moral ideals, including the ideal of the person.[1] I also agree with Brenkman when he asserts that "aesthetic 'judgment' is enabled by a material, institutionalized space of expression and criticism" and that this space is best protected by a concept of right.[2] I have named that space "the imaginary domain."[3] In order, then, to see where the difference between Brenkman's defense of Enlightenment humanism and Kant's so-called postmodern antihumanist critics lies, we need to look much more carefully at each of the positions that Brenkman defends.

First, let me begin with some cautionary remarks that stem from how I interpret the ethical effect of Kant's Third Critique, or *The Critique of Judgment*,[4] on a conception of the Enlightenment.[5] I make these remarks because my agreement with Brenkman's defense of the publicness of aesthetic form turns on a particular understanding of what that publicness entails in light of Kant's Third Critique. Clearly, Brenkman is responding to critics of Kantian Enlightenment as reactive to a representation of the project rather than to the project itself. That representation has itself been reduced to a kind of mantra. The Enlightenment subjects all categories of human life to instrumental reason so as to allow us to free ourselves from tutelage to nature and to humanity's past "backward" history. Conquerors we may be, but of a barren and destroyed natural world, which ultimately may serve its own death sentence upon us through holes in the ozone layer, the destruction of the rain forest, and the ever greater rape of our rivers, valleys, and oceans that sustain us. This mantra is often traced back to the rightfully famous work of Theodor W. Adorno and Max Horkheimer in their *Dialectic of Enlightenment*.[6]

There are many readings of *The Dialectic of the Enlightenment*, and any serious consideration of them is clearly beyond the space offered by a response. I simply want to offer here that Adorno and Horkheimer are correct to the extent that they demonstrate that any systematic conceptualization of the Enlightenment fails to be true to itself because it rejects a self-understanding of enlightenment as a self-critical process, including one that must be understood historically.[7] By true to itself, I mean faithful to its own call for continual critical reflection on the conditions of reason and the possibility of critique. In his Third Critique, Kant ultimately shows us why Enlightenment as a systematic theoretical project *must* remain incomplete. The understanding of reflective judgment that Kant develops in that Critique does not turn us to any specific object domain, such as art objects per se, but to those experiences in the subject such as pleasure and pain that do not and cannot fit either into the world of cognizable objects or into the sphere of moral freedom. As Kant reminds us again and again, there is no ultimate theoretical bridge between these two realms of the phenomenal world of scientific objects and the postulation of a sphere of our moral freedom. There is, in other words, no theoretical closure offered by reflective judgment to the breech left by the first Two Critiques between the realms of fact and value.

But nor are we simply left with the realm of individual taste—yours necessarily as good as mine—because it is completely contingent on my wholly individual sensibility. As Brenkman rightfully remarks, Kant's reflective judgment is not aestheticism. The entire project of the Third Critique turns us back to the role that affect, and with it reflective judgment, might play in healing the breech between fact and value. But this healing is not something that Kant defends as philosophically demonstrable, as something that can be actualized so as to theoretically complete the project of critique. Instead, the experience of the beautiful and the sublime can only point us toward an *ought to be,* which is symbolized from out of our experiences of pain and pleasure. The *sensus communis aestheticus* to which Kant refers always points us to a projected *ought to be* of a shared community, the enlarged mentality in which we might articulate to one another the subjective basis of our reflective judgment of the beautiful and the sublime and find it illuminated in the viewpoint of the other and echoed in the other's attempt to communicate her experience. The future nature of this community of the *ought to be* remains open as a possibility in the *sensus communis aestheticus.* It implies a "publicness" that awaits us, not one that is actually given to us, nor one that can ever be given to us once and for all in any predetermined public form. To quote Kant,

> The judgment of taste exacts agreement from every one; and a person who describes something as beautiful insists that every one *ought* to give the object in question his approval and follow suit in describing it as beautiful. The *ought* in aesthetic judgments, therefore, despite an accordance with all the requisite data for passing judgment, is still only pronounced conditionally.[8]

The *sensus communis aestheticus* relies rather on the analogical principle of enlarged mentality ("erweiterle Denkungsart"). On the reading I am giving here, Kant's theory of aesthetic reflection grapples with affect and the pleasure or pain of our bodily existence. This struggle, in turn, provides evidence that the process of enlightenment always works against itself if it attempts the arrogance that it can achieve systematic theoretical closure of the critical project. To summarize, the *sensus communis aestheticus* cannot be anchored either in the world of nature or the sphere of freedom. Indeed it cannot be anchored at all if it is to remain faithful to Kant's own conception of reflective judgment. It is this fragility of the *sensus communis aestheticus* that for me ethically and politically promotes the notion of the imaginary domain as a concept of right.

Although it is evidently not his intent, given the political place of art and literature he wishes to preserve, Brenkman can at times come close to making the same mistake as Habermas. Habermas collapses the *sensus communis aestheticus* into the *sensus communis logicus.* I mean by this collapse to indicate Habermas's presupposition that the conflict of the faculties can be overcome by reference to the order to reason. As is well known, Habermas argues that we can overcome the "dark side" of the Enlightenment through an overarching concept of *communicative reason*. Kant himself did not accept that there could be such a rational resolution of the conflict between the faculties; certainly, the Kant of the Third Critique does not think so. Just how much of a Habermasian Brenkman is remains an open question in this essay, but I would argue that any collapse of the *sensus communis aestheticus* into the *sensus communis logicus* runs afoul of Brenkman's own defense of the role of the aesthetic and of reflective judgment in a democratic culture.[9] More important, the reading that I give to the relationship between Kant's Third Critique and a defense of enlightenment humanism can help us to beware of the hubris of the Enlightenment. This hubris has often, and to my mind rightfully, been critiqued as inseparable from the imperial domination of the West. Yet we can reject this conceptualization of the Enlightenment and still embrace a more humble standpoint of enlightenment as a continual process of reflective judgment.

The Third Critique always reminds us that we are haunted and afraid by what is the Other to reason—affect—with all the joys of pleasure and all the suffering of pain. If, as Kant argues in The Third Critique, the ethical transformation of fear can only be mitigated if we seek to think from the standpoint of everyone else and develop the enlarged mentality from that viewpoint, then we can start to see how the humanism that can be constructed from that critique can help us think more fruitfully about how to articulate enlightenment in a complex, multicultural world. This understanding of how fear is mitigated and thus ethically transformed can help us reexamine what is both right and dangerous in Kant's understanding of Enlightenment as our freedom from immaturity and from the tutelage of nature. To remind the reader here, the first two sentences of Kant's famous quote on Enlightenment are: "Enlightenment is man's emergence from his self-incurred immaturity. Immaturity is the inability to use one's own understanding without the guidance of another."[10]

Brenkman's conclusion is that maturity of contemporary thought does not lie "in believing we can think beyond or post- that motto."[11] But in our complex, multicultural world, in which the dominance of the northern democracies is being challenged, we need to at least ask certain basic questions about what constitutes "maturity." John Rawls in his "Law of Nations" exemplifies the enlarged mentality of reflective judgment as applied to international law.[12] In that essay, Rawls worries about the Northern democracies endorsing a philosophical liberalism that is itself illiberal precisely because it judges as inferior or immature other cultures and peoples that may be unlike ours because they allow certain legalized hierarchical distinctions. This judgment refuses them recognition as a "decent" nation or culture. Rawls' political liberalism has been referred to as a liberalism of fear, in that it seeks to maintain the ever-waning force of liberalism by finding allies for it even if that

means making concessions to illiberal societies. But I want to give a different interpretation to the role of fear, one that is more consistent with what I
have already argued inheres in Kant's notion of reflective judgment. We
could put it this way: through reflective judgment we do not simply seek to
negate the fear of the other, but instead seek to respect the dignity of the
Other through the enlarged mentality of reflective judgment. Rawls' political
liberalism is enlightenment in an historical process that knows itself as an inevitably incomplete theoretical project. It is only such a project that can
allow tolerance on the level of philosophy itself. I am well aware that Rawls
himself does not refer to the Third Critique in his defense of a humbled enlightenment. But if Rawls is interpreted in this manner, I think we can begin
to see how Habermas and Rawls fundamentally disagree on what the conception of enlightenment entails.[13]

In a complex argument, Rawls tries to define the minimal human rights
standards that he believes would be consistent with tolerance applied to philosophy. This tolerance he defends as the hallmark of his own unique, but
still Kantian-inspired, political liberalism. For example, Rawls argues that
basic human rights must be defended on a basis that is "neutral" between
Western ideals and those of other cultures that could also serve as the basis
for an overlapping consensus on such rights. Whether one thinks that Rawls
effectively defends his argument that such a neutral perspective is possible
is not my primary point here. It is rather to emphasize Rawls' rightful moral
concern with judgments of "immaturity" of other cultures, in the name of
some strong, philosophical justification of the universality of our shared conditions as rational "men." For Rawls, such judgments paradoxically undermine the enlightened Kantian liberalism they are meant to defend. If we are
to draw a conclusion from the moral concerns Rawls addresses in this paper,
then "maturity"—Rawls himself never uses this word and I myself am reluctant to use it and therefore place it in quotation marks—is reflected in the
recognition of the complexity inherent in a political liberalism that unfolds,
at least partially, from this seeming paradox. The history of German idealism—culminating in some of Hegel's most dreadful statements about the immaturity of the cultures of the South, to the point that some of them are
erased from the spirit of humanity because they cannot "grow up,"—is not
directly addressed by Rawls but clearly haunts his work on international
human rights, and to my mind he is right to be so haunted.

For Hegel, for example, Africa and the African peoples could never aspire
to be included in humanity.[14] Hegel's moral arrogance does not mean that
we reject the tradition of German idealism, refuse to read Hegel, or write off
what is best in Kant, as Brenkman accuses cultural studies theorists of doing.
For example, he quotes an article in *Public Culture* that he argues defends
the position that some cultures can rightfully defend their right not to have
rights. But this is not what a sophisticated Kantian constructivist like John

Rawls is arguing. Nor is it an entirely fair reading of the editors of *Public Culture*, Arjun Appadurai and Carol A. Breckenridge. They are concerned to render visible in the discussion of human rights the divergent forms in which religious, social, and political ideals are articulated. In different cultures, some of those ideals are valued outside of the realm of the legal. Both Rawls and the editors of *Public Culture* can be interpreted to share a common concern that can be summarized as follows: Enlightenment humanism can turn against the political liberalism it promotes if it tries to achieve philosophical closure to the project of critique.

Brenkman, of course, is right to note that some thinkers in cultural criticism equate liberalism and the Enlightenment with imperialism, or at least worry that they cannot be effectively separated. As a result, they mistakenly forsake the enlightenment project altogether. But what Brenkman seems to forget is that we also endanger political liberalism if we do not critically examine the concept of Enlightenment itself.

To continue for a moment with Rawls' political liberalism, he also does not share Brenkman's argument that egalitarian theories of distributive justice have not survived the seeming collapse of Marxism and subsequent readjustment of the states in Eastern Europe.[15] Indeed, one of the crucial ways in which Rawls breaks with Kant's own articulation of a concept of right and justice in the modern state is through his disagreement with Kant's own defense of considerable inequality based on natural, inherited differences between people.[16] To remind the reader of Kant's articulation of the rightfulness of a modern state, it is as follows:

> The civil state, regarded purely as a lawful state, is based on the following a priori principles:
> (1) the freedom of every member of society as a human being
> (2) the equality of each with all others as a subject
> (3) the independence of each member of a commonwealth as a citizen.[17]

Through his use of the famous representative device of the veil of ignorance, which in Brenkman's sense is a good example of a political philosopher's attempt to give form to the ideal of political and moral autonomy, Rawls argues that human beings who engage in the hypothetical experiment of imagining themselves without the constraint of knowing their own hierarchical position in society, based either in nature or in socially imposed discrimination, would never accept the radical inequalities that Kant himself defended. This radical egalitarianism mandates the loosening of the hold of natural destiny on any person's fate. Such a mandate has also recently been understood to implicate questions of immigration as they relate to nationhood. Rawls, until recently, assumed that we could postulate that persons enter political associations at birth only to exit them at death. But Joseph Carens, for example, has used Rawls to argue that it is morally arbitrary, in exactly Rawls' sense, to define citizenship in a particular country or nation-state as flowing naturally from either birth on the territory or through lineage.[18] Whether or not one accepts the position that Kantian constructivism, properly conceived, would lead to the advocacy of open borders, we can at least see how powerfully enlightenment humanism challenges any easy acceptance of the nation-state as the only and basic unit of political life in a democracy.[19]

There is an important reason that Kantian constructivists can move so easily to the defense of open borders: Kant himself privileges the freedom of every member of society as a human being over the other two conditions of right that are derivative of the first. Kantian universality, in other words, cannot be in principle constrained by any appeal to a particularistic suppression of a creature of reason. Thus, even if one were to accept the nation-state for prudential reasons, for example as a necessary barrier to the encroachment of international capital and enforced programs of economic management upon emerging nation-states in the South,[20] further distinctions between membership and admission, and the suppression of linguistic diversity through the promotion of linguistic unity, would still run afoul of the commitment of Kantianism to the freedom of each one of us as a human being.[21]

Postcolonial theory, in the works of some of the most significant thinkers of our time, can be interpreted to take Kant's privileging of freedom seriously and to defend a conception of universality that can be rendered consistent with Kant's own argument that the idea of humanity as an *idea* must remain contentless if it is to remain coherent with our moral freedom. In the best tradition of Frantz Fanon, such thinkers have claimed that a universality faithful to Kantian humanism must be one that embraces the reciprocal relativism of cultures, none starting from a predetermined place in this engagement as *the mature culture.*[22] Such a universality *must* begin with a moral rejection of the colonial status. The demand for inclusion articulated in post-colonial theory is faithful to a universality that no longer takes one people or set of ideals as the hallmark of what it means to be "men." Reciprocal relativism that proceeds through an appeal to universality, may sound like a paradox, but if it is a paradox, it is perfectly consistent with Kant's own insistence that a concept of humanity as an idea coherent with moral freedom must remain contentless at least on the abstract level of philosophy. The important theoretical addition of postcolonial theory is to remind us that yes, we are always inevitably reconfiguring our humanity, substantiating our identities and identifications. But these are just configurations. None come pre-marked with a hierarchical position vis-à-vis other identities, identifications, and cultures.[23] The moral reminder of the universal is also a moral reminder of a democratic dynamic relationship that no longer reinscribes status differentiation between the colonizer and the colonized.

Judith Butler has succinctly defended this understanding of the universal as it has been relevant to her work in the advocacy of gay and lesbian human rights.

When competing claims to the universal are made, it seems imperative to understand that cultures do not exemplify a ready-made universal, but that the universal is always culturally articulated, and that the complex process of learning how to read that claim is not something any of us can do outside of the difficult process of cultural translation. This translation will not be an easy one where we reduce every cultural instance to a presupposed universality, nor will it be the enumeration of radical particularisms between which no communication is possible. The task that cultural difference sets for us is the articulation of universality through a difficult labor of translation, one in which the terms made to stand for one another are transformed in the process, and where the movement of that unanticipated transformation establishes the universal as that which is yet to be achieved and which, in order to resist domestication, may never be fully or finally achievable.[24]

In my reading of Butler's essay "For a Careful Reading," Butler is arguing that there cannot be a final form given to our humanity by any one people or culture, because that form can always be morally contested in the name of the very universality upon which it rests its privilege. It is Butler's insistence on universality and her privileging of freedom that is often missed in her theoretical and political writing. Brenkman discusses Butler as a classic example of someone who, with Foucault, avoids all the purportedly "thorny questions about the meaning of freedom and individuality and the role of the state" as these are "nested in different strands of libertarianism."[25] Yet Brenkman also argues that he is in agreement with every political position that Butler takes, for example, in her *Excitable Speech*. It is just her avoidance of the thorny questions with regard to what it means to be a "libertarian manqué" that disturbs him. But I would argue on the contrary that it is just those questions and her recognition of the need to address them that is the moral force behind her arguments in *Excitable Speech*. Butler is often read—and Brenkman seems to accept this reading—as if she were simply arguing against all forms of regulation of controversial speech, such as hate speech and pornographic representation. But this is exactly not what she is doing. If anything, her text patiently raises one thorny theoretical question after another. To quote Butler, because she is so often misunderstood on this point:

> This is not to say that subjects ought not to be prosecuted for their injurious speech; I think that there are probably occasions when they should. But what is exactly being prosecuted when the injurious word comes to trial and is it finally or fully prosecutable? That words wound seems incontestably true, and that hateful, racist, misogynist, homophobic speech should be vehemently countered seem incontrovertibly right. But does understanding from where speech derives its power to wound alter our conception of what it might mean to counter that wounding power? Do we accept the notion that injurious speech is attributable to a singular subject and act? If we accept such a juridical constraint on thought—the grammatical requirements of accountability—as a point of departure, what is lost from the political analysis of injury? Indeed, when political

discourse is fully collapsed into juridical discourse, the meaning of political opposition runs the risk of being reduced to the act of prosecution.[26]

If Butler had the Habermasian confidence that Brenkman attributes to her—that is, "that there is something in the logic of language or communication that determines the horizon of democracy"[27]—she would perhaps be less concerned with how law can potentially constrain the very freedom it purports to protect. Freedom here, certainly as it is to be understood in *Excitable Speech*, is the freedom to transform our symbolic field through what Butler calls the reiteration of words, signs, and other cultural representations so that they can take on new meanings and different forms from the ones for which their users or producers originally intended them. Butler uses the example of the word "queer" as it has been reappropriated and reaffirmed by Queer Theory as a classic example of this kind of freedom. But this freedom is fragile and relies precisely on the institutionalized publicness and space of free expression that Brenkman also insists must be protected. Brenkman seems to believe that he and Butler disagree about the need for the institutionalization of this speech. The main difference is how it is to be institutionalized and if it is to be institutionalized through law, what are the legal ideals through which it can be best protected.

There is no doubt that Butler has a Nietzschian suspicion of the articulation of legal ideals that claim a substantive universality and thus a moral closure on who should be included in the reach of universality itself. But this wariness can itself be understood as inspired by her commitment to freedom and to her Adornian-inspired romance with the heterogeneous and incommensurate materiality and singularity of our human being, which renders us humble before our necessary attempts to symbolically lay claim to our person and to consolidate the form of our appeals to the idea of humanity. This is the "romance" that it is kept alive in Kant's Third Critique.

Brenkman begins his argument with a defense of the publicness of aesthetic forms, including conceptions of the beautiful. But there is another step that I would argue he needs to take. That step is the recognition that the ideals he defends and the configurations of them that he advocates are just that—configurations, and more specifically what Kant would call aesthetic ideas. I agree that aesthetic ideas are crucial to the form we give to our legal rights specifically and to our sense of publicness more generally. But aesthetic ideas, since they are configurations, can always be contested and judged again for the moral and political effect they have in the form they give to our public life.

I leave Brenkman with Fanon's prayer at the end of *Black Skin, White Masks:*

My final prayer:
   O my body, make me always a man who questions![28]

Part II

WHY RIGHTS?

Part II

WHY LIGHTS?

6

Worker's Rights and the Defense of Just-Cause Statutes

INTRODUCTION

The tension between "private ordering" through contractual consent and governmental regulation of the employer/employee relationship has long been at the heart of the debate over the future direction of American labor law. This fundamental tension has arisen once again in the recent clash between those who defend the perpetuation of the employment-at-will doctrine as an appropriate mechanism for the "private ordering" of the employer/employee relationship, at least in those circumstances where there are no specific contractual provisions between the parties to the contrary, and those who contest the doctrine as a bad excuse for the exercise of arbitrary power by the dominant employers against their employees.[1] The doctrine of employment at will was succinctly summarized in *Payne v. Western & Atlantic Railroad.*[2]

> [M]en must be left, without interference to buy and sell where they please, and to discharge or retain employees at will for good cause or for no cause, or even for bad cause without thereby being guilty of an unlawful act *per se.* It is a right which an employee may exercise in the same way, to the same extent, for the same cause or want of cause as the employer.[3]

Prominent writers in law and economics such as Richard Epstein[4] and Richard Posner[5] have challenged those who condemn the doctrine of employment at will not only for the substance of their views but also for their seeming lack of justification. Epstein has noted that "it takes a theory to beat a theory, so it is wholly insufficient for them to belittle the use of common law arguments without some explanation as to why these arguments are wrong or why they should be replaced."[6] Once the air is cleared of condemnatory rhetoric, little is left in the way of an effective ethical argument to serve as a counterpoint to the utilitarian and/or libertarian perspective offered in the law and economics literature.

To defend and expand the inroads into the doctrine of employment at will, consequently, requires such an ethical theory. My purpose in this essay is to develop an ethical framework that allows us a coherent justification of rational-cause statutes. This ethical framework has three prongs: (1) a conception of individuality and correspondingly of freedom as a social achievement enforced by the state; (2) a view of the common will as differentiated, allowing for the disruption of the rights/duties correlation within certain areas of law, if that correlation is understood as it has been in the Hobbesian framework as a reciprocal trade-off, so that if the employer has to give reasons for the firing of an employee, so must the employee give reasons for quitting; and (3) a notion of *concrete* reciprocity that includes questions of substantive inequality within the sphere of right. I suggest that Hegel's thought is crucial in support of the first two prongs of the theory even if, ultimately, he cannot provide the third. This essay proposes that we adopt unwaivable rational-cause statutes to replace the current doctrine of employment at will. I advocate a rational-cause statute as opposed to a just-cause statute[7] because I believe that it addresses the ethical concerns of the law-and-economics movement by reducing the risk inherent in wide-ranging arbitrators' discretion through the use of established statutory guidelines.

The just-cause statutes that have been advocated mimic the language of current union contracts, which, indeed, leave the ultimate question of "just cause" up to the arbitrators. In contrast, an ethical theory in which a rational-cause statute can be situated obviates the need to rely solely on the standards of fairness developed in and through the arbitration of union contracts.[8] The need for such a theory becomes even more evident once we recognize that underlying the debate as to whether the law should explicitly reject the doctrine of employment at will—either through the legislative process or judicial decision—is the fundamental philosophical question of how we should properly conceive of the relationship between the individual and the state. Directly addressing the relationship among the individual, legal entitlement, and the larger community forms the basis of the philosophical framework necessary to challenge those who disfavor state intervention into the contractual relations between employee and employer as either a paternalistic encroachment on autonomy or an inefficient interference with the market.[9] An ethical and political theory that can successfully justify state intervention into the employer/employee relationship cannot avoid addressing the libertarian principles of individual autonomy, contractual freedom, and the related contractualist justifications for the maintenance of civil society and the state. When taken to their conclusion, as they are in writings of Richard Epstein, these principles mean that, in contract law, the only basis for assessing the fairness of any particular contract is the expressed desires of the parties.[10] Any attempt to appeal to standards of fairness other than those expressed by the parties must necessarily fail, unless such an appeal can be justified by the utilitarian argument that it maximizes efficiency.

The starting point for the development of such a theory is Hegel's understanding of the noncontractualist basis of the modern community, in which the state is a differentiated, complex unity, irreducible to the sphere of civil society or to the organs of the government, and which at the same time both delimits and protects the sphere of private right as but one aspect of the larger whole. In Hegel, the historical development of modern contract principles and of the legal person who can freely enter into contractual negotiations expresses the realized relations of reciprocal symmetry that displaced the asymmetrical legal obligations associated with feudalism. Legal personhood is understood as a social achievement, unlike theories of natural law, in which autonomous selfhood is itself grasped as an ahistoric reality. The notion that the self as a person and moral agent is a presocial reality is the ground of libertarian views of individual right;[11] modern libertarianism continues to find its roots in what Hegel called "empirical natural law."[12] In Hegel, on the other hand, it is the realized ideal of reciprocal symmetry that constitutes the collective ethical reality of modernity—what Hegel refers to as *Sittlichkeit.* Central to the *Sittlichkeit* of modernity is the principle of subjectivity. The embodied ideal of reciprocal symmetry serves to protect the conditions of legal personhood and of individual agency and, at the same time, justifies the containment of the sphere of right in the name of the ideal itself. This understanding of relations of reciprocity provides the basis of freedom and indeed, of individuality, and thus allows for a conception of state regulation as freedom enhancing rather than freedom restricting.

In contrast to Epstein's Hobbesian view, in which contractual standards of fairness have no content and defer entirely to the expressed desires of the parties, "fairness" or justice in contract in Hegel is the realized ideal that makes modern contractual relations possible. We have, then, an objective standard of fairness to which the judge can appeal in assessing the validity of contractual transactions. We need such an objective standard of fairness—here, objective is only meant to indicate an ethical conception irreducible to the subjective desires of the parties[13]—to answer Epstein's advocacy of a presumption in favor of employment at will in those circumstances where the parties are silent on the matter. The Hegelian ideal of reciprocal symmetry is particularly powerful as an objective standard of fairness in contract because it is based on the conditions for the recognition of modern personhood. This standard allows us to explain what kind of facts are relevant to the condemnation of employment at will because it allows us to explain *why* employment at will is wrong, *given* the modern conception of the person. It allows us to reject the relevance of efficiency as the wrong kind of fact.

Hegel is also helpful in another crucial respect. Hegel defends a differentiated conception of the common will, rather than an abstract unity created by a hypothetical contract. This means that Hegel allows, in certain circumstances, the breakdown of the reciprocal trade-off of duties held by the libertarians as essential to a modern legal system respectful of individual right.[14] This disruption of the correlation between rights and duties—that is, of reciprocally imposed duties—is crucial, because it provide us with *one* answer to Epstein's argument against those who have advocated just-cause statutes; this argument, although also an appeal to reciprocity, differs considerably from the Hegelian ideal of reciprocal symmetry. The argument, as such, maintains that if an employer must give "just" cause for terminating an employee, an employee must also give "just" reasons for quitting her job. The argument continues that this kind of "reciprocity" is morally repugnant because it would impose a form of indentured servitude on the employee. Just-cause statutes are therefore condemned as retrogressive, at least if advocated under the structured rights/duties correlation, as Epstein, among others, has understood it.[15] A differentiated conception of the common will is one way out of this problem. As I will demonstrate, this solution is superior to the conception of law as the defense of the weaker party that Clyde Summers advocates in support of "just cause" statutes,[16] as well as to standards of fairness in contract more generally.

Hegel, in other words, justifies state-imposed duties in which there is no corresponding right in the name of the common good. The disruption of the correlation of rights and duties is vital to the debate over the replacement of the presumption in favor of employment at will, in view of a previous attempt to displace the doctrine of employment at will through the development of the tort of wrongful discharge.[17] Hegel, as we will see, allows us to develop and defend a justification for the tort of wrongful discharge. But here again, Hegel is sensitive to the crucial importance of moral agency in any acceptable modern conception of the common good. As a result, he attempts to reconcile state-imposed duties with individual moral agency.

We all have the capacity to recognize the need for rational-cause statutes, because we would not want to live in a society where human beings could lose something as important to their sense of identity and well-being as a job without some reason. Of course, an assertion that the potential for this capacity exists requires that we believe that there is a view of dignity widely enough shared and that it informs the individual's ethical self-conception. This view of dignity is in turn implicated in relationships between employers and employees. A duty is imposed upon the employer in the name of the good of society, committed to the realization of individuality and the conception of dignity it enforces. Hegel uses this mode of legal argumentation

in his defense of good samaritan laws that, while not justifiable under the formal structure of right, are still necessary for the achievement of a good society. This good is the good of relations of reciprocal symmetry necessary for
the full development of individualism. This good within the sphere of civil
society allows for intervention into the sphere of private right. The significance of this point must be stressed. Hegel does not just leave us with the
abstract reciprocity of the sphere of right. His differentiated conception of
the common will implies a substantive view of reciprocity: the abstract reciprocity of the sphere of right is enriched as we encompass that sphere within
the state as a whole. Within the sphere of civil society, reciprocity is not
merely abstract because it comes to include certain measures that even out
the most glaring inequalities between citizens. Thus, although I criticize
Hegel for not developing the meaning of the concrete relations of reciprocity within the sphere of right itself, it would also be a serious mistake to read
him as if he left us with only the abstract reciprocity of abstract right. If, however, we are to justify rational-cause statutes as a matter of right, we must still
move beyond Hegel's own understanding of the sphere of private right, even
if in doing so we remain true to the aspiration of achieving the "good" of relations of reciprocal symmetry. I will argue for recasting the notion of the
legal person and the principle of right so that matters of substantive inequality are addressed as questions of right.

This expansion will entail a renewed focus on relations of reciprocal symmetry as *relations* between citizens, in which the ideal of horizontal equality
is emphasized so that the parties are standing eye to eye, with no one legally
recognized as subordinate and therefore necessarily on the bottom. This
view of equality cannot be reduced to equality of respect by the state, which
would only express the notion of abstract reciprocity; instead it emphasizes
the horizontal dimension of relations between citizens. The state, in other
words, must protect conditions of horizontality.[18]

As I hope to show, the expansion of the ideal of reciprocity to emphasize
horizontality as crucial to the achievement of concrete relations of concrete
reciprocity need not lead to the Marxist conclusion that the sphere of private
right must be completely obliterated. It should, however, mandate that questions of substantive inequality be addressed as crucial to the realized breakdown of the asymmetrical, legal relationships of feudalism. Absent measures
in this direction, the achievement of horizontality remains an illusion. Employment at will, in other words, can be understood as a residue of the asymmetrical structure of the legal obligation associated with the master/servant
relationship. But to show that no matter what its origin, the presumption in
favor of employment at will cannot be justified as preferable to rational-
cause statutes under modern contract principles, we must examine the actual
context of the usual employment contract, which more often than not is between the individual worker and the structure of the corporation or the firm.

This focus also stems from the insistence that the protection of horizontality must include certain substantive measures. Although my goal here is to provide an alternative ethical framework within which to justify unwaivable rational-cause statutes, I will critique Epstein's assumptions about the reality of in-firm training, which serves as the basis for his use of bilateral monopoly analysis in an unorganized setting.[19] I turn now to the contrast between Hobbes and Hegel to show how the competing approaches to individuality lead to different conclusions as to the legitimate context of state regulation.

THE COMMUNAL BASIS FOR UNIVERSAL
RECOGNITION OF INDIVIDUALITY

In Hegel, individuality is socially engendered. Human beings come to recognize the social basis of their own personhood and thus learn to participate in the life of the political community as the inner demand of their own longing for the recognition of selfhood. In Hegelian language, the "state of nature" is an immediacy that negates itself. The inevitable modality of the natural self, its striving to maintain itself as a self, demands the recognition of the person in social institutions.

The empirical basis of natural law lies in its appeal to the reality of human singularity. Each one of us is an individual at least in the sense that we have boundaries that separate us from one another. But the empirical reality of our singularity should not be confused with the assumption of particularity we associate with individual identity and self-consciousness. In Hegel, particularity is the self-enfolding of subjectivity; to observe the reality that we are singular does not necessarily lead to the conclusion that our singularity can be identified with individuality. In Hegel, the distinction between empirical singularity and the achievement of personality or self-consciousness is crucial if we are to comprehend individuality as itself a social achievement that demands community protection in and through the state's institutional structures. The collapse of particularity into singularity is the central mistake of theories of empirical natural law.[20] Empirical theories of natural law, for all of their individualist rhetoric, cannot give us an adequate account of the human conditions in which true particularity can flourish, because they assume that empirical singularity is pregiven individuality.

When Hegel speaks of empirical natural law, his main interlocutor is Thomas Hobbes.[21] Like Hobbes, Hegel asserts that natural individuality is the unlimited exercise of a "power with regard to all things," to the exclusion of all other human beings.[22] The *conatus*, or individual drive, is initially animated only by this urge to mastery.[23] In Hobbes, however, contract between individual beings in "nature" can only yield this contest of strength against strength. Even love, for Hobbes, is nothing other than power—be it power over another or a homage rendered to one's own power. There is no internal mechanism that takes us beyond this endless clash of competing strengths, except perhaps exhaustion. If the natural individual is to maintain himself, to conserve some of his energy and power, he must ultimately accept an exterior force that can successfully impose itself against the ever-battling, natural men. In Hobbes, the state is the vehicle for individual self-preservation; the power of the state is an external limitation on the natural individual. The state is a form of domination, not an enabling power that promotes the flourishing of true individuality. For Hobbes, the disjuncture between the singularity of the natural individual and the universality of political institutions cannot be overcome.

It is precisely Hegel's task to overcome this fundamental disjuncture between the particular and the universal by demonstrating that it is the dialectic of desire itself that leads to the mutual recognition that selfhood needs its other to be preserved as a self-conscious particular. The move to reconciliation with the other is, in other words, *internal* to the desiring self as it plays out its own initial longing for mastery.

The self-conception of mastery also undermines itself from within. The other, who is enslaved, becomes an object no longer able to pit her own desire against her opponent. As we will see, the achievement of mastery is self-defeating, because we can only find ourselves in the other if she remains a subject, another desiring "I." What is desired, according to Hegel, is the desire of the other, for it is her ability to reflect the other as also striving for sovereignty that provides the mirror in which the interlocutor first glimpses his own potential subjectivity. It is in the moment of mutual recognition that the self finds itself to be more than sheer physical presence. The self becomes self-conscious of her own striving, as inherent to who she is. In Hegel, the desire for mastery does not just express the individual's longing for possession of external objects and, therefore, whoever achieves mastery can possess what the other has; possession itself is a means to an end. When an individual feels herself excluded by another who takes no notice of her, as he takes possession of her things as if she were a thing herself, she experiences a gap between her knowledge of herself and the lack of knowledge the other has of her.[24] She is also one who seeks possession, not just a thing to be possessed. In the struggle for possession between clashing wills, each side wishes to surmount the lack of identity between her knowledge of herself as an individual who also can possess things and the knowledge the other seemingly has of her as a mere thing. Each seeks to be recognized as a being who can possess and not as a being who is simply identified with her possession. Only another creature who sees herself in the desire of the other can recognize the "I" for the kind of unique being she really is.

Another dimension of Hegel's discussion, often obscured, proposes that it is not possession itself that makes one a person; indeed, it is precisely the master's ability to forsake the most cherished possession, life itself, that allows him to achieve mastery.[25] What is sought is not possession itself, but recognition through the medium of possession. It is a serious mistake, then, to identify the Hegelian conception of personhood with the possession and ownership of property. What is sought is not possession but reciprocity, which is precisely why the self-conception of mastery is self-defeating. No amount of things can suffice for what he has sacrificed in the achievement of mastery, the recognition by an equal interlocutor.[26] What we seek in possession is recognition of our selfhood. But we can, at times, achieve such recognition only through the relinquishment of possession, which is what the master does when he risks his most essential possession—life itself. The insight that the striving for possession is an expression of a more basic desire for recognition is the fundamental point separating Hegel from Hobbes.

The first manifestation that the self's desire is not just for domination but for recognition is found in Hegel in the "natural" relation of sexual love. Unlike in Hobbes, where love is reduced to a homage to one's own power, love in Hegel is the first experience we have of finding one's true "essence" in the other. The one we love recognizes our being-for-self as absolute. In the moment of mutual recognition, the "I" experiences confirmation of her own self-consciousness as she, in turn, engages with the other who, like herself, is also a self-conscious being. But such recognition demands that the two parties understand one another as desiring wills, each striving to become a being-for-self. In their love, the lovers find themselves; each is for the other in an alliance that allows for the self to flourish. Love is the self's longing, not its diminution. It demands that neither one give up his or her subjectivity. It is just this recognition of her desire to become a being-for-self that is denied to the slave in her moment of submission.

The slave gains her own sense of herself as a subject in control of her own natural impulses, not through conquering of the fear of death in battle but through her labor for the master. It is through her labor that she learns of her own ability to become a subject by externalizing her capacities and, in so doing, leaving a mark on the world around her. Again, let us emphasize that in the case of both the master and the slave, the experience of engaging with the world of things does not have as its goal mere possession or assertion of control, but the imposition of one's own knowledge of oneself as an individual who can put her will into external objects and therefore claim them as her own. But to bring about the recognition that the individual is one who can externalize her will, the other must see her as more than just her possessions. The recognition of the being-for-self as absolute demands that each antagonist show that she does not identify her selfhood with her possessions. The master first awakens to his potential subjectivity through his willingness to relinquish his own bodily existence in order to win the desire of the other. The slave, on the other hand, forsakes her own natural self in her work for her master, which teaches her about her own subjectivity through the use of tools and the manipulation of the world of things. Self-consciousness is the realization that one is a subject who is irreducible to any of the objectifications that may be imposed on her because of her subordinate status. It arises in the context of a struggle with the other. She then begins the long journey down the "highway of despair," which ultimately leads to the revelation of the necessary social and political conditions for the fulfillment of the subject's desire for recognition of her own particularity. In Hegel, it is the slave's journey that culminates in the universal recognition of equal personhood, because it is only under such conditions that the slave can finally find self-realization. Universality in Hegel is not a construct. It is an historical achievement unleashed both by the inherent contradiction of mastery and the slave's longing for what the master apparently has—confirmation by the other of his being-for-himself. Once the ideal of mutual recognition as the condition for individual freedom is discovered, it can be temporarily shut out, but never again completely silenced, precisely because it is rooted in the dialectic of desire itself. Desire is the longing for freedom. As long as there is human life, there will be this longing for freedom; this longing for freedom, in turn, can be fulfilled in relations of mutual recognition. The drive for universality is rooted in desire.[27]

It is critical to note here that not only is the self-consciousness of the subject a social achievement, it is also an achievement capable of being realized only in relationships of mutual recognition and reciprocal symmetry in which each sees the other as a being-for self. Mastery is self-negating, because the master needs the recognition by the slave of his subjectivity. When he denies her subjectivity, he denies her standing to give him the recognition he seeks. It is only through the achievement of self-consciousness that what is desired is the recognition of another desiring "I," that the futility of the striving for mastery is fully grasped. Both parties must come to understand that they are symmetrically situated in their desire to overcome the other's false consciousness about their being. The individual who is recognized as another "I" is recognized as a person.

The community that embodies the conditions necessary for the achievement of subjectivity is not, then, an external force of domination, as in Hobbes, but the internal expression of the dialectic of desire itself. The stance toward the other is reciprocal in that it is mutual and synchronized in time. I recognize the other looking back at me as I recognize her. Our position vis-à-vis one another is also symmetrical. Both of us are similarly situated in our relation to other selves, who also seek the recognition from others of their being-for-self. The image is of two people looking one another in the eye, knowing the other is looking back. No one is on top. The modern legal system recognizes that no one is on top at least in terms of the judicial relations between persons. This is what I call horizontality. Horizontality demands that each one of us is guaranteed symmetry in our relations to other legal persons.

In this way the ethical substantial order has attained its right, and

> its right its validity. . . . Subjectivity is itself the absolute form and existent actu-
> ality of the substantial order, and the distinction between subject on the one
> hand and substance on the other, as the object, end, and controlling power of
> the subject, is the same as, and has vanished directly along with, the distinction
> between them in form.[28]

In Hegel, the ethical is the realized good of the actualized relations of mutual recognition and reciprocal symmetry. The realized social good over-
comes the antithesis between ego and the other, of consciousness, and between nature and spirit, which are inherent in the framework of empirical
natural law, by showing us that it is only under certain conditions that we
achieve the status of persons. In fact, it is precisely our desire to achieve such
recognition of ourselves as persons as distinct from others. The properly in-
stituted community, in other words, is the condition for the realization of our
desire; it does not pit itself against the desiring self.

THE SIGNIFICANCE OF HEGEL'S ACCOUNT OF
INDIVIDUALITY FOR THE *PHILOSOPHY OF RIGHT*

At the very heart of the modern state is the universally recognized particularity of each individual, established through the juridical definition of the
person in the sphere of private right. The state, in other words, is a necessary
power for the enabling and flourishing of personhood.[29]

The modern state breaks down the status distinctions associated with asymmetrical feudal systems of obligation as incompatible with the socially recognized value of personality, or what Hegel himself calls the principle of subjectivity. Recognition is not only the defining conception of self-identity in Hegel,
but also the ethical practice that gives validity to the institutions of right themselves. Both the law of private property and contract are justified as abstract
legal forms compatible with realized relations of reciprocal symmetry. But
again, let me stress that what makes property and contract important in Hegel
are not the legal forms in themselves, but the role they play in the achievement
of a modern conception of relations of reciprocal symmetry. To the degree that
any existing system of positive law is incompatible with the actualized ideal, it
must be reformed to meet the actualized ideal's standard.[30]

In Hegel, the tension between the actual (the realized ideal) and the mere
existent (the brute reality of social life) prevents the appeal to the realized
norms of *Sittlichkeit* from degenerating into a defense of the perpetuation of
order. All social institutions, including the sphere of private right, are to be

judged against the realized ideal. The realization of the ideal is no longer a simple unity, but instead involves the development of the complex, institutional structure we associate with the modern state. It is this institutional structure that protects the principle of subjectivity and makes individual freedom a substantial reality and not an abstract ought.[31]

In Hegel's social philosophy, even the right to property is ultimately valued as a relationship between persons, expressive of the ideal of reciprocal symmetry. As we saw in the case of the slave in the *Phenomenology*, the relationship of control over external things takes on value only because it teaches the self a sense of her own subjectivity—at least on the plane of her own self-consciousness—as one between subjects.[32] The value of property, in other words, allows each person to be recognized as a formal equal, a legal subject, capable of embodying her will in external things. We respect each other's right to her property because we acknowledge her as a self-conscious being, as a subject like ourselves.

Because it is the *relationship* that is valued, and not the fact of possession itself,[33] property is fundamentally tied to contract.[34] Property, in other words, does not recognize us as a possessive individual, but as a self tied to other selves in a contractual relation. But this contractual relation cannot serve as the basis for a social theory of the state. And why not? Here again we can see the usefulness of contrasting Hobbes and Hegel. In Hobbes's empirical natural law, the state is grounded on a social contract by which particular wills accord to a third will the status of a universal will. For Hegel, the Hobbesian notion of the social contract is a faulty representation of the relationship between the individual and the state because it cannot truly unite the particular will with the universal will. Here we are returned to the central error of empirical natural law, the conviction that the universal will is exterior to the individual will because the individual is an empirical given. As a result, a fundamental contradiction arises within the Hobbesian framework as soon as it is used to defend a justification for the common will on which law is based. In Hobbes, the only legitimate device for the generation of substantive duties and rights is contract. Yet at the same time, the form of contract must be enforced against the self-seeking individuals who, if let alone, would forsake contractual relations if it were in their interest to do so. To preserve contract as a relation, we need to enforce it from the outside; according to Hobbes, only the power of the monarchy can effectively counter the force and violence of individual desire—we have to yield to the sovereign. In Hegel, on the other hand, we realize our desire in a properly constituted relationship with others. As a result, the universal will is not created by a contract between persons who exist before the social compact.

The very idea of the right to contract depends on the recognition of a subject of entitlement who cannot bargain away her status as a rights-bearing subject. Therefore, only by virtue of the universal will embodied in the state can one own property and be secured in his freedom to contract in civil society. The very notion of freedom of contract, then, must find its roots in a noncontractualist conception of political authority in the modern state.[35] The *public* rights of individuals are no longer private property and, as a result, cannot be alienated at will. Instead, public rights are secured in and through the universalized conditions of personhood guaranteed by the state *against* the encroachment of civil society.[36] The right of the state is not reducible to the rights of the individuals. The state has a right that is more, in this specific sense, than the sum of its parts. Hegel essentially turns the Hobbesian contractualist theory of political authority on its head, but in the name of the principle of individual right, which it seeks to value above all else. It will also become apparent that this understanding of the self and its relationship to the state fuels the argument that certain forms of state intervention into the sphere of private right are needed entrances.

According to Hegel's historical account, the modern principle of subjectivity demands that the legal person no longer be considered an alienable good because the very existence of the modern market is dependent upon the existence of the free person. It is the state that "frees" the self through the universal recognition of each one of us as a legal person. Without the juridical embodiment of the free person, there would be no modern market. As a result, the market's values are to be subordinated to the relations of reciprocal symmetry in which personhood is realized. The condition necessary for the sphere of the market to continue to exist, the recognition that we are each a rights-bearing subject who cannot alienate her guaranteed public rights, also provides a limiting principle by which the market is curtailed.

Slavery and indentured servitude can therefore be understood as inherently wrong practices because the socially achieved recognition of the value of personhood is denied. To turn a person into a slave is to mistakenly reduce him to a natural entity. As we have seen in the master/slave dialectic, the reduction of a human being to someone else's property confuses her with a mere external thing that can be possessed. The crowning achievement of modernity is precisely the embodiment in right of relations of mutual recognition in which each sees the other as a self-conscious "I." The subject, as we have seen, becomes a self-conscious "I" by taking possession of itself as other than a merely natural, immediate being. It is this potential to become a personality that marks each one of us a distinctive person.[37]

Our labor power, in Hegel, is understood as capacity that can be externalized. As an externalized capacity, labor power is sold on the market as any other good. When one sells one's labor for a limited period of time, one does not give one's personality over to another. The legal person must be able to take her labor power back into her own possession. This ability to take back her own capacities is crucial if she is to remain a person whose body is her own. It is not time, in and of itself, that is crucial—although the limited time of the bargain can be understood as essential to the exercise of one's potential to take back one's externalized capacities. Rather, it is the recognition of the personhood and the employer. Here, to recognize the individual as a person is to respect her power for self-determination.

> Man, pursuant to his *immediate* existence within himself, is something natural, external to his concept. It is only through the development of his own body and mind, essentially through his self-consciousness's apprehension of itself as free, that he takes possession of himself and becomes his own property and no one else's. This taking possession of oneself, looked at from the opposite point of view, is the translation into actuality of what one is according to one's concept, i.e. a potentiality, capacity, potency.[38]

Relations of reciprocal symmetry also are not to be reduced to the reciprocity of an exchange such that if good *A* is received, payment in some kind will follow. This understanding of reciprocity of exchangeable goods in a transaction would be short term, only applicable to the exchange once the promise between the parties had been made; this understanding is dependent on the more fundamental reciprocity of relations of mutual recognition. Hegelian relations of reciprocity imply a stance toward one another over time, a stance that is objectified in the institutions of right. The actual contractual exchange takes place within this established legal framework. Hegel distinguishes a promise from a contract precisely because a contract is a legal form. What the state enforces in contractual relations, in other words, is not the individual's promise, but the obligation imposed on both parties by right as part of the legal recognition of their personhood.

Consequently, in a specific area of legal doctrine, we are alerted to the significance of Hegel's insistence that the universal will supersedes the alterable and arbitrary dispositions of the parties. The relevant legal question is not what the intent or the appetites of the parties were when the contract was made. The question is what *right* had they to the intentions expressed or violated in the contract? Contractual fairness is a matter established by law, not a matter left to be decided by the parties in each new exchange.

Theories of contract based on either *actual* consent or the moral obligation of the promise reflect the central error of empirical natural law, which holds that rights and corresponding duties arise only out of the interaction of individuals. Hegel does not deny that the entry into a contract involves individual agency, but only that the will of the person is expressed in a pregiven legal form that marks the interaction with the other as a modern legal contract. The right to contract cannot arise out of a contract.[39]

As previously seen in the discussion of the *Phenomenology*, the demand for a properly constituted community is internal to the dynamic of desire, in which the individual's longing for the recognition of her own particularity leads her to negate or supersede her immediacy as a natural being.

The recognition of right is part of the demand of the desiring self for a properly constituted community in which her particularity is allowed to develop. When an individual recognizes the universality of right as established by the state, this recognition expresses the true aim of her constituted subjective will.[40]

The modern state, then, which is not based on contract, still rests on the potential of consent of individuals who recognize the truth of their "desire." The acknowledgment that the individual truly demands a properly constituted community in which the individual can flourish is itself an historical achievement. For Hegel, reconciliation with the community in modernity is always mediated by the subject who comes to understand her community as a response to her own demand. Hegel's communitarianism does not postulate a simple immediate unity of the individual and the state. We cannot jump over our shadows and return to the time in which the force of the principle of subjectivity had not been brought into history. The simple immediacy between the individual and the state that Hegel associated with Greek life has been lost forever; however, this loss is not cause for endless mourning, because the Greek state could not satisfy the individual's desire for the recognition of her own particularity because Greek culture did not have an adequate concept of the person.

Only a state based on principle of subjectivity can adequately embody the conditions necessary for the flourishing of the particular person. The demand for recognition is a demand that "I" be recognized. The universal will embodied in the state, in other words, does not simply obliterate the subjective individual will.[41] It expresses its desire in and through the protection of the sphere of private right and of moral conscience. I am obligated to the state only because it provides me with the conditions for the flourishing of my particularity.[42]

As we have seen, Hegel's state, if it is a properly constituted community, is not imposed against the individual as an external force but instead enables her own self-realization by embodying the conditions in which personality is universally recognized in juridical definition. This understanding of the state has significance for the debate over the legitimacy of state regulation of civil society, and more particularly for the defense of the replacement of the doctrine of employment at will.

Focusing on one dimension of the debate concerning the state's role in the protection of the right of contract, I want to suggest that the libertarian perspective adopted in the law and economics literature, which remains deeply influenced by Hobbes, does not so much *reject* state regulation as adopt a Hobbesian approach to the *content* of regulation. The state can regulate to protect against violence. That is, the debate between the Hobbesian and the Hegelian is not simply over whether state regulation should ever be allowed in civil society. The debate is instead over the extent of the justification for and the content of that intervention. For instance, Epstein offers a Hobbesian justification for state regulations of labor picketers. What is at stake is not the question of whether the state should regulate relations in civil society, but what view of regulation truly promotes individual freedom. The second and crucial point is that for Hegel state regulation is done in the name of the ideal reciprocal symmetry. It is the ideal which gives us an objective stand of right. We now turn to the question of what regulation in the name of that ideal means for the specific justification of the tort of wrongful discharge.

THE HEGELIAN ETHICAL FRAMEWORK FOR OPPOSING THE DOCTRINE OF EMPLOYMENT AT WILL

As we have seen in Hegel, the substantive rights and duties imposed by the law do not arise out of the postulation of a hypothetical contract between presocial individuals. The rights and duties we associate with a modern legal system are established as a matter of objective right in and through the state that embodies the common good as it incorporates the conditions of individual flourishing. My discussion of the tort of wrongful discharge in the context of these notions considers first how, according to Hegel, the subjective understanding of our interconnectedness in civil society provides the basis for individual consent to state-imposed duties even where there is no corresponding right. Under the rubric of Hegel's justification of the "police"— what we would now think of as the welfare state—I suggest that we can develop a justification for the tort of wrongful discharge as a state-imposed duty. Of course, Hegel did not actually seek to justify the tort of wrongful discharge, so we must extrapolate from his argument about the need for the police or welfare administration within civil society.

The second part of my discussion returns to explain why Hegel cannot expand the conception of *right* to embrace rational-cause statutes. We will see that Hegel's "internal" restrictions on the definition of the right to contract are extremely limited because his concept of the legal person follows that of Roman law. Only contracts that violate the conditions of personhood in an abstract sense are forbidden. If we are to justify rational-cause statutes as a *matter of right* rather than as a state-imposed duty, then we have to expand Hegel's own understanding of abstract right to comprehend the way in which horizontality demands measures to mitigate against extreme inequality within the sphere of right.

The Defense of a State-Imposed Duty and the Tort of Wrongful Discharge

For Hegel, the appearance of civil society as the sphere in which radical individualism remains supreme is deceiving. In civil society, each one of us is *free* to pursue our own particular self-interest. But as we have seen in the discussion of contract, we can only do so because of the established universality of relations of mutual recognition. In other words, we can only be free to pursue our individual needs as long as others recognize our freedom to do so. Otherwise, we would not only not have civil society, but also not have society at all—we would have only the war of each against all. Civil society, despite its minimal appearance, is still order. Civil society only survives as long as individuals recognize their fundamental tie to one another in the exercise of their selfish interests.[43] The recognition that even in civil society we are interconnected leads Hegel to argue that the public authority (or the police) is indeed a part of the civil society. The mechanism of civil society constantly threatens the very order on which it depends.[44]

Hegel's rhetoric is often as condemning as that of his successor, Karl Marx. Hegel's difference with Marx does not lie in the competing pictures of civil society they offer, but in their program for what can be done to change the situation. As we have seen, for Hegel the recognition of the sphere of private right was crucial for the expression of personality and therefore could not be wiped out without fundamentally violating the individual's claim to personhood. Marx, on the other hand, believed that the sphere of private right was itself a reflection of the relations of subordination that characterized class society. For Hegel, we cannot abolish either the sphere of private right or the textuality of exchange in civil society. However, we can, indeed we must, intervene against the consequences of civil society left to operate on its own. For Hegel, the police or the welfare administration serves to alleviate the distress inevitably created by the working of civil society. Yet, because the individual of civil society is a particular self pursuing his or her own needs, and not the universal subject of abstract right, the welfare apparatus is not part of the structure of right. Indeed, according to Hegel, it cannot be, because it is the "specific" as opposed to the universal aspects of distress that the welfare administration must handle.

Hegel believes that there are two ways to handle the distress created by the mechanisms of civil society. The first is through direct legal intervention. The second is through the spontaneous organization of the members of civil society (for example, through charity). In both cases, the subjective willingness to accept and to participate in such measures stems from the awareness that arises out of our experience in civil society. We perceive the interconnectedness of our relations in civil society as we also recognize one another, not only as abstract subjects of right but also as particular persons with needs. To see another's distress awakens my identification with her. I develop empathy through the recognition of myself as an individual of need. Poverty is objectively created, but it also creates the desire to alleviate the worst distress.[45]

But, of course, poverty is not the only kind of distress that the individual suffers. For Hegel, what we would now think of as tort law is necessary in the modern state precisely because of the need to alleviate the distress that even the best community cannot help but inflict. Ernest Weinrib has noted that what we think of as modern tort law would not be justifiable under Hegel's understanding of the sphere of abstract right.[46] Yet even though Weinrib correctly points out that Hegel's conception of abstract right does not allow us to take into account advantage, harm, or substantive inequality, since these aspects of the person relate to her particular existence, he makes Hegel's own conception of law and the differentiated common will more rigid than it is. Weinrib interprets Hegel to offer us only an abstract conception of reciprocity. But this abstract conception of relations of reciprocal symmetry is the limited meaning reciprocity has within the sphere of right. As we move through the *Philosophy of Right*, we see that what relations of reciprocal symmetry mean is progressively enriched and concretized. Although the progressive concretization of relations of reciprocal symmetry does not take us to the point where we can justify rational-cause statutes as a matter of right, it is still a mistake to suggest that Hegel *ultimately* leaves us with only the abstract reciprocity between legal persons in the sphere of abstract right. To so argue is to fail to see that the differentiated common will itself involves the progressive concretization of what relations of reciprocal symmetry mean in different spheres of the society. The relations of reciprocal symmetry that underlie the sphere of private right also define our interactions in civil society. Those relations in the different spheres of the state are also differentiated in that reciprocal symmetry takes on new meaning in civil society, beyond what it has in abstract right. Relations of mutual recognition within civil society mean that I recognize that you are a person of need, a physical striving creature who also must suffer and die. This is another approach to recognizing that the drive to universality is inherent in the dialectic of desire. We understand that each one of us is a subject of desire and need. Our reciprocity, in other words, can be understood to demand the mutual recognition of suffering. Only then are we truly on the same plane with one another—an image that is crucial to the achievement of horizontality. If my suffering could be completely disregarded because of my position of subordination, then I would be denied my claim to be recognized as a person like yourself. The objective recognition of horizontality has a subjective dimension that we can identify as compassion. Hegel, in other words, allows us to give an answer to how and why human beings can be ethically motivated to seek a just society and the promotion of the general welfare.[47] Mutual recognition, thus, can lead the individual of civil society to promote the general welfare as a component aspect of the achievement of relations of mutual recognition. This experience of mutual recognition is what allows the individual to accept state-imposed duties, such as good samaritan laws, in which there is no corresponding right. Under this interpretation of the Hegelian understanding of civil society, tort law remains a crucial aspect of the modern state. The same kind of argument that Hegel made in defense of good samaritan laws can also be made in favor of the tort of wrongful discharge. The tort of wrongful discharge has become a judicial mechanism adopted in some states as a way to undermine the doctrine of employment at will.[48] Although Hegel himself did not speak to the issue of wrongful discharge, he certainly testified to the damaging effect of an ever-increasing division of labor on the worker's sense of self-respect and self-worth.[49]

It is easy to conclude from Hegel's remarks on the damaging effect of poverty and unemployment on the self-conception of the person that the distress of factory work should be minimized through the public authority. I am arguing that, under our common-law system, the Hegelian framework serves nicely to justify the tort of wrongful discharge. Here we see the advantage of Hegel's insistence on a differentiated common will in the modern state. Law cannot and should not be reduced to the sphere of private right in which the correlation of duty and right would always hold. This would reduce relations of reciprocal symmetry to the abstract reciprocity of the sphere of right. It would deny our responsibility to the greater whole. Given the modern state's complex nature, we need to supplement the sphere of private right through state-imposed duties in the name of the common good. The limitation on the employer's "right" to fire at will, without imposing a corresponding duty on the employee's "right to quit," constituting a state-imposed duty done in the name of relations of mutual recognition as these relations are concretized within the sphere of civil society so as to incorporate the "subjective" realization of compassion into the general welfare. This, in turn, is expressed in the apprehension of the common good embodied in the law.

I would also suggest that the Hegelian framework provides the best justification of Clyde Summers's position that law must "protect the weaker party."[50] But note: This is not the case as a matter of contractual right, but as a matter of the common good, which is precisely why this argument allows us to sidestep the question of abstract mutuality or reciprocity in modern contract law. Relations of reciprocal symmetry mean that the symmetrical aspect of our standing with regard to one another cannot be completely ignored if horizontality is to be other than an illusion that completely belies the reality of the effects of the free reign of the market in civil society.

The Hegelian framework allows us to show why law *should* protect the weaker party. Law should promote the general welfare in the name of the relations of mutual recognition and reciprocal symmetry that lies at its base. I have deliberately replaced Summers's phrase "protect the weaker party" with "promote the general welfare." The weaker party is an empirical designation that, as we see in the next section, cannot provide us with an objective standard of fairness. The promotion of the general welfare is an explicitly ethical appeal that must be present if we are to normatively justify intervention into the sphere of private right in the name of the common good. The common good in modernity is the relation of reciprocal symmetry embodied in a modern legal system. To the degree that the operation of civil society undermines these relationships by creating gross inequality, it must, at the very least, be thwarted by the law.

The Limits of Hegel's Own Understanding of the Sphere of Abstract Right

Although I believe that Hegel's account of civil society can provide us with a powerful defense of the tort of wrongful discharge, we cannot directly rely on Hegel if we are to justify unwaivable rational-cause statutes as a matter of right, although we might use his definition of the legal person to render employment at will as legal doctrine inconsistent with a modern legal system. In Hegel, questions of substantive inequality *must* be irrelevant in the sphere of right, although it should be noted that the Hegelian framework would not necessarily allow the perpetuation of employment at will. To see why this is the case, we must turn to how Hegel's analysis of the judicial definition of the person stems from his understanding of the break between Roman law and a modern legal system.

Hegel rejects the Roman law distinction between *jus ad rem* and *jus ad personam* as incompatible with the modern principle of subjectivity. In Roman law—and Hegel uses this fundamental principle as his starting point in the *Philosophy of Right*—it is personality alone that can confer a right to things, and therefore *jus ad personam* is encompassed in *jus ad rem*. But *jus ad personam* in Roman law connects the right of personality with the possession of a certain social status.[51]

Legal recognition of the person means that we no longer recognize in law the hierarchical status associated with an individual's particular capacity or social role. It is incompatible, in other words, with the normative demands of a modern conception of personhood. Employment at will, however, can be traced back to the master/slave relationship in which the Roman tradition of *jus ad personam* had not yet been effectively undermined. The status differential between the master and the servant was reflected in the master's absolute power over the servant's livelihood. Indeed, it was his legally recognized power over the servant that marked him as a master. Therefore, the servant was subjected to the master's every wish; his legal status was defined in the subordination to the master. To force the master to give reasons for the termination of the relationship with the servant would violate his status.

But once we have "depersonalized" the legal relationship between the employer and the employee by completely rejecting the *jus ad personam* of Roman law, both parties are to be subjected only to the impersonal legal norms of the law. The subordinate status of one person to another is no longer to be recognized by the law. Employment at will, since it continues to reflect the Roman law doctrine of *jus ad personam*, is incompatible with the legal recognition of each of us as an abstract personality and not as a capacity or social role. As legal persons, each legal subject is to be recognized as having attained a *symmetrical* relationship to all other persons. This is what it means to stress that a modern legal system breaks down the legal embodiment of status distinctions in the name of relations of reciprocal symmetry. To justify the judiciary's striking down of employment at will, we need only demonstrate that precedent is incompatible with the modern legal recognition of each one of us as a personality who stands, at least before the law, in a symmetrical relationship to all others. Employment-at-will doctrine should be struck down, in other words, because it violates the prohibition of a modern system of right, based on the idea: "Do not negate me as a personality by legally reducing me to my particular capacity." This far Hegel can take us.

To note that the doctrine of employment at will is Roman in origin serves to weaken the "functionalist" defense of employment at will, which defends the doctrine on the basis that it must have some merit or it would not have survived so long.[52] The question becomes: For what kind of legal system does the doctrine function? Alan Watson has shown that the fact that a legal doctrine is borrowed by a later system is not necessarily indicative that it is functional for that system.[53] Watson emphasizes the haphazardness of the process of borrowing from one legal system to the next. He shows us that what is actually borrowed from Roman law can be explained by the legal profession's structure in a particular society, together with its bureaucratic and political needs. Exposing the origin of the employment at will doctrine is important because it reveals that, at least as initially conceived, it is in conflict with the normative, modern conception of the person. The "fact" of origin, in other words, is significant within the ethical framework developed.[54]

Although Hegel explicitly rejects distinctions in Roman law he found to be incompatible with the modern juridical definition of the person, such as the distinction between *jus ad personam* and *jus ad rem*, he accepts the divide between the abstract person of right and the concrete self of need he associates with Roman law. Abstract rights are negative in that they protect against the infringement on personality. But they do not and cannot *as rights* give to the person what she thinks she needs to actually develop her personality. The *structure of right* cannot protect against the inevitable contingency inherent in the individual's pursuit of satisfaction. But as we have seen, the state and the law itself must protect against the full force of the mechanism of civil society. Hegel finds this kind of intervention absolutely necessary.

Limitations in the sphere of right can only be accepted if they are consistent with the juridical definition of personhood. We can expand the Hegelian conception of right, however, if we comprehend that it is relations of reciprocal symmetry that are expressed in the juridical recognition of personhood. As we have seen in Hegel, it is our symmetrical situation as legal persons that breaks down the vertical dimension of our social relations. We are returned to the image of symmetrical relations as involving each citizen standing on the same level with the other so that she can look the other in the eye and see the other looking back. Thus, I argue that horizontality is crucial to the achievement of concrete relations of reciprocal symmetry. It is this image of reciprocity as looking at one another in the eye that demands the symmetry of the parties. If relations were asymmetrical, one party would be looking down on the other. The modern legal system recognizes that at least as legal persons we are symmetrically situated. The law is no longer allowed to recognize that one person is on top of another. It is this legal guarantee of relations of reciprocal symmetry that yields what I call the principle of nonsubordination. The principle of nonsubordination, in turn, demands that we expand the Hegelian conception of the sphere of abstract right.

The Need to Expand the Hegelian Conception of Right to Include Questions of Substantive Inequality

As we have seen, in Hegel's view, the dismantling of the feudal hierarchies through the legal protection of each individual as a person does not reach substantive questions of inequality, at least not within the definition of right. Bruce Ackerman has argued, however, that it is this need to justify the substantive inequalities that distinguishes the liberal state and its system of right from other modes of social ordering. Ackerman states, "The fundamental problem for liberal political theory is to determine what you could possibly say that might convince me of the legitimacy of your claim to power."[55] The state must give me reasons and, I would argue, protect my right to be given reasons by others who assert their power over me to justify substantive inequality between us. If our legal system, in essence, is to allow inequalities that violate full substantive equality, it must ensure that we are given reasons that justify the reinstatement of asymmetry.

Ackerman contends that the authority of the modern liberal state, with its system of right, must rest on this dialogic structure for the justification of the perpetuation of the state. If the state did not give me reasons for inequality it would treat me as a mere means to its end—to do so would violate my personhood. Absent this reason-giving, the state would not protect my horizontal standing vis-à-vis other citizens. Ackerman attempts to develop a dialogic and neutral mechanism for the determination of justice. In the Hegelian approach I am advocating, however, the dialogic "image" does not function as a mechanism for legitimation. Instead, "dialogism," if understood as the demand for reasons from the state to justify inequality, is seen as a necessary expression of the modern conception of personhood. What I am offering, then, is a Hegelian understanding of the significance of the image of dialogism, based on a normative conception of the person. Such a conception is not neutral. Instead, it rests on a substantive good—the good of personhood itself.

Only by giving us reasons does the state demonstrate respect for our personhood. The authority of the universal will depends on a justificatory structure, which demands that reasons be given for every substantive inequality that potentially undermines fully actualized relations of reciprocal symmetry. If I am a person and therefore as good as you are, then my claim must be heard. Accepting the silencing of another person violates relations of mutual recognition. If you believe that you need not listen to me to take my ethical claims seriously, then you are refusing to grant me mutual recognition. You are implicitly declaring that I am not a person, as you are, and therefore I am not your equal. Legal relations of reciprocal symmetry include this dimension of horizontality. As we have seen, within the Hegelian framework, what the state protects in its rights is precisely the horizontal plane of our relations. Horizontality, however, can be interpreted to demand a dialogic structure of justification so that each of us is considered as good as the other; no one is reduced by law to a subordinate status so that her voice and claim can be silenced on the basis that she does not deserve to be heard because of her role in society. This dialogic structure of justification also means that the individual must be given the right to answer and to participate in the deliberative process of self-government.[56]

I want now to distinguish dialogism as I have just defined it from one version of the "new civic republicanism."[57] The new civic republicanism emphasizes the *central* role of law in the protection of the process of political deliberation. The substantive rights to be adopted emerge from the process of deliberation between citizens. Although the new civic republicanism is not against rights, it minimizes the central importance of a normative conception of the person protected by law.

With Hegel, I want to emphasize that this conception of the person is essential in a modern legal system. Certain basic substantive rights, in other words, should be protected as a matter of legal personhood. As we will see, I am suggesting, unlike Hegel, that the right to participate in the political process is part of that conception of the legal person. But I am also arguing against one version of the new civic republicanism that reduces the role of right to the protection of the conditions of political participation. What is right is not what arises out of conditions of dialogue; what is right is the reallocation and protection of personhood.

The Secularization of the Hegelian Conception of the State through Dialogism

The dialogic turn in Hegelian interpretation explicitly recognizes that the community is rooted in the finitude of our actual interconnectedness. Spirit is grasped as the *Mitte* of our primordial, internal inner-relatedness.[58] Hegelian dialogism, however, in no way denies the communitarian basis of the self or the ontological basis of community. It simply recasts the Hegelian insight that the Ethical Idea is not produced or constituted through the rational consent of individuals. The Ethical Idea presupposes the achievement of shared values that command our rational consent. The Ethical Idea is accessible to the individual reason of actual human beings because it has been substantially realized in state-organized social institutions. Without this state actualization, the Ethical Idea would bear no reality. Our membership and allegiance to *Sittlichkeit* norms demand not blind allegiance, however, but critical assessment. This understanding of the critical moment of evaluation inherent in the acceptance of our *Sittlichkeit* norms takes on significance for how we justify state regulation in civil society. Such justification is twofold. First, regulation is accepted as necessary to the achievement of freedom, because "true" freedom is not given in a state of nature but only found in relations of reciprocal symmetry. Second, state regulation goes beyond the Hobbesian correlation of rights and duties and is accepted as part of our responsibility to one another, which we come to understand through the achievement of horizontality.

No matter how one reads Hegel, there is undoubtedly a profound tension between his own deconstruction of the logic of identity, which I have traced in this essay through his critique of the self as a positive substance, and his own tendency to reinscribe it in a reified notion of *Geist*, or spirit. Under the traditional reading of Hegel's absolute, which politically has become associated with right-wing Hegelianism, the state or the universal will becomes a higher subjectivity identified as the unified substance of the people. In Hegelian language, the modern state is understood as the fully adequate and completely determined representation of the infinite or *Geist* in history. As is well known, Hegel defended the monarchy. The monarch becomes the symbol of the Infinite's self-expression in history, embodied in the realized sovereignty of the Ethical Idea.[59]

On this reading of Hegel, his rejection of social contract theories stems not from his communitarian understanding of the development of the legal person, but from his conception of the state as the representation of the Absolute Subject. We have seen that such a communitarian perspective is crucial if we are to understand state regulation as freedom enhancing rather than freedom restricting. State regulation is freedom enhancing insofar as it promotes the realization of substantive relations of reciprocal symmetry. If freedom could be found in a state of nature, then regulation would always be restrictive of that freedom. But if freedom and individuality are social achievements because, as communal creatures, we can only find freedom in and through the proper structure of our relations, then we do not have to justify, as Hobbes does, state regulation as a necessary evil but instead as a "good." So we want to maintain Hegel's communitarianism even if we reject his understanding of the state as the expression of the Absolute. For Hegel, a state based on a contract is contaminated by contingency and finitude. Participatory institutions, even those as moderate as universal suffrage, reduce the state to the interplay of the citizens themselves; therefore, such participatory institutions must also be condemned for introducing finitude into the state. A reformulation of Hegel's Absolute, then, is crucial to render Hegel's institutional analysis of modernity consistent with participatory democracy and, more specifically for the purposes of this essay, with an understanding of right as an open-ended, because indeterminate, intersubjective practice.

Such a reformulation can be found in the deconstruction of the subject as a positive substance that Hegel initiates but does not take to its conclusion. We need such a deconstructive account[60] of the subject to adopt an understanding of the universal will of political institution as the *Mitte* of reciprocally constituted subjects that enables their freedom. This Hegelian view I have suggested can be captured in the image of dialogism. Only on the basis of such an account can we both continue to answer the Hobbesian challenge by maintaining the distinction between singularity and particularity, and at the same time avoid reifying *Geist* into a deified subjectivity. The *Mitte* of reciprocally constituted subjects is still not reducible to the sum of its parts. The universal will is not reduced to the aggregation of individual wills, as it is in Hobbes. Nor does the reformation of Hegel let the state come full circle as a self-contained entity that successfully tears itself away from finitude. As a result, this reformulation maintains a communitarian perspective that allows us to justify state regulation of civil society as a good, without "deifying" any particular set of social institutions as the complete expression of the Absolute.

The dialogic turn in Hegelian interpretation allows us to give a dialectical account of the relationship between the universal and the particular will that is not endangered by completely collapsing the particular into the universal. The account that I have given is also important because it proposes that the universal will does not simply arise out of dialogue. This is the axis of my disagreement with both civic republicanism and Ackerman's own understanding of his project. Such a view of the universal will would be a re-endorsement in dialogic form of contractual justifications of the state. The universal will is an expression of our primordial relativity. In this sense, the narrative of the modern legal community cannot escape ontology. Law demands synchronization of persons and rights, and synchronization, in turn, demands an account of our belonging together. In Hegel, this synchronization process takes place within the substantively realized Ethical Idea. It is only because the Ethical Idea is present in our community that we can rationally access and critique our institutions. Reason is not just a formal cognitive process in Hegel. Reason is made actual in social practice. Indeed, if reason did not leave its mark on our actual social institutions, it could not guide us at all. Reason, in this sense, is always circular, because it must be presupposed as the beginning of the movement of thought that finds its starting place at the communitarian standards in which the individual comes to herself. Hegel rejects all neo-Kantian procedural notices of reason as the contractual basis of the state, because such conceptions must remain empty and formal. They can, in other words, only generate a procedural notion of right that cannot effectively synchronize the right and the good in the actual substance of a concrete legal system. It is only because the "life-world" is, to a limited extent, organized rationally that we can develop a concrete institutional jurisprudence that allows for a differentiated system of law. Procedural notions of communicative reason cannot give us such a jurisprudence, which is precisely why Hegel remains so important in modern legal debates.

Of course, the standard response to Hegelianism is that we have much more to lose than we have to gain by adopting any philosophical view that privileges the good over the right in law, even when the good is understood as the protection of conditions of personhood. We stand to lose individual freedom itself, since the individual will can be subordinated to the objective ethical order. Indeed, the individual will is only given meaning within the context of this objective order. A neo-Kantian dialogic approach to cooperative will formation would, on the contrary, always have to take the existence of individuals into account since the universal will can only arise out of their consent. Therefore, such an approach seems more compatible with the liberal insistence on individual freedom from the imposition of an outside "good."[61]

But as we have seen in Hegel, the very structure of right is given concrete content through the realized good of relations of reciprocal symmetry. It is only through our appeal to the good that the normativeness of the right is guaranteed. But does that mean that the right has no independent standing in Hegel since it is conceived within the whole of the Ethical Idea? In the later Hegel, the right is a *necessary* appearance that is constitutive of any modern conception of the good. The very idea of modernity rests on the principle of subjectivity. The good, in other words, if it is to be rendered consistent with the principle of subjectivity, must be internalized as my good. The Ethical Idea, then, does not just subsume the right as an illusion of the false consciousness of individualism.[62]

As a necessary appearance in the objectification of the good in its particularly modern form, the right has both positive significance and ontological stability. The ontological stability of the sphere of right—which is not to say that it cannot be "destabilized"—is due in some measure to the kind of subjects we are constituted to be in a modern society. In the *Philosophy of Right*, each of the stages of the objectification of the Ethical Idea is ultimately given its meaning through the whole. But at the same time, each stage remains as a necessary instantiation of the whole. The general will is differentiated in Hegel. There can be no simple recovery of a lost unity. What makes Hegel's voice unique in the current debates is the way in which he synchronizes the right and the good, so that the autonomous appearance of the right is part of the good itself. By so doing, he avoids the vacuousness of a purely procedural conception of the right, and the libertarian perspective that reduces the good to a question of individual taste and preference. He also avoids the danger of an appeal to an undifferentiated community as the only basis for ethical meaning. State regulation of the sphere of private right and of civil society can only be justified if it protects the good of relations of reciprocal symmetry that give the right its normative dimension in the first place.

Of course, if we do not accept Hegel's system as Absolute Knowledge, we can only justify Hegel's synchronization of the right and the good through an appeal to its pragmatic power. We cannot say this is the truth and has been shown to be so. A better interpretation of how the synchronization of the right and the good should be accomplished may be offered. Hegel remains important, however, because he understands that the two must be synchronized once we give up the illusion that the right cannot stand on its own, since it and not the good can be grounded in a reconstructive science.[63] If the right cannot claim to be grounded any more than a conception of the good in first philosophy or in a reconstructed science, then we are left with pragmatic justifications for our competing visions.[64] Hegel's synchronization of the right and the good allows us to think beyond the dead-end of the either/ors that have characterized recent debates between the "liberals" and the new "communitarians." For that reason alone he should be heard.

But Hegel did not develop his own understanding of the necessary place for self-assertion against the community as crucial to a modern conception of the good into a political view of the individual's involvement in the state. Independence from the community is protected by the sphere of private right; state regulation cannot simply erase that sphere, for it expresses the unique modern aspect of relations of reciprocal symmetry. But what about interdependence with the community exercised as critical participation in it? Here Hegel cannot help us. In Hegel, the constitutional government allows participation only through the corporations. Even so, nothing forbids us from bringing Hegel's conception of the principle of subjectivity and of relations of reciprocal symmetry into the world of political deliberation. We need to argue that the very idea of personhood not only demands the recognition of right but also the recognition of the powers of citizenship. These powers include the right to participate in the deliberative processes of a reconstructed political life as part of the achievement of horizontality, in which no one can claim that an individual should not be heard because her social role renders her inherently subordinate to another. Participation in this understanding would be protected as a matter of the person's right to assert herself in the political process and not merely against it. But the right to participation would also be understood as essential to the realization of the good of relations of reciprocal symmetry between citizens. The element missing in the later Hegel is a normative conception of the person as a citizen as well as a rights-bearing subject.

The dialogic turn in Hegelianism, then, allows us to expand Hegel's own understanding of what the ideal of relations of reciprocal symmetry should mean in the sphere of right. As we have seen in Hegel, "do not violate my personhood," the central principle of right, is a purely negative prohibition. But "do not violate my personhood" can be translated to mean "you must give me a reason for your power," and then the prohibition is no longer simply negative. However, the prohibition does not demand full substantive equality in the name of reciprocal symmetry. Full substantive equality would be inconsistent with the principle of subjectivity, which recognizes the distinction between myself and the community. I have the right to pursue my good, in civil society, otherwise individuality would have no meaning. But my subjective preferences are not the last word, because to be a true subject, I must be in a properly constituted community. My obligation to the state is justified because of its need for my freedom, which can only be found in relations of reciprocal symmetry. Yet, if the state is to be justified only to the degree that it embodies relations of mutual recognition, then the state must rest on dialogic structure in order to legitimate its claim to obligation. We each have the right to be given reasons in the face of inequality, since under the Hegelian framework, it is not the "appetites" of the parties that determine fairness in contract, but instead the objectified relations of reciprocal symmetry.

The Problem of Contractual Mutuality

The law and economics challenge to those who advocate that we replace the presumption in favor of employment at will with unwaivable rational-cause statutes relies on the normative significance of a particular rendering of modern contract principles, a rendering rooted in conceptions of contractual mutuality and individual freedom. Within the context of this essay, we can understand the conception of contractual mutuality to reduce to the abstract reciprocity between persons in the sphere of private right. The power of this challenge requires us to address these limitations as an abstract reciprocity. Abstract reciprocity cannot provide a normative defense of unwaivable rational-cause statutes. As I have suggested, to develop a normative defense of such statutes, we must move beyond Hegel's own understanding of abstract reciprocity in the sphere of right, because it is the realization of horizontality that is crucial for relations of reciprocal symmetry.

As we have seen, for Hegel the right to contract depends on the achievement of certain objective conditions. These conditions, at least on the formal level of abstract right, embody relations of reciprocal symmetry. The relations of reciprocal symmetry provide the "ideal" that justifies contract. They also provide a standard of objective "fairness," which can, in turn, be used to fill in the silent gaps of an actual contract. This objective standard thus provides the basis for the presumption in favor of "implicit fairness" that has served as the contractual basis for judicial intervention into employment relations. This ideal of reciprocal symmetry is not a pie-in-the-sky notion but a valid interpretation of the legal reality of contract. So far, the structure of the Hegelian understanding of the objective ideal inherent in the contract relation can serve us well, precisely because Hegel shows us the basis for implicit fairness.

We can see this by reference to Ian Macneil's hypothesis of the actual functioning of common law contractual principles. Macneil's hypothesis reads as follows:

> American legal institutions, common law and others, limit unilateral power in contractual relations of all other kinds, whatever may be its source, overcoming all policy considerations, including economic efficiency, where other policy considerations are deemed to lead to excessive unilateral power.[65]

Macneil's hypothesis describes the actual functioning of contract law; it is about the *is* of contract. And if contract operates to limit unilateral power, following Macneil, it does so in order to realize the *normative* ideal of relations of reciprocal symmetry.

Macneil also recognizes that contract law not only limits unilateral power but also creates it. There is a real sense in which rational-cause statutes create unilateral power in the workers if they are not to be subjected to the corresponding duty to give reasons for terminating employment. But if we understand that the disruption of unilateral power is justified in the name of relations of reciprocal symmetry, we can distinguish between the breakup of the employer's unilateral power and the seeming creation of power in the employees. We intervene into the sphere of contract to secure the normative conditions of reciprocal symmetry on which contract in fact rests. Mutuality or reciprocity in contract, in other words, is not something essential only to discrete transactions between equally situated persons. All contractual transactions express the achievement of certain substantive conditions vis-à-vis our relationship to one another as legal persons over time: this relationship involves not only reciprocity but also symmetry. Here we see the importance of horizontality, in which relations of reciprocal symmetry are envisioned as placing citizens on an equal plane.

The Hegelian vision is significant because it reminds us of the psychodynamics of subordination. Employment at will is not problematic simply because it leads to the unfair distribution of things. Instead, the problem is that it reduces the person to a position of subordination because she cannot assert her personhood. To argue that the assertion of personhood is always possible because the individual can quit misses the point. If an employee is fired, he obviously has not quit. The circumstances in which an employee would need protection by rational-cause statutes are precisely those circumstances under which she has been fired. In such circumstances, we have to ask the question: What are the minimal conditions necessary for her respect as a person? I have argued that dialogism as understood within the Hegelian framework insists that, at the very least, the person must be given reasons before she is dismissed. Of course, there are situations in life in which we are dismissed and we would not want to impose a legal duty to give reasons. What makes the firing from one's job so important? Here, again we are returned to the Hegelian insight, later developed by Marx, that work is crucial for the development of personality because it allows us to externalize our creative capacities in the world. When our ability to externalize our capacities is challenged, so is our personhood. Of course, to merely give reasons for the firing cannot completely take away that harm. What it does is recognize just how important work is to personality. It demands that a firing be seen as the serious assault on personality that it is. To impose this harm without reasons is to belittle the damage done.

A key aspect of domination is the capacity or power of one person to refuse to respond in the face of the demand for reasons. Rational-cause statutes essentially serve to emphasize this enforced breaking of the silence in the relationship. Once one understands the harm of subordination as the denial of the desire for recognition, it follows that the problem would not be solved even if the employee were given a cash settlement. By insisting that the employer give the employee reasons, we are only demanding that conditions of mutual recognition be resolved. Mutual recognition does not mean that the employee and the employer are literally required to do the same thing—if the employer must give the employee reasons before firing her, then likewise the employee must give the employer reasons before quitting. Instead, mutual recognition expresses a normative relationship in which the conditions of personhood are fulfilled. To return to the discussion of Macneil, relations of mutual recognition can be understood to demand some degree of symmetry between the parties. Mutuality, therefore, demands the development of unilateral power in the very name of the achievement of symmetry.

Even Epstein, in his discussion of bilateral monopoly, premises his discussion of the system of mutual coinsurance, which he believed to prevent the abuse of employment at will, on the achievement of some kind of *symmetry* between the employer and the employee. In other words, his view of reciprocity is not as purely abstract as he thinks. There must be some "equalizing" of the stance in one party vis-à-vis the other for reciprocity to be meaningful. To Epstein, the symmetry that creates the mutual coinsurance depends on the employer's investment in firm-specific training. This investment serves as a disincentive to irrational firing. Epstein's justification of employment at will, however, implicitly recognizes the need to grapple with the differential of power between the employer and the employee. In terms of the philosophical framework developed here, this means that Epstein focuses on "reciprocity" in the exchange and not on the guaranteed symmetrical status of the persons involved. Yet even Epstein recognizes that to introduce reciprocity in bargaining, there must be some sort of symmetry: "So long as it is accepted that the employer is the full owner of his capital and the employee is the full owner of his labor, the two are free to exchange on whatever terms and conditions they see fit, within the limited constraints just noted."[66]

This bargaining model of wage determination allows Epstein to introduce the notion of bilateral monopoly, a conception usually associated with relations between unions and employers, into a discussion of the relationship be-

tween the individual worker and her employer. Nevertheless, the conception
raises obvious difficulties. Whatever power a union might have in negotiating
with an employer, a nonunionized worker would not have the same position
of symmetry. To assume such symmetry exists, Epstein must and does make
the assumption that labor markets are committed to firm-specific training, and
that sunk costs in firm-specific training are a crucial disincentive to employers to abuse the doctrine of employment at will.[67] But empirical studies show
that the Epstein assumptions that "workers are not fungible" and that the cost
of training is time do not apply to the labor market as a whole but only to a
segment of the labor market—that segment primarily including skilled and
semiskilled, white males. Women and national minorities do not face the
same labor conditions as white, male, semiskilled and skilled workers. One
way in which the segmentation of the labor market calls into question Epstein's central assumption of firm-specific training is that there are certain
kinds of employment situations in which no training is provided and the cost
of replacing a worker is low. Obviously, in those job situations in which on-
the-job training is not a reality, the employer has little disincentive to avoid
abuse of the employment-at-will doctrine. There, workers are indeed fungible. Therefore, Epstein implicitly believes that symmetry established through
job training is undervalued, at least for certain sectors of the labor market.[68]

Once we recognize the need to consider the basis of contract in relations
of reciprocal symmetry, we can also reinterpret contractual mutuality consistent with rational-cause statutes. If rational-cause statutes are to be defended as a matter of right, they must be rendered consistent with contractual mutuality. According to the law-and-economics argument, if an
employer is to have the duty to give notice, employees must also have the
duty to give reasons for quitting. Without the imposition on both parties,
there would be no mutuality because abstract reciprocity between the parties would be violated. Duties arise on the basis of an exchange for a corresponding duty or a corresponding right. Only then is there reciprocity. Summers, however, has asserted that mutuality is a "spurious concept." As he has
stated in his attempt to understand why courts have been reluctant to imply
standards of fairness into employment contracts:

> The rationale is often rooted in mutuality—for the employer to be bound, the
> employee must be bound, and this would bar the employee from seeking a bet-
> ter job: As the court in *Simmons v. Westinghouse Electric Corp.* said, "'[I]n this
> land of opportunity it would be against public policy and the spirit of our insti-
> tutions that any man should thus handicap himself . . . .'" There is, therefore, an
> almost conclusive presumption that employment is not permanent but at will.
> Mutuality in this context, however, is a spurious concept, neither required as a
> legal principle nor acceptable as a social principle, and it can scarcely explain
> the courts' decisions.[69]

This is slight of hand. Summers denies the validity of contractual theories
of justice widely accepted in modernity precisely because they root duties

and rights in a hypothetical choice and in a mutually beneficial exchange. Summers does not tell us why mutuality is a "spurious concept," when indeed the very opposite seems to be the case. It is not that mutuality is spurious; it is instead that mutuality properly conceived does not forbid rational-cause statutes. Indeed, as we have seen, it can be reinterpreted to demand them. The abstract view of reciprocity may be preferred because it appears consistent with the protection of subjectivity, allowing the individual the freedom to pursue her own good. But as we have seen, in Hegel freedom is not a given in nature but a social achievement made possible through the realization of the horizontal dimension of modern law. The enforcement of horizontality, then, is not against pregiven freedom. Rather, it forms the very basis for that freedom, including the freedom *to* contract. The Hegelian framework I have offered helps us to recast mutuality within the ideal of reciprocal symmetry. Mutuality or reciprocity is not simply a device for imposing norms peculiar to discrete exchanges on more complex relationships. It is instead a necessary incident of an achieved relationship of reciprocal symmetry. Symmetry is necessary if the horizontality of the contractual relationship is to be preserved. Given this as the basis of modern contract, in cases where power differentials between the parties become so great as to threaten the freedom to contract, the law must intervene in the name of the horizontality. This is precisely Macneil's point when he insists that law limits unilateral power.

An understanding of the role of contract is also crucial to the justification of unwaivable rational cause statutes. To insist on unwaivable rational-cause statutes is to argue that such statutes are a "bottom" line that cannot be bargained away. Unwaivable rational-cause strategies obviously remove from the preference of the parties the decision of how to render their relations. Such intervention in the parties' decision making is based on the belief that this degree of symmetry is necessary between the employer and the employee if the relationship is not to degenerate into one of systematic subordination of the employee. It is consistent with the principle of nonsubordination as necessary to the realization of legal relations of horizontality.

The ideal of reciprocal symmetry should guide us in legal interpretation, not the empirical designation of who is the weaker party. Summers argues to the contrary, contending that principles of fairness of contract can be justified as the protection of the weaker party. It is difficult, however, to translate "protecting the weaker party" into a workable legal principle, because this notion is based in an empirical designation and not in a normative determination. This designation of weakness cannot be a matter of presumption only. We would have to determine in each case who the weaker party actually is. Sometimes, it might indeed be the employee or the union. Obviously, this is not always the case. If the teamsters union strikes a small printing company, can we really assume that it is the organized workforce that is the weaker party? And if we were to do a case-by-case, empirical study of who was actually weaker, the transaction costs would be outlandishly high in every litigation. Therefore, to achieve a universally and more easily applicable principle, we need a normative determination, which we can arrive at through the principle of nonsubordination.

Yet Summers's language does help to remind us of the power relations contained in the actual employment contract. This reminder is particularly important in light of the reality that the employment contract is usually between an individual and a corporation or firm. It is a fallacy to believe that the employment contract can be taken out of this relational context. Of course, some writers associated with law and economics, most notably Alchian and Demsetz,[70] and Jensen and Meckling,[71] have argued that there are no meaningful corporate structures. Instead, the corporation is merely a nexus of discrete contracts between economic agents. From this interpretation it follows that attention to corporate power and corporate hierarchy is misguided. Accordingly, the employment contract is just another transactional exchange that takes place in the "nexus of contracts" that we call the corporation. One could return to the strong realist or communitarian notion of the corporation that Hegel offers. But alternative conceptions of the corporation permit us to address the power differential between the corporation and the individual worker. One can instead develop a "functionalist" argument that the corporation cannot be automatically reduced to a nexus of contracts. The corporation functions as an entity irreducible to the very sum of its parts. Consent through delegation plays a role in the creation of the corporate hierarchy, but on the level of day-to-day management, the hierarchy still exists.

I emphasize this debate within the corporate literature to defend the legitimate concern with a differential power in the employment relation. Indeed, one of the earliest advocates of the replacement of employment at will, Lawrence Blades, based his argument not only on the ethical ideal of individual freedom but also on observations of the reality of corporate power.[72] Focusing on the relational context of the employment contract at least serves to call into question the empirical accuracy of the assertion that workers actually consent to the regime of employment at will. One can wonder how many workers even know what regime they have entered. If we accept Macneil's relational analysis of contract, which when normatively restated can be understood to follow from the Hegelian ethical framework I have elaborated, then it makes sense to argue that the law should imply standards of contractual fairness so as to limit unilateral power in the name of the achievement of relations of reciprocal symmetry.

Yet even if I believe that the problem of mutuality can be addressed so as to disfavor the presumption in favor of employment at will, I, like Summers, would advocate a statute rather than a judicial solution. My reasons for preferring a statute, however, differ from those of Summers, as does the content of the statute I would advocate. I prefer a rational-cause statute because it can be more easily tailored to the ethical relationship of dialogic reciprocity.

The doctrine of employment at will holds that the employer does not have to give me reasons for firing me from my job. But for another to control his property by denying me my job creates a great inequality between us. If the state allows this inequality to be established without the giving of reasons, it undermines its authority since its authority is based on its protection of relations of reciprocal symmetry. At the very least, the state must provide procedures that allow me to demand reasons for this inequality and that allow me to contest it. And why should we demand statutes in the employment area when there are all sorts of harms that we perpetuate against one another on a day-to-day basis that do not seem to warrant legal redress? The answer, I believe, lies in the importance to the individual of his or her job. As both Hegel and Marx remind us, our personal identity is profoundly tied up in our employment. This is not connection by coincidence, but instead stems from the need for human beings to externalize their talents in the world if they are to be recognized for the unique human beings they are. To force the employer to give me reasons for my termination is to force him or her to recognize me as a human being whose identity is fundamentally tied up with my work. The personal humiliation caused by individual firing is well documented. An essential aspect of the humiliation is one's feeling of being erased as individual. Rational-cause statutes would insist that the employee at the very least be addressed. To the degree that the humiliation of being fired is intensified by the experience of being erased, rational-cause statutes can help to minimize the psychic damage.

As should be evident by now, I believe that we should adopt rational-cause statutes and not the just-cause statutes advocated by Summers. And why do I think there is a distinction between these two statutes that makes a difference? Clyde Summers has argued for the creation of an arbitration structure that would allow workers to contest their firing. He favors an arbitration system to enforce just-cause statutes for several reasons:

> Unlike other countries that have used equally flexible phrases as statutory standards, we have a large body of precedent and general understanding as to what "just cause" means. Perhaps more importantly, our arbitration system has developed a substantial cadre of individuals who are experienced in hearing discipline cases and applying the "just cause" standard. No other country, when it enacted its unjust dismissal statute, had available such a trained judiciary. Finally, the customary arbitration procedure provides the flexibility and informality most suitable for the handling of these cases.[73]

I agree with Summers that we have the advantage of an already trained set of arbitrators, experienced in handling the issue of unjust dismissals. But there are drawbacks to too much flexibility and informality. Therefore, I would want to spell out as explicitly as possible a list of illegitimate reasons to serve as guidelines to be incorporated into the statute itself. The problem with leaving what does and does not constitute just cause to the arbitrators is twofold. First, it is difficult for either side to accurately calculate the risk in arbitration. Summers has noted that, at least within the union context, about half of all dismissal cases are decided in favor of the employee and that this fact alone would make employers wary of arbitration and careful in their exercise of the power to terminate employment. While this may well be true, such guidelines would still facilitate the calculation of the transaction costs involved in the termination of employment if illegitimate reasons for termination were incorporated into the statute. I would favor the adoption of the model statute of the International Labor Organization, Recommendation No. 119, "Concerning Termination of Employment at the Initiative of the Employer."[74] This provides a preliminary list of reasons that have been continually expanded to meet changing social perceptions since the Recommendation was first proposed in 1963. The second advantage to a rational-cause statute is that it does not require that we define justice. Summers is satisfied to let the arbitrators decide what justice is in the employment arena. I am less sanguine about leaving such crucial definitions up to the wisdom of the arbitrators. With a list of illegitimate reasons, both sides can better conceptualize the parameters in which they are operating.

Although I would distinguish individual termination from layoffs, I would still argue that we need statutes that provide a notice requirement in the case of layoffs. In the case of layoffs, I would suggest that we adopt Watcher and Cohen's sunk cost loss rule to guide us generally in the bargaining between the employer and the employee.[75] The sunk cost loss rule is, of course, an economic rule, not a legal rule. I would want to add that a legal limit on the exercise of that rule should, at the very least, be a notice requirement. This legal limit does not put the question of layoffs outside of the bargaining process, but it does put one significant limit on that process.[76]

I have argued that an ethical theory that can adequately answer Epstein's Hobbesian framework, which justifies state regulation in the market only against unwarranted violence, must have three components. The three components of a competing framework are: (1) a conception of individuality and individual freedom as a social achievement only possible within a properly constituted community that is protected by the laws of the state as the guardian of freedom; (2) an objective standard of right that gives us an ideal both to justify and delimit the sphere of contract so that we can defend a standard of "implicit fairness" in contractual relations; and (3) a conception of a differentiated common will that allows us to justify the suspension of the rights/duties correlation in certain circumstances so as to defend the tort of wrongful discharge.

As we have seen, Hegel can help us in developing such a framework, because he offers a conception of the communal individual who is only free in a properly constituted community. State regulation is necessary to protect the very freedom that is the justification for the sphere of private right. State regulation, in other words, is not purely negative. In addition, Hegel can help us to develop a justification for the tort of wrongful discharge because his philosophy of right unfolds the whole of the state, as differentiated in the various spheres of social life. But, as we have also seen, we must move beyond Hegel if we are to defend rational-cause statutes as a matter of right. We do so by reinterpreting what relations of reciprocal symmetry should mean in that sphere by emphasizing a new version of what horizontality entails within contractual relations.

7

Hegel and Employment at Will

Richard A. Posner

A towering figure not only in general philosophy but also in jurisprudence, Hegel, like James Fitzjames Stephen whom he otherwise does not resemble in the least, is too little known to Anglo-American legal scholars. Drucilla Cornell is one of the handful of such scholars who are trying to domesticate him for American legal thought.[1] Particularly noteworthy, because it has a concreteness seldom encountered in Hegelian jurisprudence, is Cornell's effort to apply Hegel's thought to the important common-law doctrine of employment at will.[2] That effort is the focus of this chapter. As in other chapters, I try to clear away thick theoretical underbrush to create a space for empirical inquiry. The question we ought to be asking about employment at will is not whether it is un-Hegelian, but what would be the likely consequences of abolishing it.

Employment at will means employment terminable by either party, employer or employee, at any time and without grounds. Cornell uses several strands in Hegel's thought to argue, primarily against Richard Epstein,[3] that employment at will should be outlawed. Every employee would be entitled after successful completion of a brief probationary period to retain his or her job for life unless economic adversity required layoffs or an arbitrator or some other neutral adjudicator determined that the employer had good cause to discharge the employee. This is the type of job security enjoyed at present by tenured college and university teachers, civil servants (including public school teachers), and workers covered by collective-bargaining agreements. Cornell's particular proposal is that statutes be enacted that would specify forbidden grounds for discharging an employee, so that all discharges would be for "rational cause." The list of forbidden grounds, on which Cornell is surprisingly casual, must be specified precisely before one can be sure whether her proposal would curtail the freedom of action of employers substantially. But probably it would; and assuming it would, I am against it; it is inefficient and regressive. And I doubt whether Hegel can be squeezed hard enough to yield persuasive reasons for it.

I grant the force of Hegel's argument, which Cornell emphasizes, that individualism, upon which Epstein founded the ethical part of his argument for employment at will,[4] is socially constructed rather than presocial. Individuals do not have "natural" rights to make contracts. The natural state of human beings is one not of equality but of dependence on more powerful human beings. Economic freedom, including freedom of contract, in the classical liberal sense is one of the luxuries enabled by social organization. The long life, wide liberties, and extensive property of the average modern American are the creation not of that American alone but of society—that is, of a vast aggregation of individuals, living and dead—and of luck—in geography, climate, natural resources. To this extent, Robert Halle and Morton Horwitz are right to question the distinction between the public and the private spheres. If there are two equally able and hard-working people, one living in a wealthy society and the other in a poor one, the former will have a higher standard of living; and the difference will be due to the efforts of other members, living and dead, of the wealthier society and to other factors external to the character, capacity, and efforts of the two individuals. The individual's "right" to property in such a society is not "natural," because, even if we ignore the role of luck, his possessions are a product of social interactions rather than of his skills and efforts alone, and those skills may be, in part or whole, a social product too. I thus stand with Hegel and Cornell, and against Hobbes and (1984 vintage) Epstein, in believing that freedom of contract—the principle that undergirds the institution of employment at will—cannot be defended persuasively by reference to natural liberty.

But this concession will not carry the day for opponents of employment at will. To knock down one of the doctrine's philosophical struts is not to show that the doctrine should be abandoned. It would be odd to conclude—although this is the character of Rawls's famous "difference principle"—that because individual well-being is, in an important sense, a social product, the state ought to be empowered to take away the difference between my income and that of the average resident of Bangladesh. That would be the same *reductio ad absurdum* as supposing that recognition of the artificiality of the distinction between private and public action makes all private property, such as the computer keyboard on which I am typing this sentence, public property. Employment at will is a corollary of freedom of contract, and freedom of contract is a social policy with a host of economic and social justifications, even though nature is not one of them. Employment at will happens to be the logical terminus on the road that begins with slavery and makes intermediate stops at serfdom, indentured servitude, involuntary servitude, and guild restrictions. That should be a point in its favor. Hegel himself, as Cornell notes, would have thought employment at will a fine idea. Just the pragmatic success of free markets in "delivering the goods"[5] warrants a presumption in their favor, preventing Cornell from resting her case with Hegel's demonstration that rights are social rather than natural.

She knows she cannot stop there, and she is therefore led to place great emphasis on Hegel's belief that the possession of property is an element of a person's sense of himself as a person.[6] Taken literally (but Cornell does not take it literally), this is an odd and implausible idea. But what is true or at least plausible is that we are scarcely persons unless we are able to intervene in the external world. An individual who cannot have any effect on his environment may not be aware of himself as a person—that is, aware of himself as being distinct from his environment. These interventions constitute personality in the further sense that our sense of ourselves as persons is a function in part of our recollections of past experience, and, as Proust taught us, those recollections are kept fresh by the objects and activities associated with them. That is why it can be a terrible wrench (over and above the inconvenience) to lose one's house and personal possessions in a fire even if they are fully insured.

It may therefore be the case empirically that a person who has no property has a fainter awareness of himself as a separate person than one who does have property—is it not a purpose of monastic life to make its adherents feel themselves a part of a larger organism? To Margaret Jane Radin, Hegel's analysis of property implies that heirlooms should receive greater legal protection than cash or other fungible property.[7] This may seem a curious suggestion, but insolvency law does place some of the bankrupt's personal property—including, in some states, his heirlooms—beyond the reach of his creditors. Radin also suggests that Hegel's theory of property provides support for entitling tenants to renew their leases indefinitely, provided they behave themselves.[8] This suggestion is far more problematic. Carried to its logical extreme, it would destroy the institution of tenancy by giving the tenant a right almost as extensive as outright ownership. It is difficult to see how the interests of people who cannot afford to own their homes would be helped by the destruction of tenancy. Existing tenants would benefit, but what of persons who will be seeking rental housing in the future?

Cornell's version of Hegel's theory of property rights is less literal than Radin's version, although neither has much bearing on employment at will. The employee at will can quit whenever he wants and go work for someone else. He can also, it is true, be fired at will. But the consequences of being fired, in our society at any rate, do not include becoming someone's slave. Given unemployment insurance and welfare, they do not even include becoming a poor person, in the sense of someone utterly destitute and without property—the sort of fell consequence that we recall Fitzjames Stephen associating with the loss of a job (see chapter 10 of *Overcoming Law*). Poor people in the United States have enough goods to retain a lively sense of themselves as persons. It is patronizing to suggest otherwise.

But by pushing a little harder the idea that our sense of personality is embodied in our accustomed possessions and activities, we can begin to see a loosely Hegelian argument for job tenure, as for tenant rights. The person who has had the same job for a long time, like the tenant who has lived in the same place for a long time, albeit under a succession of one-year leases, may develop such an attachment that termination is wrenching. But we are now a long way from the idea that people who lack any property (the monk, the conscript soldier, the pauper) may in consequence have a precarious sense of self. We are now saying merely that everyone dislikes losing what they have grown accustomed to having. We have turned Hegel into a superficial utilitarian, who does not consider the long-range consequences of his happiness-maximizing proposals.

The right of property, moreover, implies the right of alienation. If I own my labor I should be entitled to rent it on whatever terms I see fit. We shall see that the employee at will is likely to have a higher wage than he would if he had a term employment contract or any other form of job tenure, including Cornell's proposed "rational cause" protection. With the higher wage he can acquire additional property. To force him to forgo his preferred wage-tenure package and accept a lower wage in exchange for greater job security is, one might think, a denial of his personhood. This analysis would fail if employees did not *realize* they were employees at will. But especially nowadays, with so many well-publicized mass discharges by large employers, few employees at will think they have job tenure; being dismissed from a job is not, or at least is no longer, such a low-probability event that people have trouble thinking rationally about it. Maybe we need heavier sanctions on employers who mislead their employees into thinking they have job protection when they don't. But this would be far different from abolishing employment at will.

To suggest that one's right in one's labor should be freely alienable may seem inconsistent with the fact that people are not allowed to sell themselves into slavery. The ban against self-enslavement is connected with notions of essential personhood, but an additional, pragmatic consideration is that most of us cannot think of any reason why a sane person in our affluent society would make a contract to become a slave. However generous the price were for surrendering his freedom, as a slave the person would derive no benefit unless he were intensely altruistic toward his family or others *and* they were either truly desperate or did not reciprocate his concern—for if they did they would suffer from seeing him a slave, and his altruistic gesture would fail. And if they are so indifferent to his own welfare as to be untroubled by seeing him a slave, he is unlikely to be so altruistic toward them as to be willing to make that sacrifice for them. The surprising implication is that sacrifice is likely to be more rational, the less grateful the person for whom the sacrifice is made is to the person making the sacrifice.

I would not put too much weight on utilitarian arguments pro and con allowing self-enslavement. Our reaction to slavery is both culture-bound and semantically influenced. We are unlikely to say that a captive in ancient times who chose slavery over death surrendered his personhood. And today when a person does outwardly rather similar things to self-enslavement, but for what is considered a good reason—joins the army, becomes a Catholic priest, or even, having robbed a bank, becomes a "slave" of the state, maybe for life—we do not say that he has surrendered his essential personhood. Slavery has become the name of the forms of involuntary servitude that we abhor, and what those are owes almost everything to the history of Negro slavery in the United States. The word does not signify the abhorrence of all forms of involuntary servitude. And none of this has anything to do with employment at will, which lies at the other end of the spectrum of labor contracts from slavery.

Cornell emphasizes the importance of reciprocal symmetry in personal relations: "The image is of two people looking one another in the eye, knowing the other is looking back. No one is on top."[9] This is not a bad description—of the regime of freedom of contract. The employer and employee meet as free individuals and can strike any deal they want; presumably it will be mutually advantageous. It may or may not involve job tenure, as the parties prefer. If, perhaps by virtue of a statute, the employee could dictate the terms, he would be on top, and this would violate reciprocal symmetry.

Cornell understands reciprocal symmetry differently, as entitling each of us to demand that someone who proposes to harm us, as by firing us, must have and give us a compelling reason for doing so. Carried to its logical extreme, this is an unworkable principle. Each of us is harmed every day by the actions of unknown others and harms unknown others by our own actions, if only through the operation of competition in economic and other marketplaces. It would be absurd to require that all the harmed—the jilted boyfriend, the writer whose book is reviewed unfavorably, the consumer faced with an increase in the price of anchovies, the loser in a tennis match—be given notice and a hearing. Granted, losing one's job is apt to be a greater blow. But it is a known risk, and anyone who desires—and is willing to pay for—protection against it can negotiate for an employment contract; or, more realistically (because asking one's employer for a contract may signal to the employer that one is apt to be an unsatisfactory worker), can enter the sector of the workforce where such protection comes with the job.

Let us pause for a moment to consider conditions in that sector. For the truth is that millions of American workers have job tenure. Does their experience suggest that universalizing the practice would improve human relations? Does the union worker have a greater sense of personality than the nonunion worker? Does the civil servant have a greater sense of personality than his counterpart who works without tenure in a private-sector job? Do public school teachers have a greater sense of personality than private school teachers? Even if there is something to the Hegelian notion that property is a part of personality, or to the notion that people should interact on terms of reciprocal symmetry, it is far from clear that Cornell's proposal would, if adopted, cause these notions to be more fully actualized than they already are. What it clearly would do is curtail freedom of contract, an important part of Hegel's notion of freedom.

Another objection to entitling a person to demand a reason for being fired is that it logically entails giving the employer the right to demand of the employee a reason for quitting—and if this seems to be pushing logic too hard, consider that in the Netherlands neither party to an employment relationship can terminate the relationship without cause, and workers can be sent to jail for trying to do so.[10] The resemblance of the just-cause principle to slavery is nowhere clearer than in this example: the employee who could not show just cause for leaving his employment might be forced to spend his whole life in a job he hated. This is unlikely, of course; the costs of monitoring the effort of an unhappy worker would be too high. That is one reason why slavery has gone out of fashion. Nevertheless, what is sauce for the goose should be sauce for the gander. Cornell does not deny that an employee can sometimes hurt his employer, and hurt him badly, by quitting without notice or just cause. She thinks a discharge will on average hurt the employee more than a quit will hurt the employer, but this is not clear, as we are about to see. Even if she is right, this would not provide a compelling justification for denying the employer a remedy in those cases where he *was* hurt by the resignation of a key employee.

She makes one good argument against employment at will (or at least against an argument made in favor of employment at will), and it would be petty to object that the argument owes nothing to Hegel. The economic defense of employment at will builds on the fact that an employment relationship is often one of bilateral monopoly.[11] (This was implicit in my reference to quits by key employees.) The employee develops skills that are specialized to the particular job he is doing for his particular employer. As a result, he would be less productive working for another employer; and knowing this, his current employer may be able to threaten him, explicitly or implicitly, with discharge if he demands a wage equal to his marginal product for this employer. But precisely because this employee is more productive than his replacement would be, he can threaten the employer with quitting if the employer does not pay him his full marginal product. It is a game of chicken, likely to end in a stand-off, in which case both parties are protected, to some extent anyway, against over-reaching by the other.

There is an alternative path to this conclusion. Suppose a worker would be more valuable if he developed skills specialized to this employer. If the employer incurs the full costs of developing these skills, the worker can hardly complain if the employer refuses to pay him the higher marginal product made possible by the employer's own investment in the worker's skills; and to the extent that the worker (by threatening to quit) can extract any part of that higher marginal product in the form of a higher wage, the employer has been "had." Conversely, if the worker pays for the acquisition of these skills himself (maybe by accepting a lower wage initially), he will be at the mercy of the employer, who can expropriate the worker's investment by refusing to pay him his full marginal product. If the worker quits he will have lost his entire investment, since by definition the skills are worth nothing in another employment. Consideration of these alternatives leads to a prediction that the costs of developing specific human capital (as skills specialized to a particular employer are called) will be shared between worker and employer.[12] Then neither party has as much to gain or lose from a termination of the employment relationship, so there is less incentive to engage in bluffing and other gaming, and less turnover, even if neither party has contracted protection against termination by the other.

But the assumption is that the worker develops specialized skills; and, as Cornell rightly points out, not every employee is so fortunate. This is a good point, but incomplete. If the employee lacks specialized skills, he loses a club over his employer's head, it is true, but by the same token the employer loses a club over the employee's head. The employee's wage will be as high in another job as it is in this one, since his skills, such as they are, are by hypothesis mobile. Were there a vast labor surplus, the wages of unskilled labor would be very low, but this situation would not be alleviated by job tenure.

There are other reasons for doubting whether employment at will is exploitative. The employer who encourages employees to develop a specialized skill and then takes advantage of their resulting immobility by refusing to compensate them adequately will find that he has to pay higher wages to induce people to work for him in the future. (A similar concern with reputation may restrain key employees from taking advantage of their employer's vulnerability by walking off the job without notice, or by demanding a raise not to do so.) The employer will also find that his employees are highly susceptible to the enticements of labor unions. One of the curious by-products of the universal "rational cause" rule that Cornell proposes is that it would weaken labor unions by giving every worker the kind of protection that could be got through a union only at the cost of having to pay union dues. I had thought that Cornell, a former union organizer, was a supporter of unions for reasons that went beyond the tenure provisions in collective-bargaining contracts. But I said she is a *former* union organizer. She may have come to regard unionization as a lost cause.

Although not every employer in the United States is an effective profit-max-imizer (and hence cost-minimizer), a free-market institution as persistent and widespread as employment at will is presumptively more efficient than an alternative imposed by government would be. The reason it might be more efficient is not hard to find. Litigation, even when conducted before arbitrators rather than before judges and juries, is costly. To these direct costs of legally enforceable tenure rights must be added the indirect costs from the weakening of discipline in the workplace when workers can be fired only after a costly and uncertain proceeding. The sum of these costs should not be underestimated. If they did not outweigh the benefits to workers, why would employers not offer just-cause protection voluntarily, the way they offer other fringe benefits? Are the employers that do offer such protection—government agencies, unionized firms, and universities—the most efficient producers in the marketplace? Do law professors know more about the efficient management of labor than business people? One is amused to be told by another advocate of abolishing employment at will that we need not be afraid that it would be inefficient, because "under the British system, for example, industrial tribunals determine whether an employee has been improperly discharged."[13] The "British system" of employment regulation is no more promising a model for our economy than the employment practices of our nonprofit and governmental sectors are. And while it is plausible that cooperative relations between labor and management are more conducive to increases in productivity than antagonistic relations,[14] it is implausible that granting workers tenure is an efficient method of fostering that cooperation. If it were, why would not companies adopt it without prodding by government?

We must not neglect the *incidence* of the costs of a just-cause or rational-cause principle. Consumers would be hurt to the extent that the employer passed on any part of these costs to its customers in the form of higher product prices. Workers would be hurt the most. In figuring what he can afford to pay, an employer considers not only the direct costs of labor but indirect costs as well (such as the employer's social security tax, unemployment insurance premiums, and workers' compensation insurance premiums), of which the costs of tenure would be one. The higher the indirect costs of employment, the lower the wage the employer will be willing to pay.[15] Since just-cause protection is itself a fringe benefit (like severance pay or unemployment compensation), the worker does not lose out completely. But if he had preferred such protection to a higher wage, the employer would have offered it to him. Just-cause protection may force employers to provide what from the average employee's standpoint is an inferior compensation package.

If, because of union contracts, minimum-wage laws, custom, inertia, or other factors, employers were prevented from charging back the full cost of job protection to workers in the form of lower wages or fewer (other) benefits, unemployment would rise because the cost of labor would now be higher.[16] Employers would have an incentive to hire less, automate more, and relocate plants to foreign countries that do not have such protection. Since, as we saw in chapter 3 of *Overcoming Law*, job tenure causes people to work less hard, the employer might actually need more workers under a just-cause regime to get the work done; but this prospect would accelerate his flight to automated and foreign plants.

Some workers would keep their jobs who would have lost them under a regime of employment at will, but presumably not many. A rational employer will not fire an employee without cause. Although most dismissals are made by lower-level supervisors, who may not be perfect agents of the enterprise, irrational firing of workers does not appear to be widespread,[17] especially in profit-making enterprises, which are penalized by the market for making mistakes. (This may be the reason why employment at will is so much less common in the nonprofit and governmental sectors.) At all events, it is not one of the grounds on which Cornell defends her proposal.

In a regime of universal tenure, a rational employer would search longer before hiring a worker,[18] because the cost of firing the worker if he did not pan out would be higher. This effect would be mitigated but not eliminated by postponing just-cause protection until the worker had completed a probationary period of employment.

The brunt of any disemployment effect of just-cause laws would be borne by newcomers to the workforce and other marginal workers.[19] In the United States, most of these newcomers would be women, nonwhites, or handicapped—the very people whom Cornell would most like to protect in the interest of reciprocal symmetry. Employers would be less willing to take chances on problem workers or on workers who lacked an impressive job history, because it would be harder for an employer to correct mistakes in hiring than it is under the system of employment at will. They might therefore prefer encouraging overtime work by their existing workers to hiring additional ones, and this too would reduce employment.[20] And if, as has been the pattern with European job-protection laws, temporary and part-time workers were exempted, employers would tend to substitute them for full-time workers, creating a tier of second-class workers.[21]

The short of it is that the adoption of Cornell's proposal might move the United States farther down the road of "Eurosclerosis"—high long-term unemployment due to excessive regulation of labor markets.[22] Or might not. I shall not pretend that all economists would accept the analysis that I have presented, or even that, if all did, this would show it was correct. My objection to her proposal is not that it is demonstrably wrong, but that it is irresponsible, because if adopted it might very well impose immense social costs—and costs born mainly by workers themselves, the intended beneficiaries of the proposal—that she has not considered. She has tried to substitute political theory, in the person of Hegel, for the study of consequences. She illustrates the flight from fact so characteristic of even the ablest academic lawyers.

8

Spanish Language Rights: Identification, Freedom, and the Imaginary Domain

In the traditional story of immigration to America (the "assimilation story"),[1] the most motivated, talented, and intelligent of the world's dissatisfied people—our ancestors—came here to seek success in the world's largest, freest, and deepest national marketplace. The American system, we are told, was demanding but fair, holding out equal economic opportunity in exchange for two things. First, the system required hard work on the job. Second, the system required hard work on the identity: to avoid consignment to America's lower economic caste, immigrants had to root out the linguistic and cultural components of their old-world selves and substitute the less affected, more facilitative incidents of American identity. Eventually, the immigrants' self-reliant efforts would bring the reward of Americanization. This transformation, however, called for patience. Only the most clever and ambitious could reconstruct themselves completely within a few years of arrival. The rest had to be content with life as quasi-Americans of foreign origin. Their children, however, would go on to achieve a full American identity and its accompanying economic opportunity.[2] The third generation would complete the process of Americanization; internal ties to the antecedent language[3] and culture[4] would not burden the immigrants' grandchildren.

The assimilation story, while always normative,[5] has taken a particularly sharp normative edge in recent tellings. These versions set the assimilation pattern of early twentieth-century European immigrants as a standard against which one should measure the social success of more recent arrivals. This usage of the early twentieth-century pattern, not coincidentally, has accompanied a thirty-year decline in the proportion of immigrants coming from Europe and a concomitant increase in immigration from Latin America and

Asia.[6] Critics argue that new arrivals of Latin American origin, hereinafter "Latinos and Latinas," or in abbreviated form, "Latinos/as,"[7] in particular have fallen short of this standard because too many have remained in a handful of large, Spanish-speaking enclave communities and have failed to disperse across the continent. Critics contend that the resulting concentration of non-English speech and other incidents of foreignness pose a threat to the nation's social, economic, and political cohesion.[8] Among other remedies,[9] proponents advocate regulation to protect and enhance the status of the English language and thereby hasten (or force) the assimilation of Latinos/as and other foreign-born and foreign-language residents.

The American public has heard similar "scare talk" before. Nativists[10] have been characterizing foreign-language speech as a threat for as long as non-English speakers have been settling in this country in large numbers.[11] Despite American civilization's unscathed survival, the nativist impulse powerfully continues to influence law and policy,[12] even in sophisticated quarters where skepticism usually greets such predictions of social disaster. Nativism derives part of its power from the negative reactions that some English-speaking Americans ("Anglos") experience upon encountering foreigners in traditionally Anglo neighborhoods.[13] Its remaining power derives from the widely held assimilation norm. The assimilation story ties the English language to American national identity, asserts the primacy of both, and implies a concomitant duty of submission for this country's non-English speakers.

This essay critiques English-Only statutes and defends Spanish language rights by defending the moral, ethical, and legal meaning of the free person pursuant to an existentialist interpretation of the Kantian idea of equal worth. I use the concept of the free person of equal worth to locate both the intrinsic and extrinsic wrong inherent in the suppression of Spanish.[14] In doing so I expand the conventional liberal framework, which has difficulty accommodating a complex understanding of individual identity, to discuss the formation of identity out of basic identifications, one of which clearly is language. To lay the groundwork for this discussion, I revisit the communitarian-liberal debate as well as the critique of the liberal person that feminist and race-critical theories articulate. I ultimately hope to show both that one can reconcile a more complex understanding of identity with a concept of rights, and that the ideal of the person need not rely on an individualistic anthropology. The mainstay of this case for a revived ideal of the person is the aesthetic idea of the imaginary domain.

I defend the ideal of the imaginary domain to connect the Kantian ideal of the free person to the contemporary notion that identifications play a constitutive role in each person's life. My theory of right follows from an interpretation of what it means to treat each individual as a free person with equal dignity—an interpretation grounded in a description and defense of the ideal of the imaginary domain. This theory of right demands that each individual receive the moral and psychic space to evaluate, to represent, and, ultimately, to integrate the complex realities of culture, linguistic origin, national affiliation, ethnic identity, and religious heritage. Two points logically follow from this theory of right. First, the legal system should treat language as a fundamental identification encompassed by each person's right of personhood. Second, a legal system that treats Latinos/as as equals[15] recognizes and respects the value they bestow on the Spanish language. In contrast, an English-Only regime designed to force Latinos/as to speak the majority tongue in public life or in the workplace treats Latinos/as as something less than free persons, thereby degrading them and violating their imaginary domains.

While articulating this position, I also address the recent, general debates on cultural rights. This discourse teaches that identifications are both constitutive of the person and, to some extent, embedded. Human beings cannot just step out of their identifications. This teaching in turn destabilizes assumptions basic to the traditional metaphysical defense of the fully autonomous subject. I accept this result[16] but nevertheless define my project as Kantian because it focuses on freedom. To understand the subject as symbolically or socially constructed is to imply that freedom is fragile. If who we are is profoundly rooted in our identifications, then we cannot know for certain whether any of our judgments, evaluations, or actions are truly self-determined. A need to thematize anew what freedom can mean for us arises from this uncertainty.

The ideal of the imaginary domain renders this thematization consistent with the Kantian ideal that the individual person, as opposed to the state, must be legally designated as the responsible source of judgments and evaluations. This approach makes no attempt to claim, in the strong Kantian sense, that we can make our evaluations and judgments freely and solely in accordance with the moral law.[17] It nevertheless insists that our actions and judgments inevitably engage us in the practice of self-responsibility. Even though our own histories profoundly determine our decisions, we still make them and, in so doing, make ourselves who we are. Self-responsibility re-emerges on this interpretation as a practice by which we constitute ourselves as unique beings who over time shape identities indissociable from the evaluative designs we give to our identifications. On this view, our value as free persons is independent of both our particular value and of the uses we make of our judgments and evaluations. This approach thus maintains the distinction, central in Kant, between the worth of our freedom and personhood and the value we make of them in particular cases. It offers, in sum, Kant with an existential twist.[18]

In conclusion, I apply the idea, which George Fletcher developed, that a culture or a nation can have a right to linguistic self-defense, which justifies protective measures to ensure the survival of its majority language including, in extreme circumstances, regulation like Official English.[19] I conclude that the conditions for this right do not exist in the United States at this time. Indeed, if here and now any group could make a case for such a right, it would be Latinos/as in the Southwest.

After establishing a right to personality at a general level, I argue that the suppression of Spanish controverts the freedom of Latinos/as reasonably to design, by developing their own sense of culture and heritage, unique lives. This argument does not rely on metaphysical or foundational notions of the subject.[20] My assertions depend instead on a simple, direct interpretation of the normative organizational ideal of political or ethical liberalism—the state and our basic social institutions should treat everyone as free and equal persons.[21] At the same time I contend that this interpretation survives the contemporary critique of the autonomous subject. I begin my analysis by reconsidering the ideal of the person.

THE IDEAL OF THE FREE PERSON

All forms of liberalism start with a simple premise: the state should treat us all as if we are free persons of equal worth.[22] Critics of liberalism attack this moral, legal, and political ideal of the person, charging that it is out of touch with reality. In real life, they contend, we are not the abstract persons that the liberal model deploys; we are not beings who in any meaningful sense actually can be self-determining.[23] Some of these criticisms, however, fail to recognize the reason why Kantian liberalism stresses the significance of the ideal of the free person. My interpretation of the Kantian ideal of the person is not meant to be a full picture of the lives of actual human beings; rather, it is tailored to enshrine our freedom as a practice of self-responsibility for the lives we lead.[24]

The Kantian Idea of Equal Worth of Free Persons

Kant defended the simple idea that the state should treat all human beings as "ends in themselves," because as rational beings they are the ultimate source of the value they give to their ends.[25] This idea is Kant's Formula of Humanity.[26] For Kant, an end is an object of free choice. Ends are by definition at least partially "set" by practical reason. I want to stress *partially*, because Kant does not mean that an "end" may not also be an object of desire or inclination. But it is reason that is responsible for the unique human characteristics that translate an object of desire into an end. It is a misreading of Kant, however, to argue that the Formula of Humanity demands respect only for our capacity for choosing morally obligatory ends. When we take a rational interest in something, we do so by deeming it valuable or important and, in that sense, good. In this sense, we do not value our ends as objects of desire, but because they are good. It is this capacity that the Formula of Humanity demands that we treat as an end in each person. This is why it is completely illegitimate to force someone to take up an end, because to do so denies her dignity as someone with this capacity. As beings that assume responsibility, including self-responsibility in the practice of moral and ethical judgment, each is of equal worth because each bestows value on those decisions.[27]

Kant's argument for our equal worth is based on his argument that the good will—or our rational nature (which, to Kant, is synonymous to the good will)—is the only thing that can have unconditional value, meaning it can be recognized as the source of all value.[28] For Kant, something has unconditional value if it has intrinsic value under all conditions, and the only "thing" that can meet this condition is the good will.[29] Even something like happiness and the search for it, at least according to Kant, is conditional and not valuable in all conceivable circumstances.[30] As beings who ultimately confer ethical value around us through setting our ends at least partially by reason, we are the source of what makes things important or deemed good. Objects have value because they have value for individuals who bestow value on objects rationally by making them their ends. It is this value-conferring capacity as rational beings that human beings recognize in one another. This recognition creates the mandate that Kant claims is basic to both morality and, in an impure form, politics.[31] An individual respects the equal worth and dignity of all others because she shares in the humanity that makes them the source of value they give to their own ends. Hence, it is as free persons that we all have equal worth, and it is this equal worth that law must recognize.

It is beyond the scope of this essay to rehearse all the criticisms of Kantian moral theory or, alternatively, to review the efforts to render his moral theory coherent without ontological dualism.[32] I note only that I agree with those who argue that a strong Kantianism offering a comprehensive view of the self is indefensible, because it relies on an outdated concept of causality.[33] Yet I still want to defend the Kantian conception of our equal worth as free persons who possess a value-conferring capacity, partially setting our ends by reason. I do so by adding an existentialist twist to Kant's insight into the assertiveness of our value-conferring capacity whenever we judge an object of desire to be an end.

In his book on Kant, Heidegger argues that the factual dimension of lived experience makes judgment and evaluation inevitable.[34] Moral freedom is a praxis of self-responsibility that we must assume as part of our moral awakening to the inevitable reality that we do make judgments and evaluations, bringing forth a moral self when making those judgments and evaluations. Self-responsibility is a practice in and through which we constantly are becoming who we are as we individuate ourselves by evaluating and re-evaluating our actions, evaluations, and judgments as we make them our own ends.[35] In this understanding, we exercise our freedom as a narration that makes the value-conferring moment in our actions and judgments one that we ourselves understand as called upon rationally or reasonably to justify to others. This understanding of our moral freedom as a practice of self-responsibility for our ends as moral beings suffices to defend the idea of our equal worth, even though it temporalizes the way in which the moral self is brought into being.

The Kantian Standpoint of Practical Reason

As persons with a life, which is ours alone to lead, we all ask the question, "What should I do?" By posing this question, each one of us takes up the stance of practical reason. From this standpoint, an individual cannot be the object of another because each individual is existentially positioned to ask and answer that question through moral reflection only for herself; her actions still will be hers as she reflectively takes them on as such. Each of us has her own moral and ethical options and reacts to her own set of external demands, although some of us are much more constrained by law and circumstance than others.

Liberal political philosophy, particularly when informed by the tradition of critical idealism,[36] demands that any just societal order begin with the treatment of each individual as an equal in the sense that we must view each as equally worthy to pursue her own answer to that fundamental question, "What should I do?" The state should treat each of us as if we are rational in a specific sense—as if we are capable of assuming responsibility for our own ends. We are *reasonable* in that we realize that we are capable of recognizing and harmonizing our pursuit of the good with creatures who are like us in that they have equal dignity.[37] Both notions, rationality and reasonableness, must operate in the law. The law should recognize persons as the source of ethical value that they give to their own life's decisions when they take these up as ends through moral reflection. But it also should accord individuals the capacity to decide that other human creatures are, like themselves, worthy of that same recognition and respect. We therefore are reasonable only when we recognize in others their worthiness to pursue their own lives and recognize that we must try to organize both our own lives and a system of social life and of political organization that is consistent with the equal dignity of all persons.[38]

The person as a legal and moral ideal must remain abstract if that ideal is to denote the freedom on which it is based. Because each individual undertakes her own practice of self-responsibility, the state must not impose definitions of how one can or should realize that potential for self-definition. Of course, we are more, much more, than this abstract free being. The political and moral point of abstracting the ideal of the person from the substance of any one individual's concrete life is to protect the freedom—the potential—of forming ourselves into a unique being—a being immersed in a life to be lived in all the relational complexity we associate with any actual living human being.

The Ideal of the Imaginary Domain

On this understanding, a person is not just a given, but implicates a practice in and through which the person is constantly engaged, a process of assuming self-responsibility through moral reflection on the question, "What should I do?" As persons, then, we inevitably are implicated in the working through of personae. Since these are not just given or imposed on us but have to be assumed, it also turns us toward culture. In this sense, culture tends to be a condition of personhood. The personae in and through which we come to ourselves are both culturally expressed and a fundamental expression of culture.

This understanding of the relationship between person and persona is crucial to my defense of the ethical, political, and legal ideal of the person against the legitimate and powerful criticisms of this ideal that both feminists and race critical theorists have made. In crude summation, these critiques argue that the liberal ideal of the person is too "thin" to provide political or legal insight into the embodied concrete concerns of everyday life.[39] Significantly, the criticisms do not reject the idea that all persons have equal worth. They instead turn on an ethical mandate to provide a "thicker" and thus truer conception of the self as the basis for legal reform.[40] I address these criticisms and simultaneously maintain as central to my defense of language rights the ideal of the free person.[41] To do so, I defend the ideal of the imaginary domain.[42]

The imaginary domain is an aesthetic idea that illuminates what freedom demands of creatures that inevitably are shaped by their own identifications. I understand freedom as a practice of assuming responsibility for our evaluations of our basic identifications as we make them our own in the course of shaping our individual lives.[43] Aesthetic ideas configure the moral dimension of experience.[44] The moral dimension is crucial to articulating the construction of the wrong- and right-making characteristics of any particular social fact—in the present case, the legal suppression of Spanish. More particularly, the aesthetic idea of the imaginary domain helps us to imagine and to articulate the cross-references by which our case for language rights follows from the liberal ideal of the free and equal person.

The imaginary domain expresses an essential right of personality by recognizing both our equal dignity and our potential to assume our special responsibility for ourselves.[45] We cannot assume this responsibility, however, unless the moral and psychic space is protected, allowing us to engage in the practice of self-responsibility through which we come to terms with the ethics of our own identifications. We may either embrace these identifications, keep them fluid, or struggle to discard them altogether. These possi-

bilities are what makes way for our ethical responsibility for our identifications. When we make an identification, such as being a Latina, a conscious
end, then we clearly can see why respect for how that identification is articulated is crucial to the respect for the person. But even if we are not so explicit in making an identification an end, in Kant's sense, we cannot entirely
escape our responsibility for how we live with these identifications because
they always are being reshaped by us as we take them on, even if we think
we only are doing so by following tradition. As persons who can never entirely escape self-responsibility, we need the moral space in which to exercise it. The imaginary domain mandates that the moral community of persons include each of us and provide us this space.

The imaginary domain operates on two levels within the moral community
of persons. At one level, the imaginary domain allows each of us to demar-
cate a space for self-evaluation through moral reflection. This space must
have protection prior to the beginning of a conception of proceduralist justice, such as the one John Rawls defends. In a famous analogy, Rawls uses the
representational device of "the original position" and "the veil of ignorance"
to engage in a hypothetical experiment in the imagination that guides our
moral reflection.[46] The veil of ignorance forecloses knowledge of our gender,
our ethnic identity, our linguistic origin, our race, or our class position.

The veil of ignorance helps us envision a procedure for moral reflection
that, by virtue of its very articulation, forces us to question social hierarchies,
and at the same time, challenges their hold on our imaginations. But how
does one take into account gender, race, nationality, and ethnic and linguistic background in the hypothetical experiment of the imagination? Certainly
we should take into account these fundamental aspects of each person's life.
But the solution is not to assert that "facts" concerning the meaning of these
realities about ourselves should reside behind the veil of ignorance.[47] Because these so-called facts are intertwined with basic social hierarchies in the
real world, placing them behind the veil of ignorance frustrates the purpose
of the exercise of imagining ourselves as free, equal, and unbound by our hierarchical place in society. This difficulty, however, does not mean that we
should forget these realities; instead, we should imagine ourselves as persons free to morally evaluate these hierarchies. Behind the veil of ignorance,
in other words, the idealized situation of the representative includes the postulation of the self as free in the terms described earlier. The imaginary domain, in which we conceptualize all persons in the moral community as possessed of the right to represent and evaluate what these realities mean to
them, provides a space for that prior evaluation of our equal worth.[48]

At a second level, the imaginary domain extends to each person a right to
self-representation—a right to establish herself as her own representative of
whom she is because she must take responsibility for her own life.[49] To be
included in the moral community is to be recognized as having the potential

to shape and to reshape one's identifications out of the symbolic material they present. This right to self-representation subsumes the right to privacy, at least when interpreted as the demand to be left alone. This subsumption is because the right to self-representation insists that each person must have the psychic and moral space to experiment with the personae through which culture is expressed so that she may have the chance to resignify what culture means to her. By demanding this psychic and moral space for each of us, the right to the imaginary domain takes us beyond hierarchical definitions of the self, whether caste, class, race, gender, national origin, or linguistic descent imposes it. Some have thought that these socially and symbolically constructed identifications determine the person.[50] But as persons with the right to self-representation, women, African Americans, and Latinos/as cannot be reduced to naturalized classes whose entitlements and duties flow from their status positions. This right demands that the state and our basic social institutions recognize the person as worthy of being who she is as a member of the moral community of persons and, as such, treat her as the legally authoritative source of any moral or ethical meaning she gives to her basic identifications.

THE DYNAMIC NATURE OF IDENTIFICATION AND MY DISAGREEMENT WITH THE COMMUNITARIANS

I now turn to a detailed response to the several critiques of the liberal person that communitarians, feminists, and race-critical theorists make. My conceptualization of identifications as central to the shaping of identity answers these divergent critiques of the liberal person. For me, a person's identity is inseparable from her identifications; as a result, the moral self is inseparable from an ethics of identification through which the person engages the practice of self-responsibility. I have no quarrel with communitarians, feminists, and race-critical theorists when they criticize the phenomenology of the individual, often implicit in liberal thought.[51] But I argue that they are wrong to the extent that they denigrate the significance of freedom due to its purported use in a misguided phenomenology or anthropology in liberal theory.

Our basic identifications are fundamental aspects of our lives. We internalize these basic identifications initially as essential to ourselves, often even without recognizing, let alone rationally assessing, the fact that we do so. We cohere into a self only by making sense of these basic identifications, whether we consciously question them as contestable or not. We inevitably engage these inheritances when we acknowledge ourselves, whether as a Jew, a woman, an African American, a Latino, or a Latina.

"No one chooses her parents," goes the old saying, and indeed, our parents' identity is only one of an array of life circumstances we do not choose.

As soon as we are born, we are stamped with a sex. Our racialized culture racially designates our parents (or parent) and us with them. We are placed in their arms and delivered into their realities—their country, their culture, their class position, their religion (or lack of it), their lived sexualities, and whatever other basic identifications that have shaped them. We are immersed into a world thick with meaning, meaning that is passed on to us in language. We rely on this language to give ourselves form slowly to distinguish ourselves from our surroundings. We inherit a world that at least to some extent comes to us framed by the language of those who engage us in intimacy; they are the ones who first teach us, consciously and unconsciously, what it means for them, and in turn for us, to be human.

Communitarians continually remind us that our inheritance of language, our country, our culture, and our tradition constitute us.[52] We do not, they say, make ourselves up from scratch. This argument is true enough. But it is just as true that we revise ourselves, even if some of us experience ourselves as already imbued with an identity, "man" or "woman"; "white" or "of color"; "Jewish" or "Christian"; "gay" or "straight"; "Anglo," "Latin American," or "Asian." As I stressed before, when we take up these identifications, we become responsible for them and for the ethical meanings they receive.[53] Some of us may experience our identifications as if ancestral tradition, religious conviction, national origin, or the nature of our sexuality carved them out in certain forms. For people who experience themselves in this way, it makes little or no sense to separate themselves from these basic identifications. Who they are is for them identical to their constitution as Jewish, African American, or Asian. But consciously or not, they still exercise moral and ethical responsibility when they take up a life associated with a particular identification.

For example, there are many meanings of what it means to be Jewish. Anyone who simply claims that her Judaism mandates acceptance of a particular institutionalized form of Judaism still must confront responsibility for this associational decision. Clearly, members of the Jewish community constantly exercise this responsibility or freedom, as many different meanings of being Jewish have been both expressed and institutionalized. Still, other people do not experience themselves as identical with their origins, whether national, ethnic, or religious. Indeed, the entire immigrant story, particularly as it emphasizes battles between the generations, stems from what it means for the members of the next generation to revise their sense of themselves by re-evaluating for their own lives the basic identifications of their parents.

Many believe the debate between the liberals and the communitarians to be over whether or not individuals can revise these basic ends and identifications or for that matter rationally assess these at all.[54] As generation after generation of immigrants have shown, even the deepest identifications are open to both re-evaluation and re-representation. Thus, the communitarians clearly are wrong about what people can do. The real debate is over what people should do and should take responsibility for and, more specifically, what the state should be allowed to do to enforce people's allegiances to specific ends and identifications. If, as some communitarians have argued, people's ends and identifications constitute and thus are identical with them,[55] the state can enforce fidelity to these ends and identifications without trampling on individual freedom and on the practice of self-responsibility. The individual is the ends and identifications; she only can be as free as those specific ends that already constitute her. As I have suggested, this conception of the self may indeed be a true description of how some people experience their identities, but even then it does not relieve them of responsibility. It also suffers from overinclusion: the state still can trample on other people's freedom by reinforcing all people's allegiances or by limiting the space in which people's basic identifications can be re-evaluated and re-represented.

What body should we recognize as the source of moral value for these moral allegiances and identifications when they are defined as ends? Can the state bestow value on them in its own name or even in the name of the "true" interests of the individual? For a communitarian, if the individual truly knows who she is, she would understand that the state-imposed allegiances are truly her own ends.[56] She would exercise her practice of self-responsibility in the only way she truly ethically can: by living a life in allegiance with her community.[57] I argue, on the contrary, that the *person* must be recognized as the source of the ethical or moral value she gives to her basic identifications. To make this argument in no way implies that human beings, like persons shedding clothes, simply can detach themselves from the ends and identifications that have shaped who they are as persons. My argument presupposes only that people can revise and readjust ends and identifications, and that even if we accept them as passed down to us, we remain responsible for the form in which we accept them. It emphasizes that the communitarian insight that human beings grow into individuals only in and through webs of relationships also should remind us that freedom is fragile. Indeed, the degree to which persons actually can revise identifications and ends depends in part on whether the state and basic social institutions provide them with the moral and psychic space to do so. This responsibility is why the equal protection of the imaginary domain is so important. Protecting the imaginary domain ensures that the person and not the state is the source of the evaluations and representations of her fundamental ends and identifications. It is precisely *because* we initially do not choose the primordial relationships and identifications through which we pattern a self and become a person that we need morally and legally provided psychic space to incorporate them, to re-evaluate them, or to contest them through the evaluations and meanings we give them. How one does so is inevitably a part of the exercise of self-responsibility.

Once we see that identifications are not just stamped on us, we begin to comprehend the ideal or idealized element of identification. This element often is made explicit as an ethical or political ideal. This is the case with Latinos/as. The identification of Latino/a carries an ethical and political message due in part to the historical basis of its usage in the United States. The identification implies that the person can trace roots to a Latin American country and is ensconced in the Spanish language, but is not trying to pass as Spanish—as a white European. Identification as Latino/a also is relational: an historical interpretation of the Southwest, Puerto Rico, Mexico, and Cuba, as well as the significance of the economic and political domination of South America for Latin culture and for the Spanish language, defines in part the meanings of Latino/a.[58] The definition of what it means to be a Latino/a thus is partially an act of the political imagination. To enhance this identification can be to take it as an end through moral reflection. In like manner, Gloria Anzaldúa describes the political and ethical process by which Chicanos/as came to imagine themselves as bound together as a people:

> Chicanos did not know we were a people until 1965 when Ceasar [sic] Chavez and the farmworkers united and *I am Joaquín* was published and la *Raza Unida* party was formed in Texas. With that recognition, we became a distinct people. Something momentous happened to the Chicano soul—we became aware of our reality and acquired a name and a language (Chicano Spanish) that reflected that reality. Now that we had a name, some of the fragmented pieces began to fall together—who we were, what we were, how we had evolved. We began to get glimpses of what we might eventually become.[59]

THE DIFFERENCE BETWEEN PARAMETERS AND LIMITS

The fact that the boundaries of an identification have political and ethical dimensions does not mean that anyone can take on any identification. I am not Latina, and if I were to insist that I am, you would be right either gently to prod me to see a psychiatrist or, once you had heard me speak Spanish, to make reference to this essay and accuse me of moral hubris. The communitarians are correct that the inheritance of language, culture, and country sets parameters for our lives.[60] But they are just that: parameters. They are not necessarily imposed limits that so rigidly define us, that we cannot develop a personal response to the full particularity of our situation.[61] As Ronald Dworkin has argued, ultimately, each of us personally should make the distinction between parameters and limits, even if the historical situation in which we find ourselves in turn indexes it.[62]

At this point, another important difference with the communitarians becomes manifest. It is a *limit* on our lives that, under the above definition of Latino/a, I cannot embrace that identification or gain acceptance as those who identify themselves as Latinos/as, even if I desperately seek to do so.[63] But what if I were to marry a Mexican, move to Mexico, become a Mexican citizen, achieve fluency in Spanish, and raise children of the marriage as Mexicans? Assume that I took on that overwhelming project of transformation and later told you, "At this point in my life I identify myself more as a Mexican than as an American." My life *parameters* substantially would have changed. Identification as Latino/a would no longer seem like simple craziness or hubris, despite the fact that many if not all Mexicans would continue to identify me as an Anglo.

Even though we cannot completely escape our Anglo context, we certainly can change its meaning for ourselves—despite the fact that other members of society may not recognize the change.[64] Freedom demands that the individual should be the only entity empowered to set, ethically and politically, the divide between limits and parameters. The imaginary domain gives the person the moral and psychic space to determine which historical circumstances are limits and which are parameters. Concomitantly, the imaginary domain gives the person space within which to embrace the parameters of her life, thereby enabling her practice of self-responsibility.

LANGUAGE, CULTURE, AND IDENTIFICATION WITHIN THE PARAMETERS OF THE IMAGINARY DOMAIN

Language as a Parameter

In response to the question of whether or not he was "influenced" by the Spanish language, the great novelist Jorge Luis Borges exclaimed:

> I am inseparable from the Spanish language. My dreams, my aspirations as a writer are formed in Spanish. It's no exaggeration to say that the man I am would not "be" who he is without Spanish. The writer I have become is unthinkable without the shape it has been given by the great traditions of Latin culture.[65]

For Borges, the Spanish language is a personal, ethical, and aesthetic parameter of his life both as a man and as an artist. In Dworkin's sense, Borges makes judgments about whether he has met his own standards for an effective life as an artist and as a person within the parameters of Spanish language and of Latin American culture.[66] Spanish language and culture are, at least for this one writer, what Dworkin calls "hard" parameters.[67] Borges can imagine himself only within these parameters. The person outside those parameters would no longer be the man or writer, Borges.

Toni Morrison makes a similar point when she writes:

> The question of what constitutes the art of a black writer, for whom that modifier is more search than fact, has some urgency. In other words, other than melanin and subject matter, what, in fact, may make me a black writer? Other

than my own ethnicity—what is going on in my work that makes me believe it is demonstrably inseparable from a cultural specificity that is Afro-American?[68]

Morrison answers her question through a careful analysis of the first sentences of several of her novels, noting that one can find the answer in "the ways in which I activate language and ways in which that language activates me."[69] The parameter of her writing that gives it the specificity of the work of a black writer is a practice of language, "a search for and deliberate posture of vulnerability to those aspects of Afro-American culture that can inform and position my work."[70] Morrison's writing, in other words, is inseparable from her assumption of the identification of African American in the form of a search—a search conducted in part by her self-responsibility for the articulation of the cultural difference of her people.

For Morrison, it is through language that we try to fathom cultural difference and try to give shape to "Unspeakable Things Unspoken."[71] How does a writer tell the story of a young African American girl's unbeing? How does one tell this and other horror stories that block the "rememoration," which is, in turn, a representation of the previously unrepresented past? Writing, for Morrison, is explicitly an act of self-responsibility before the stories that haunt the historical present of her life—a life that she deliberately has assumed as that of an African American writer. The opening phrase of *The Bluest Eye* is, "Quiet as it's kept."[72] This phrase was a familiar one from Morrison's childhood, one she heard again and again, listening to adult black women talking among themselves. The hope in this phrase, from the perspective of the adult women looking back on the young girlfriends who lived through the character Pecola's undoing, is that the "us" that is keeping the secret can admit to it and therefore confirm that this "us" has the power to confront even the most horrible reality. Telling a story gives a possible new meaning to the "us" that is formed, even if the secret that made us can never be fully revealed, not only because it is too horrible, but also because the story comes too late to save Pecola. As Morrison writes,

> The words are conspiratorial. "Shh, don't tell anyone else," and "No one is allowed to know this." It is a secret between us and a secret that is being kept from us. The conspiracy is both held and withheld, exposed and sustained. In some sense it was precisely what the act of writing the book was: the public exposure of a private confidence. In order fully to comprehend the duality of that position, one needs to think of the immediate political climate in which the writing took place, 1965–69, during great social upheaval in the life of black people. The publication (as opposed to the writing) involved the exposure; the writing was the disclosure of secrets, secrets "we" shared and those withheld from us by ourselves and by the world outside the community.[73]

The "we" is in quotation marks because this group is not just there but is also formed in part by the secret and the effort to fathom the meaning of the rape of a young black girl who only can be there when she hallucinates a white self with the bluest eyes. How can "we" make sense of that? Of a young black girl who cannot see herself until she becomes mad enough to see herself as the idealized white girl with the bluest eyes? She strives to take on her own version of the idealized identification of "white girl." Then she becomes what everything in the racist world in which she grew up told her she could not be. The young girl's hallucination of herself is madness because she must extinguish herself to see herself as "worthy" of her existence. Psychosis is the only way for her to dream up a self because she lives her "blackness" as an absolute limit on any attempt to fill herself in and become a person. The adult women who tell the story stumble before they make the identification with her that they must to reveal the secret, an identification they did not make when they let her go to the abyss of her madness. Pecola is not alone in the brutal limitations imposed upon what she could make of herself as a black girl in a racist society. The story proceeds through rememoration of what it means to be an African American.

How does the writer find the language to tell this story? What is it about this story and the language in which it is told that makes it an expression of identification and re-identification of the difference of Afro-American culture? Morrison explains:

> The points I have tried to illustrate are that my choices of language (speakerly, aural, colloquial), my reliance for full comprehension on codes embedded in black culture, my effort to effect immediate coconspiracy and intimacy (without any distancing, explanatory fabric), as well as my (failed) attempt to shape a silence while breaking it are attempts (many unsatisfactory) to transfigure the complexity and wealth of Afro-American culture into a language worthy of the culture[74]

It might seem strange to use Morrison and Borges as if they are making the same point. Borges is speaking of the unsunderable connection between himself and the Spanish language and culture. He implicitly draws the connection between Spanish language and Latin culture. But the Spanish language also embodies the culture of Spain, which is not Latin American. Morrison writes in English, but hers is an English that among other things expresses the colloquial practices of black folklore and the day-to-day expressions encoded in Afro-American culture. Both writers articulate the insight that who they are is inseparable from the way they are "activated" in language and that their language is inseparable from both the culture that brings it to life and their own identification with that culture. Morrison and Borges describe language as an essential parameter of their lives, but one that the complex relationship language has with culture, ethnicity, nationality, and race shapes. As is the case with all parameters, the very attempt to articulate its significance reworks its meaning.

Language and Culture

The exact relationship between the person, language, and thought remains a matter of dispute, as does the precise connection between language and culture. Steven Pinker, for example, has argued that we all think in a prelinguistic medium called "Mentalese."[75] As a result, the mode of linguistic expression has no real bearing on our thoughts and on our access to reality. Pinker could imagine a world in which we all speak in the same universal language.[76] Perhaps James Joyce in *Finnegan's Wake* came closest to realizing such a world, undoing the boundaries of historical human languages. But to do so, Joyce also had to imagine the dissolution of the rigid ethnic, national, and sexual identifications.[77]

For human beings living today, however, language differentiation is inseparable from the lived experience of ethnicity, national conflict, and racism. This is not to say that Pinker is right or wrong, although other thinkers and linguists strongly disagree with him. For example, Benjamin Lee Whorf, who has devoted his life to studying the unique syntax of the Hopi language, argues that different structures of language can shape our conceptualization of basic parameters such as space and time.[78] And yet, if we listen to Morrison, to imagine the English language is not to imagine the form of life of African American culture, even though African Americans speak English.[79]

Culture is more than language. Not all culturally embedded communication is verbal. Many ways of signaling to one another mark our connection or our identification with a group. Signs—a way of pointing a finger, raising the eyebrows, sighing in church, nodding to each other on the street, and shaking hands—allow others to identify the signaler as a member of a particular group.

These nonverbal personae are crucial to how actual human beings express culture. But personae are lived only as the people who are the members of the culture and who bring it to life assume and re-imagine them. Because human beings are the entities that express themselves and their cultural identifications through these personae, the meanings of those personae always are changing. At the same time, one can both misinterpret and stereotype the cultural personae of others. This misinterpretation and stereotyping is one of the many ways in which people convey racism and ethnic disparagement within a culture. Sometimes it takes the subtle form of mistakenly thinking that only other cultures have personae, while white Anglos simply represent the moral and decent mode of behavior.

The proposition that language and culture are not coterminous does not imply that language is not a basic parameter of culture. A person who has no access to the language of a culture is severely, if not entirely, limited in her access to that culture. I may dance *salsa*; I may love Mexican food; I may be obsessed with the tradition of hyper-realism found in many of the great South American novels; I may be completely convinced that Puerto Rico is economically and politically disadvantaged because of its commonwealth status.[80] More profoundly, I may have thrown in my lot with people who are Latino/a and find in these loves the most important relationships of my life. But neither my love for Latin music, my appreciation of South American literature, my deep sympathy for the political concerns of the Latin American community, nor even the profound love and respect I feel for Latino/a members of my family will make me part of that culture. Similarly, learning to speak Spanish, while undoubtedly enhancing my access to the culture, alone cannot make me a part of it. Language for most of us is more of a limit than a parameter, precisely because attaining fluency in another language is a truly formidable goal.

One cannot easily draw with exactitude the relationship between language and culture. If we are monolingual, to what extent are we enclosed in our culture? George Fletcher, who fully recognizes the complexity of this question, convincingly draws a clear connection between language and culture when he examines the relationship between the English language and the subculture of law.[81] Fletcher, in one of his several examples, argues that the different meanings of reason in English, German, and French make it virtually impossible to translate accurately the term "reasonable person" and to convey to participants in other legal systems the place it holds in our legal system.[82] Fletcher writes:

> In contrast to a single rule based on reasonableness, European lawyers start their arguments with broad, sweeping rights. They would say, for example, that you have the right to use all the force necessary to protect your interests regardless of the costs that fall on others. But this is only the first step of a structured argument. If it appears that the defensive force imposed a disproportionate cost on others, European lawyers would apply the doctrine of *abus de droit*—the principle that defeats the exercise of absolute rights in particular situations. Not surprisingly, in view of the doctrine of reasonableness, English-speaking lawyers have no need for the doctrine of "abuse of rights."[83]

In Fletcher's view, this variance in the definitions of reason reflects an important difference between the subcultures of Anglo-American and European legal systems.[84] The use of the word "reasonable" suggests an Anglo-American preference for pluralism in legal thought as opposed to the stronger notion of rights that some European legal systems defend.[85] The word and the meaning it has acquired over time, including the preference for pluralism that comes to be a part of what reasonableness encodes as a word of art in the subculture of law, pass down through the generations and blend into the traditions of legal scholarship. For Fletcher, thought, language, and culture have a reciprocal relationship.[86]

I think Fletcher is exactly right. The relationship between thought, language, and culture is both reciprocal and dynamic. But we would make one important addition, addressing the question of whether or not there is a determinative or constitutive relationship between thought and language and between language and culture: this is not the *right* way to think about these relationships because languages and cultures live only through persons and personae. It is not the right language because human beings also fabricate the cultural personae in which they express themselves. Fabrication disrupts the causal chain that we need to show a determinative relationship between language and culture and leaves us with the potential to shape and reshape ourselves.

Turning Limits into Parameters: Language, Culture, and Individual Choice

We have seen that it is hard to learn a new language well enough to make another culture accessible, and it is harder still to revise oneself to identify with that culture, whether psychically or in one's outward relations with others. Yet we also know that this learning and revision is just what generation after generation of immigrants, including those from the Caribbean, Mexico, and Central and South America, have achieved. Although the high degree of difficulty diminishes the potential occurrence of cross-cultural movement, it by no means erases that potential. It follows that freedom is deeply implicated in the potential's realization. I repeat my central argument: Each of us—those experiencing that difficult process of linguistic and cultural access, as well as natives—should receive the legal freedom to re-evaluate and re-represent our basic identifications, including the moral, ethical, and political significance we give to our mother tongue. Different people will value this freedom differently.

For me, this distinction between the freedom and the value of the freedom is crucial in the case of language rights. Consequently, I disagree with the terms that define one current of the multicultural debate: the current that poses a choice between a liberal nationalist—rooted in and contained by linguistic and cultural context—and a cosmopolitan conception of the subject—surmounting context to construct an independent, personalized identity. In my view, the choice between those two conceptions is false when posed either to defend or to undermine the importance of cultural or language rights.

Jeremy Waldron views cosmopolitanism as an ethical and political ideal that best expresses the value of the freedom to make sense of our basic identifications.[87] Waldron describes the cosmopolitan as follows:

> [One] may live all his life in one city and maintain the same citizenship throughout. But he refuses to think of himself as *defined* by his location or his ancestry or his citizenship or his language. Though he may live in San Francisco and be of Irish ancestry, he does not take his identity to be compromised when he learns Spanish, eats Chinese, wears clothes made in Korea, listens to arias by

Verdi sung by a Maori princess on Japanese equipment, follows Ukrainian politics, and practices Buddhist meditation techniques. He is a creature of modernity, conscious of living in a mixed-up world and having a mixed-up self.[88]

Waldron bolsters his appeal to the ideal of cosmopolitanism by arguing that liberal nationalists are wrong to emphasize the importance of defining oneself through a specific culture and language.[89] Will Kymlicka counters, correctly in my view, that the sort of cultural melange that Waldron describes does not actually involve moving between cultures.[90] For those who do attempt such a move, language fluency will be a first, necessary step. Waldron exaggerates how easy it is for us, particularly as adults, truly to escape our "mother" tongue.[91]

Yet Waldron certainly has a right to his imaginary domain and deserves the psychic and moral space to define himself as a cosmopolitan.[92] Indeed, one can understand Waldron as being an immigrant identity—one that has fluid parameters because many different social and historical forces constitute it.[93] Gloria Anzaldúa makes a similar point when she describes what she calls the consciousness of the new *mestiza*:

> The new *mestiza* copes by developing a tolerance for contradictions, a tolerance for ambiguity. She learns to be an Indian in Mexican culture, to be Mexican from an Anglo point of view. She learns to juggle cultures. She has a plural personality, she operates in a pluralistic mode—nothing is thrust out, the good the bad and the ugly, nothing rejected, nothing abandoned. Not only does she sustain contradictions, she turns the ambivalence into something else.[94]

Both Waldron and Anzaldúa are describing processes by which an individual comes to terms with a complex historical web of relationships. The new mestiza consciousness is in part a political act that turns limits into parameters and thereby challenges the meaning of being Indian in Mexico. Yet in Anzaldúa's description, cultures continue to operate as both limits and parameters in part through the personae they make available to the individual seeking to make sense of her complex identifications. No Anglo could access the Mexican persona from the Indian point of view in the same way that Anzaldúa does. Both Anzaldúa and Waldron not only are describing piecing together identities (and in the case of Anzaldúa, playing with cultural personae to expand their meaning), but also are telling us how they morally and ethically value their identifications. This process of evaluation is that which freedom demands be left to the individual.

For these reasons, I need not choose between liberal nationalism and cosmopolitanism in the context of defending language rights. Each principle accurately describes how some individuals come to value their freedom to make sense of their identifications. Consider, as an example, individuals who identify themselves as both Quebecois and liberal nationalists. For these individuals a commitment to the French language is essential to their self-definition, and they should be free to identify with their inherited language in this strong manner. Waldron's real rebellion is not against these people, at least not on my reading of him. Rather, Waldron argues against the idea that my heritage rigidly predetermines my identity so as effectively to undercut the moral or ethical dimensions of whom one might become.[95] On this point, I agree with him. People must be morally free to make sense of their identifications in their own way. Sometimes this means a brutal uprooting of oneself from one's culture and linguistic background. Again to quote Anzaldúa:

> To this day I'm not sure where I found the strength to leave the source, the mother, disengage from my family, *mi tierra, mi gente,* and all that picture stood for. I had to leave home so I could find myself, find my own intrinsic nature buried under the personality that had been imposed on me.[96]

It is precisely because the relationship among languages, cultures, ethnicities, class, and race is complex that it is difficult to draw the kinds of causal claims that tell us what determines what. But this difficulty actually is a good thing. The intractability of grasping exactly how these relationships affect one another leaves open a space for our freedom to practice self-responsibility. To put the argument more strongly, one even can understand the intractability as a result of our freedom to re-imagine ourselves and to re-evaluate our fundamental identifications and what they mean to us.

"Put simply," Kymlicka argues, "freedom involves making choices amongst various options, and our societal culture not only provides these options, but also makes them meaningful to us." For example,

> whether or not a course of action has any significance for us depends on whether, and how, our language renders vivid to us the point of that activity. And the way in which language renders vivid these activities is shaped by our history, our "traditions and conventions". Understanding these cultural narratives is a precondition of making intelligent judgments [sic] about how to lead our lives. In this sense, our culture not only provides options, it also "provides the spectacles through which we identify experiences as valuable."[97]

I agree with Kymlicka on this point. He shows again that the way in which language "activates" someone who in turn activates her language is basic to the process of forming a unique person. But we need to address two tensions in his formulation. The first is a technical point: Kymlicka writes of autonomy while defending the proposition that our autonomy is dependent upon the phenomenal world. In other words, he is not using autonomy in the strict Kantian sense.[98] In contrast, I address this problem with an existential re-interpretation of Kant's notion of moral freedom, the only kind of freedom open to us, according to Kant. Second, a tension remains between us and Kymlicka that also lies at the heart of Waldron's disagreement with him on the question of how culture, and more specifically homogenous culture, *frames* our choices. If our culture effectively bounds our choices, then the very culture that purportedly serves our freedom limits it, regardless of the culture's contents (including, for example, its protection of individual rights). By postulating a kaleidoscope of cultures, Waldron in part tries to keep us from being limited and predetermined.[99] Waldron does not want his national origin or linguistic descent to capture his imagination.[100] This predetermination is inconsistent with most strong conceptions of freedom.

Kymlicka recognizes that cultures are open-ended phenomena, yet at times he lapses into the language of determinism: "familiarity with a culture determines the boundaries of the imaginable."[101] In other words, because persons construct culture through their identification with (or against) it, a "culture" always changes. Toni Morrison describes a dynamic relationship: language activates the person, but the person also activates language by stretching the limits of the meaning of her identifications.[102] True, language is a basic parameter of our lives, but even if a person remains monolingual, it is a cultural parameter whose meaning changes for her as she struggles to articulate its unspoken possibilities.

Yet, like Kymlicka, I defend the connection among culture, language rights, and individual freedom. Dworkin's distinction between parameters and limits aids this defense. As Dworkin reminds us, our lives are indexed; the true particularity of anyone's situation will include a whole host of limits and parameters.[103] I would argue that this indexing occurs because given sets of identifications form all of us. Because there *should* be no precise way to determine which are limits and which are parameters, and because that "determination" is part of a person's freedom, some people will seek to break out of their language and national background by assimilating into another language and culture. To make this break, some may interpret their language as a "soft parameter."[104] Others, like Borges, define their language as a "hard parameter,"[105] which gives them a fundamental sense of themselves. Borges's definition of language as a hard parameter provides him the most basic sense of himself as a man and as a writer. We experience our freedom in large part through our endeavor to determine which are limits and which are parameters in our lives. Furthermore, we try to determine how we understand exactly how the parameters bind us to a tradition and to the cultural narratives contained therein and how they enable us to tell new stories, including stories about ourselves.

To confront this substantial challenge, we must have our imaginary domain protected. Part of Anzaldúa's struggle to become a person involved her effort to free herself from the stereotypical personae in and through which the majority Anglo culture defined the meaning of her Chicana identification. But her struggle did not just involve inversion, affirming the features of the stereotypical personae imposed by Anglo culture. Instead, her struggle involved a complex re-working of the metaphor of the borderlands in which the mestiza can recreate the complex being that is herself. This process involved not only the celebration of the Spanish language but also the affirmance of Spanish as a living tongue, which the Mexican American Spanish with which she grew up changed and enriched. "But Chicano Spanish is a border tongue which developed naturally. Change, *evolución, enriquecimiento de palabras nuevas por invención o adopción* have created variants of Chicano Spanish, *un nuevo lenguaje. Un lenguaje que corresponde a un modo de vivir.* Chicano Spanish is not incorrect, it is a living language."[106]

EQUALITY, LANGUAGE, AND RIGHTS

Chandran Kukathas suggests that the right to "exit" appropriately resolves tensions among language, culture, and individual freedom.[107] I disagree because this negative option does not provide the measure of freedom demanded here. First, the right to exit implies that cultures have sharper boundaries than those existing in the real world. Second, it implies that "exit" is possible. It is almost impossible to exit a first language, like it or not. One may learn new languages, but the "mother" tongue stays with a person forever. Third, and more importantly, many people do not want to exit. Instead, they want to push against or re-interpret the meanings of their culture.

In place of the right to exit, I propose the right to the imaginary domain. This right furnishes the person with the moral and psychic space to come to terms with the full particularity of her situation, with language, with culture, with gender, and with sexuality. It does so in part by insisting that how we live with and define the parameters of our life is basic to our freedom. People differ, and profoundly so when it comes to their desire to be rooted in their native language and culture. But they certainly should have the right to affirm their language as an end because it inevitably is, at a minimum, a basic parameter that is crucial to how they shape an identity of their life. At the same time, we should never undermine the freedom to re-imagine ourselves.

Only the "degradation prohibition" limits the right to the imaginary domain.[108] The degradation prohibition forbids the characterization of someone as unworthy because of how she has constituted herself from her basic identifications.[109] One degrades a person in my sense if one does not allow her to bestow value on her language.[110] Again I quote Anzaldúa:

So, if you want to really hurt me, talk badly about my language. Ethnic identity is twin skin to linguistic identity—I am my language. Until I can take pride in my language, I cannot take pride in myself. Until I can accept as legitimate Chicano Texas Spanish, Tex-Mex and all the other languages I speak, I cannot accept the legitimacy of myself. Until I am free to write bilingually and to switch codes without having always to translate, while I still have to speak English or Spanish when I would rather speak Spanglish, and as long as I have to accommodate the English speakers rather than having them accommodate me, my tongue will be illegitimate.[111]

This freedom to use one's own tongue is crucial to equal dignity. By denying someone the freedom to affirm her linguistic origin as she ethically interprets it, one robs from her the basic freedom to practice self-responsibility for her identifications. If the state instead imposes its evaluation of her language on her, it denies her equal worth as a free person.

People still will ask who, as between natives and immigrants, should have to accommodate whom? We should resolve this question by reference to the concept of reasonableness, which helps us determine what we should expect in social relations with others, viewed as free and equal persons. I repeat the definition of reasonableness I offered earlier in this essay—we are reasonable when we realize that we are capable of recognizing and harmonizing our pursuit of the good with creatures having equal dignity. Applying that definition, it is unreasonable for Anglos to treat Latinos/as as anything other than free persons who bestow value on their language. It follows that both Official English and Workplace English are unreasonable. We can make a similar argument by reference to Kant's own understanding of external right. The suppression of Spanish is a maxim that cannot be made a universal law without suppressing the form of rightfulness.

Of course, some still might say that Latinos/as remain free persons no matter how Anglos view their language and despite any measures Anglos take to denigrate or more directly to suppress it. A strong Kantian answer would be that such particularistic suppression of a creature of reason always falls afoul of the moral law, with its universalizability requirement. That would be the end of the story. But even if we do not stop there, we can see how these measures impose a cost on the exercise of that freedom. The imposition of that cost cannot be reasonable in Rawls's sense of the word, because Anglos impose it pursuant to the view that the linguistic valuation that Latinos/as make is less worthy than that which Anglos make. The state's imposing the assimilation norm controverts the legal freedom the state must authorize as the source of the evaluative design of one's life. It is unreasonable to expect people to give up their freedom to affirm their lives as they see fit to "Americanize" themselves.

Furthermore, Official English clearly degrades people because of their linguistic descent.[112] By degradation I mean a grading down—because of ethnicity—of one's ethnic background or linguistic origin. In a world of Official English, Spanish speakers are "picked out" because of their language and marked as not belonging to the majority group.[113] To belong, they have to become "American" and assume an identity that others imagine to be bound up with the imposition of the English language.[114] Workplace English similarly degrades Spanish-speaking workers and accordingly is invalidated.

Discrimination against Spanish speakers affects the way they view their own language. Speaking Spanish becomes an imposed limit. This imposed limit not only violates a person's freedom, but also subjects her to a serious inequality by turning her language into a mark that determines how to meet her life prospects. Accordingly, courts should legally mark this discrimination with the status of a "suspect classification." In the analysis of David Richards:

> In each case its irrationalist object is not some brute fact that cannot be changed, but central features of moral personality—identifications that make one a self-respecting member of a community that one reasonably values. The suspectness of the underlying prejudice in each case is its irrationalist interpretation of central aspects of human personality and the unjust degradation of the culture (moral slavery) with which a person reasonably identifies.[115]

Spoken language obviously is central to the identity of many Latinos/as. We should consider steps taken to force a person to forsake that identity altogether or significantly to repress it as "moral slavery" in Richards's sense.[116]

CONCLUSION: ENGLISH-ONLY AND THE RIGHT TO LINGUISTIC SELF-DEFENSE

Could there be a situation compelling enough to accord a group the right to impose its language or to ask for significant state reinforcement of it? The Quebecois, arguing that French can survive only if it insures that the next generation will learn it, have sought to keep English from being taught in the schools that have a majority French population.[117] Can English-Only statutes that demand the suppression of other languages have similar defenses?

George Fletcher, analogizing to the criminal law doctrine of justification, argues that a people has a right to linguistic self-defense in some cases. Recall that, for Fletcher, language and culture have a close causal connection. Fletcher further argues that, given a conflict between two languages over which language should govern, there can be no "neutral" perspective from which to judge which language is better for any culture. He explains: "It is better to think of the struggle to retain a language as an expression of a localized imperative to survive against an external threat. Thus it seems that the principle of self-defense provides a better framework for justifying measures of defense than does the neutral standard of necessity."[118]

Fletcher emphasizes historical priority as a key factor in the determination of who should receive this right of self-defense when two peoples and two languages fight for pre-eminence. Using Kant's famous example that who got on the plank first can determine who has the right to push the other off, Fletcher argues that priority in time should be determinate.[119] In addition, says Fletcher, only a serious and demonstrable challenge to the survival of the language can trigger the right to self-defense.[120] Finally, Fletcher stipulates three ancillary requirements: first, the defensive measures should be effective; second, they must be reasonably necessary, for that is the cheapest means available for linguistic survival; and third, there must be a sense of proportionality.[121]

I take seriously the proposition of a right of linguistic self-defense.[122] But, using Fletcher's standards, it is crystal clear that such a right cannot justify English-Only. No serious threat to the survival of the English language exists, because there are and will continue to be high-powered economic incentives for immigrants to learn English. The assimilation process of today's immigrants, like that of every previous immigrant group, indeed has triggered a *Kulturkampf*, but not one that threatens the survival of our language. Under the economic theory of language, and in light of the emerging role of English as a global lingua franca, the very suggestion of a threat is absurd.

Furthermore, even if a threat were to cause the issue to be joined, it would not be at all clear that English should have a priority entitlement nationwide. In the Southwest, where most of the Title VII cases have arisen, Spanish was first in time. That Anglos conquered these Spanish-speaking areas, and that the Spanish speakers gradually lost their language rights[123] presumably would create an issue under Fletcher's standard. I would take seriously the proposition that Spanish-speaking people in the Southwest (and Puerto Rico) have this right to linguistic self-defense, although the articulation of that case is beyond this essay's scope.

Absent a plausible case for a right to linguistic self-defense, no plausible case for English-Only mandates arises because they controvert the equal dignity of free persons. Indeed, if the meaning of "American" turns on identification with a political culture based on legal recognition of the equal dignity of free persons, then to repudiate English-Only is to do something quintessentially "American."

Notes

INTRODUCTION

1. To take any of these specific arguments I make in defense of feminist programs of legal reform, or justifications of a new ethics of social arrangements, out of the political realm to which I meant to apply them would demand that I explicitly address the ethical limits of Western feminism. This topic deserves a book in itself. I will discuss the relationship of Western feminism to imperialism, national liberation struggles in the South, and international law in more detail in my forthcoming book on ethical feminism (Sage Publications, London).

2. See "Pornography's Temptation," in Drucilla Cornell, *The Imaginary Domain: Abortion, Pornography and Sexual Difference* (New York: Routledge, 1995), 95–163.

3. For my defense of the right to abortion see "Dismembered Selves and Wondering Wombs" in *The Imaginary Domain* (New York: Routledge, 1995), 31–91.

4. For my discussion of how we should interpret Kant's own understandings of right within feminist theory, see "Feminism, Justice and Sexual Freedom," in Drucilla Cornell, *At the Heart of Freedom* (Princeton: Princeton University Press, 1998), 18–19.

5. *Roe v. Wade*, 410 U.S. 113 (1973).

6. See generally G.W.F. Hegel, *The Philosophy of the Right*, trans. T. M. Knox (Oxford: Oxford University Press, 1967).

7. I put postmodernism in quotes because it has become such a vague term used to cover up so many strands of criticism and genealogy in contemporary political theory. For my own critique of the vagueness of the term, see "What is Postmodernity Anyway," in *The Philosophy of the Limit* (New York: Routledge 1992).

8. For an excellent deconstruction of Foucault and Deleuze's appeal to the direct politics of the people as implicitly underwriting a new positivism, see Gayatri Chakrovorty Spivak, *A Critique of Postcolonial Reason: Toward a History of the Vanishing Present* (London: Harvard University Press, 1999) 255-256. See Spivak also for a discussion of the relationship of the two meanings of representation in German idealism, particularly her discussion of *darstellen* and *vertreten,* at 259–266.

9. Jürgen Habermas has coined this phrase to sweep up everyone who has not adopted his own unique conception of the socialized general other constructed in the

universal pragmatics inherit in linguistic communication. There are many of us, however, who are ethically worried about Habermas's understanding of the socialized subject particularly as that subject is socialized into actual existing legal systems. For Habermas's understanding of language, law, and the socialized subject, see *Between Facts and Norms* (Cambridge: MIT Press, 1996).

10. Kant defines the faculty of desire that "by means of its representations is the cause of the actuality of the objects of those representations," *The Critique of Judgement*, trans. James Creed Meredith (Oxford: Clarendon Press, 1952), 16 n. 1.

11. Many feminists who strongly disagree about everything else share the insight that the struggle over representation in both senses that I have used it is at the heart of feminism. See my letter in response to Martha Nussbaum in "Martha Nussbaum and Her Critics: An Exchange," *The New Republic* (April 19, 1999): 43.

12. *Cornell Law Review* 84 (3) (March 1999).

13. Thomas Nagel, *Equality and Partiality* (New York: Oxford University Press, 1991), 21.

14. Although I would no longer defend just-cause statutes, on the basis of the appeal to the Hegelian concept of reciprocal symmetry, I would still do so from the appeal to legal ideals. The central disagreement with Posner therefore still remains key to the debates even though the specific ideal to which I refer would no longer be the same. That debate is over the meaning of postmodern pragmatism. The debate is between Posner's strong defense of the idea that there is no interest in human activity other than the technically practical and that that is the only interest that should be recognized in jurisprudence. I continue to defend the distinction between the morally practical and the technically practical as this is relevant to jurisprudence. For a discussion of Kant's own distinction between these two interests, see Kant's *The Critique of Judgement*, 9.

15. Kant, *The Critique of Judgement*.

CHAPTER 1

1. I put "spaces" in quotation marks because these spaces were not just literal, but also moral and psychic.

2. See chapter 2 in Drucilla Cornell, *At the Heart of Freedom* (Princeton: Princeton University Press, 1998).

3. For a more elaborate discussion of what I mean by psychic laws and their relationship to actual legal law, see "Feminist Hope," the introduction to the new edition of Cornell, *Beyond Accommodation* (New York: Rowman & Littlefield, 1999). Psychoanalytic theory, in all of its diversity, shares one thing in common: the elaboration of psychic laws that are ethically justified in the name of achieving adequate separation and individuation. I am aware that many psychoanalytical theorists would not put it this way because these laws, such as the incest prohibition, for example, are explained as an inevitable part of enculturation or as part of what it means to be a sexually differentiated individual. It is beyond the scope of this essay to defend my argument that psychoanalysis should defend these laws ethically, rather than try to show their inevitability through "scientific explanation."

4. Marilyn Friedman, "Beyond Caring: The De-Moralization of Gender," *Justice and Care: Essential Readings in Feminist Ethics*, ed. Virginia Held (Boulder, Co.: Westview, 1995), 70.

5. It is legitimate to write that we were fired for union organizing because the National Labor Relations Board found union organizers to be the reason for the firing.

6. See Drucilla Cornell, *Beyond Accommodation* (New York: Routledge, 1991), 147-152; and Luce Irigaray, *This Sex Which Is Not One,* trans. Catherine Porter (Ithaca: Cornell University Press, 1985), 76.

7. See Cornell, *At the Heart of Freedom*, 34–37.

8. See Cornell, *Legacies of Dignity,* ch. 3 for more on this notion of aesthetic knowledge (forthcoming).

9. Friedman's argument that gender is moralized is as follows:

Morality, I suggest, is fragmented into a "division of moral labor" along the lines of gender, the rationale for which is rooted in historic developments pertaining to family, state, and economy. The tasks of governing, regulating social order, and managing other "public" institutions have been monopolized by men as their privileged domain, and the tasks of sustaining privatized personal relationships have been imposed on, or left to, women. The genders have thus been conceived in terms of special and distinctive moral projects. Justice and rights have structured male moral norms, values, and virtues, while care and responsiveness have defined female moral norms, values, and virtues. The division of moral labor has had the dual function both of preparing us each for our respective socially defined domains and of rendering us incompetent to manage the affairs of the realm from which we have been excluded. ("Beyond Caring," 64).

10. See Midge Decter, *The New Chastity and Other Arguments Against Women's Liberation* (New York: Coward, McCann & Geoghegan, 1972).

11. For a longer discussion of how I have defined and used the phrase, "recollective imagination," see Drucilla Cornell, *Transformations: Recollective Imagination and Sexual Difference* (New York: Routledge, 1993), 23-24, 31-32.

12. I have defended such a moral and legal right to personality and named it the right to the imaginary domain. See Drucilla Cornell, *The Imaginary Domain: Abortion, Pornography, and Sexual Difference* (New York: Routledge, 1995).

13. For example, Katie Roiphe makes this mistake by arguing that laws against sexual harassment and date rape require the remoralization of gender. See Roiphe, *The Morning After: Sex, Fear and Feminism on Campus* (Boston: Little Brown & Co., 1993).

14. See Wendy Brown, *States of Injury* (Princeton, NJ: Princeton University Press, 1995). Also see Judith Butler, *Gender Trouble* (New York: Routledge, 1990).

15. For example, neither Judith Butler nor myself is comfortable in calling ourselves postmodernist, although we are often taken as such. Both of us have questioned whether there is a unique historical period that could be meaningfully designated as postmodern, let alone that we are in it and that it further describes a certain kind of feminist politics. See Judith Butler, "Contingent Foundations," in *Feminist Contentions* by Seyla Benhabib, Judith Butler, Drucilla Cornell and Nancy Fraser (New York: Routledge, 1995). Also see Drucilla Cornell, "The Ethical Message of Negative Dialectics," in *The Philosophy of the Limit* (New York: Routledge, 1992), 13–38.

CHAPTER 2

1. See Crenshaw 1988.
2. *Hurley et al. v. Irish-American Gay, Lesbian and Bisexual Group of Boston,* 115 U.S. 2338 (1995).
3. For a discussion of synchronization, see Cornell 1993a.
4. Published by Princeton University Press, 1998.
5. Judith Butler has pushed me to confront the ontologizing of sexual difference in Lacan. See Butler 1995.

CHAPTER 3

1. Charles Taylor, "The Politics of Recognition" in *Multiculturalism: Examining the Politics of Recognition,* ed. Amy Gutmann (Princeton, NJ: Princeton University Press, 1994).
2. Lionel Trilling, *Sincerity and Authenticity* (Cambridge, MA: Harvard University Press, 1972).
3. "I have resolved on an enterprise which has no precedent and which, once complete, will have no imitator. My purpose is to display to my kind a portrait in every way true to nature, and the man I shall portray will be myself. . . . Simply myself. I know my own heart and I understand my fellow man. I am made like no one I have ever met; I will even venture to say that I am like no one in the whole world. Whether nature did well or ill in breaking the mould in which she formed me is a question which can only be resolved after the reading of my book." (Jean-Jacques Rousseau, *The Confessions,* translated and introduced by J. M. Cohen [London: Penguin Books, 1953], translation slightly amended.)
4. See Georg W.F. Hegel's *Phenomenology of Mind,* trans. J. Baillie (New York: MacMillan, 1931). For a critique of Hegel's *Philosophy of History* for his uncritical acceptance of the colonial imaginary, see Enrique Ducell, "Eurocentrism and Modernity," in *The Post-Modern Debate in Latin America,* ed. John Beverley, Jose Oviedo and Michael Aronna (Durham and London: Duke University Press, 1995).
5. Gayatri Chakravorty Spivak, *The Post-Colonial Critic: Interviews, Strategies, Dialogues,* ed. Sarah Harasym (New York and London: Routledge, 1990), 59–60.
6. Frantz Fanon, "Racism and Culture," in *Toward the African Revolution: Political Essays,* trans. Haakon Chevalier (New York: Grove Press, 1967), 34.
7. See Ella Shohat/Robert Stam's discussion on the political significance of confounding the colonizer to unreadability in *Unthinking Eurocentrism: Multiculturalism and the Media* (New York: Routledge, 1994), 44.
8. Immanuel Kant, *Groundwork of the Metaphysic of Morals,* trans. H.J. Paton (New York: Harper & Row, 1958), 118–120.
9. We put this word in quotation marks not to be precious, but to remark that its sense is not only what is at stake in Glazer's and other recent discussions of cultural identity in North America. The appropriation of the word by citizens of the U.S. as if it could belong only to them has been challenged fiercely by those who live in Central and South America, for example.
10. K. Anthony Appiah, "The Multiculturalist Misunderstanding," *New York Review of Books* 54 (15) (October 9, 1997): 30–36.

11. See Drucilla Cornell, *Transformations: Recollective Imagination and Sexual Difference* (New York and London: Routledge, 1993).

12. Although there is much support in the literature for Appiah's conclusion about "Hispanics," there is also a countertrend. Many Latino/as are seeking to maintain the Spanish language through the generations. It should also be noted here that one aspect of this is the use of Latino and Latina in the place of "Hispanic" in order to signify and affirm the political and ethical aspiration to maintain a cultural identity that includes an affirmation of identification with the Spanish language, while at the same time maintaining a historically blurred distinction between the cultures of the Americas and that of the Iberian peninsula. There are other factors that also seem to be influencing a trend counter to that which Appiah rightfully notes has been true of most groups of Latinos and Latinas. Many Cubans have defined themselves as exiles with the historic mission of returning to Cuba; therefore they have worked to keep their children bilingual, succeeding in keeping the language alive into the third generation. Other factors influencing the tendency to break with the immigrant pattern of loss of the mother tongue by the third generation are the rise of the South American community and the establishment of nation-states in the Americas that seek to break from the economic dominance of the U.S. More immigrants are returning to their homelands as a result—or are anticipating it as an eventuality. Some, following recent examples of Mexican Americans, retain dual citizenship when possible. For a detailed discussion of the pattern of Latino/a assimilation, see William Bratton and Drucilla Cornell, "Deadweight Costs and the Intrinsic Wrongs of Nativism: Freedom and the Legal Suppression of Spanish," *Cornell Law Review* 84 (3) (March 1999). The point that we would like to stress is that economic and political factors shape the ways in which ethnic groups constitute their identifications.

13. Appiah, "The Multiculturalist Misunderstanding," 34.

14. Appiah, "The Multiculturalist Misunderstanding," 34.

15. We borrow this term, "pervasive culture," from Avishai Margalit and Joseph Raz: "The group has a common character and common culture that encompasses many and varied aspects of life, a culture that defines or marks a variety of forms or styles of life, types of activity, occupations, pursuits and relationships. With national groups we expect to find national cuisines, distinctive architectural styles, a common language, a distinctive literary and artistic tradition, national music, customs and dress, ceremonies, holidays, etc." See "National Self-Determination," in *The Rights of Minority Cultures*, ed. Will Kymlicka (New York: Oxford University Press, 1995), 83. For Margalit and Raz, the existence of a pervasive culture is one of the conditions that should be met in a case for self-determination. While they are specifically addressing the conditions under which a people can legitimately demand self-determination, we think that their definition describes the kind of ethnic identity Appiah believes either to have been lost or significantly diluted in the U.S.

16. Appiah borrows the term "cultural geneticism" from Henry Louis Gates, *Loose Canons* (Oxford and New York: Oxford University Press, 1993). See Appiah, "Race, Culture, Identity: Misunderstood Connections," paper presented to the Program for the Study of Law, Philosophy, and Social Theory, New York University Law School, October 9, 1997.

17. K. Anthony Appiah, "Cosmopolitan Patriots," *Critical Inquiry* 23 (3) (Spring 1997): 617–639.

18. Appiah, "The Multiculturalist Misunderstanding," 36.

19. Toni Morrison, *Jazz* (New York and London: Penguin, 1993), 79.

20. See Appiah, "Race, Culture, and Identity: Misunderstood Connections," esp. 2–24: "We have followed enough of the history of the race concept and said enough about current biological conceptions to answer. . . . the question of whether there are any races" (23).

21. Morrison, *Jazz,* 57.

22. Morrison, *Jazz,* 57.

23. Morrison, *Jazz,* 59.

24. Morrison, *Jazz,* 221.

25. Morrison, *Jazz,* 58.

26. Homi Bhabha, *The Location of Culture* (New York: Routledge, 1994), 134.

27. Of course, the story of jazz' reception is a notoriously long and complicated one; in fact, the course of the development of many modern musics is unthinkable without it. But as a salient example of the racialized complexity of that reception among musical minds, one can think of Adorno's peculiar position on jazz in *Prisms* (Cambridge, MA: MIT Press, 1981); see also Juliet Flower McCannell, "Race/War: Race, War, and the Division of Jouissance in Freud and Adorno," *Journal for the Psychoanalysis of Culture and Society,* vol. 2 (fall 1997) 2, for an interesting reading of Adorno's trouble with jazz.

28. Marie Cardinal, *Words to Say It* (Cambridge, MA: Van Vactor and Goodheart, 1983).

29. Toni Morrison, *Playing In the Dark: Whiteness and The Literary Imagination* (Cambridge, MA: Harvard University Press, 1992) viii.

30. Morrison, *Playing In the Dark,* 5.

31. Morrison, "Unspeakable Things Unspoken," *The Tanner Lectures on Human Values,* vol. 11 (Salt Lake City: The University of Utah Press, 1990), 135.

32. Morrison, "Unspeakable Things Unspoken,"150.

33. Shohat and Stam, *Unthinking Eurocentrism,* 359.

34. Morrison, "Unspeakable Things Unspoken," 150.

35. In certain instances, we would even recognize the right of a group to something like linguistic self-defense, as in the Quebecois in Canada and Chicanos/as in the southwestern U.S.; See Bratton and Cornell, "Deadweight Costs and Intrinsic Wrongs."

36. See Appiah's reading of Taylor, "Identity, Authenticity, Survival: Multicultural Societies and Social Reproduction," in Gutmann, *Multiculturalism,* 149–164.

37. See Frantz Fanon's *Black Skin, White Masks* (New York: Grove Press, 1967), 44. See also Homi Bhabha's lectures.

38. Fanon, "Racism and Culture," 33.

39. Stuart Hall, "Cultural Identity and Cinematic Representation" in *Black British Cultural Studies: A Reader,* ed. Houston A. Baker Jr., Manthia Diawara, and Ruth H. Lindenborg (Chicago: University of Chicago Press, 1996), 211.

40. See Benita Parry, "Resistance Theory/Theorizing Resistance or Two Cheers of Nativism," in *Rethinking Fanon: The Continuing Dialogue,* ed. Nigel Gibson (Amherst, N.Y.: Prometheus Books, 1999), 215.

41. Stuart Hall, "New Ethnicities," *Stuart Hall: Critical Dialogues in Cultural Studies,* ed. David Morely and Kuan-Hsing Chen (New York and London: Routledge, 1996), 441–449.

42. Acknowledged by Toni Morrison, personal communication, March 1999.

43. Taylor, "The Politics of Recognition," 63–64.

44. The imposition of such pre-established values is also inconsistent with the understanding of the social basis of self-respect as a primary good. See Cornell, *The Imaginary Domain* (New York: Routledge, 1995), 10: "It should go without saying that hierarchical gradations of any of us as unworthy of personhood violates the postulation of each one of us as an equal person called for in a democratic and modern legal system."

45. Hall, "New Ethnicities," 443.

46. Hall, "New Ethnicities," 447. Hall's evocation of the "transparency" effected by the hegemony of British national identity recalls for us Conrad's *Heart of Darkness*, particularly the novella's ambivalent imperialist narrator, Marlowe, who famously begins his shipboard story with a glance at the banks of the Thames: "And this, too, has been one of the dark places of the earth."

47. Hall, "New Ethnicities"

48. Hall, "New Ethnicities," 448.

49. Taylor, "The Politics of Recognition," 66–67.

50. See Cornell, "Spanish Language Rights" in this collection for further discussion of the implications of this.

51. Another approach to the problem of the relations of representation and the crisis in traditional conceptions of an aesthetic observer is presented by John Guillory in his excellent *Cultural Capital: The Problem of Literary Canon Formation* (Chicago: University of Chicago Press, 1993). See especially chap. 3, "Aesthetics," 269–340.

CHAPTER 4

1. David Richards, *Women, Gays, and the Constitution* (Chicago: University of Chicago Press, 1998), 458.

2. The task of current feminist and lesbian and gay activists can be characterized as one of recollective imagination. This is the phrase I use to describe the relationship between the past and the future in legal interpretation. For a description of this process, see Drucilla Cornell, *Transformations: Recollective Imagination and Sexual Difference* (New York: Routledge, 1993), 28–29. The term is meant to capture how what is recollected in law—the embodied norms and values—are never just "there" but are always represented to us in interpretations. When we seek an account of our legal history, we do so in part by reference to how it guides our future conduct because we cannot validate its truth as a purely descriptive manner. Hence, we are reimagining our legal values and norms when we re-collect them into a new interpretation. Richards' constitutional history, as I interpret him, proceeds through recollective imagination and should be evaluated for its contributions to contemporary dilemmas over sexual freedom.

3. Richards, *Women, Gays, and the Constitution*, 62.

4. Richards, *Women, Gays, and the Constitution*, 88, 92.

5. Richards, *Women, Gays, and the Constitution*, 34.

6. Richards, *Women, Gays, and the Constitution*, 34

7. Richards, *Women, Gays, and the Constitution*, 84.

8. Richards, *Women, Gays, and the Constitution*, 42.

9. Richards, *Women, Gays, and the Constitution*, 53, 55.

10. See Richards, *Women, Gays, and the Constitution*, 40–55.

11. Richards, *Women, Gays, and the Constitution*, 56 [citing Lydia Maria Child's, *An Appeal in Favor of Americans Called Africans* (New York: Arno Press, 1968), 169 originally published in 1836].

12. Richards, *Women, Gays, and the Constitution*, 55–57.

13. Richards, *Women, Gays, and the Constitution*, 18–22.

14. Richards, *Women, Gays, and the Constitution*, 59.

15. Richards, *Women, Gays, and the Constitution*, 38–45.

16. Richards, *Women, Gays, and the Constitution*, 50–54.

17. For a discussion of Richards' distinction between internal and external criticism, see David Richards, *Conscience and the Constitution* (Princeton, NJ: Princeton University Press, 1993).

18. Richards, *Women, Gays, and the Constitution*, 91.

19. Richards, *Women, Gays, and the Constitution*, 99.

20. See Lacan, *Feminine Sexuality*, ed. Juliet Mitchell and Jacqueline Rose, trans. Jacqueline Rose (New York: W. W. Norton, 1982), 47–50.

21. Richards, *Women, Gays, and the Constitution*, 100.

22. Richards, *Women, Gays, and the Constitution*, 188.

23. Richards, *Women, Gays, and the Constitution*, 189.

24. Richards, *Women, Gays, and the Constitution*, 120–124.

25. Richards, *Women, Gays, and the Constitution*, 224.

26. Richards, *Women, Gays, and the Constitution*, 262–263.

27. Richards, *Women, Gays, and the Constitution*, 190.

28. Richards, *Women, Gays, and the Constitution*, 107.

29. Richards, *Women, Gays, and the Constitution*, 138.

30. Richards, *Women, Gays, and the Constitution*.

31. See Richards, *Women, Gays, and the Constitution*, Chapter 5 (discussing Stanton's capitulation of her earlier principles).

32. Richards, *Women, Gays, and the Constitution*, 32.

33. Richards, *Women, Gays, and the Constitution*, 463–464.

34. Richards, *Women, Gays, and the Constitution*, 71.

35. See generally Mary Wollstonecraft, *The Works of Mary Wollstonecraft*, ed. Janet Todd & Marilyn Butler (New York: New York University Press, 1989).

36. Richards, *Women, Gays, and the Constitution*, 156.

37. Richards, *Women, Gays, and the Constitution*, 73, 156.

38. Richards, *Women, Gays, and the Constitution*, 172.

39. Richards, *Women, Gays, and the Constitution*, 156.

40. Richards, *Women, Gays, and the Constitution*, 294–297.

41. Richards, *Women, Gays, and the Constitution*, 297–310.

42. Richards, *Women, Gays, and the Constitution*, 324.

43. Richards, *Women, Gays, and the Constitution*, 346–354.

44. Richards, *Women, Gays, and the Constitution*, 353–354.

45. Richards, *Women, Gays, and the Constitution*, 15.

46. Richards, *Women, Gays, and the Constitution*, 263.

47. Richards, *Women, Gays, and the Constitution*, 3.

48. Richards, *Women, Gays, and the Constitution*, 3–4.

49. Richards, *Women, Gays, and the Constitution*, 4.

50. Richards, *Women, Gays, and the Constitution*, 267-268.

51. Richards, *Women, Gays, and the Constitution*, 459.

52. Richards, *Women, Gays, and the Constitution*, 357.

53. See, for example, "Testimony of Congressman Steve Largent before the Senate Comm. on the Judiciary on the Defense of Marriage Act," July 11, 1996 (WL 10829445, 1996), 6.

> If our law determines that homosexual marriage is permitted, the law is actually declaring to society and to our children that homosexual marriage is desirable and good. I've always tried to live my life with love and tolerance toward individuals. Unfortunately, the practice of homosexuality is not healthy and is actually destructive to individuals. I do not want my children to falsely believe that homosexuality espouses what is chaste, desirable and good in our society.

54. I use the term "sexuate being" to indicate that all human beings are sexual creatures who must orient themselves to their sexuality. This "must" of orientation, however, does not imply that sex be given the form of gender identity, as we now understand gender identity to in turn dictate appropriate love and sexual objects. See Drucilla Cornell, *At the Heart of Freedom* (Princeton, NJ: Princeton University Press, 1998), 34–37.

55. See Immanuel Kant, "On the Common Saying: 'This May Be True in Theory But It Does Not Apply in Practice,'" in *Political Writings*, ed. Hans Reiss, trans. H.B. Nisbet, 2nd ed. (1991), 74–75.

56. Kant, "On the Common Saying."

CHAPTER 5

1. See Drucilla Cornell, *The Philosophy of the Limit* (New York: Routledge, 1992); *The Imaginary Domain* (New York: Routledge, 1995); and *At the Heart of Freedom* (Princeton, N.J.: Princeton University Press, 1998).

2. John Brenkman, "Extreme Criticism," *Critical Inquiry* 26 (1) (Autumn 1999): 9.

3. See Drucilla Cornell, "Introduction: Feminism, Justice, and Sexual Freedom," in *At the Heart of Freedom*.

4. Immanuel Kant, *The Critique of Judgment*, trans. James Creed Meredith (Oxford, U.K.: Clarendon, 1952).

5. I capitalize Enlightenment to indicate both representations of the project repeated in the postmodern mantra and to separate this representation from the open-ended process of critical enlightenment, which I argue inheres in the Kantian notion of reflective judgment in the Third Critique. It is this project of enlightenment, with a small "e," that I endorse.

6. Theodor W. Adorno and Max Horkheimer, *Dialectic of Enlightenment*, trans. John Cumming (New York: Continuum, 1944).

7. For those interested in Adorno and Horkheimer scholarship, I am readily aware that I am offering an interpretation tempered by my own reading of Kant's Third Critique as it effects their own demonstration of a "dark" side of Kantian En-

lightenment. For an excellent discussion of the relationship between Adorno and Horkheimer's concept of the "Enlightenment" in the *Dialectic of the Enlightenment*, as it can and should be tempered by Kant's own insight into reflective judgment in the Third Critique, see Anthony J. Cascardi, *Consequences of Enlightenment* (Cambridge: Cambridge University Press, 1999).

8. See Section 19 of Kant, *Critique of Judgment*, 82.

9. For an excellent discussion of how and why Habermas wrongfully collapses the *sensus communis aestheticus* into the *sensus communis logicus,* see Anthony J. Cascardi, "Communication and Transformation: Aesthetics and Politics in Habermas and Arendt," in *Consequences of Enlightenment*, 132–174.

10. See Brenkman, "Extreme Criticism," 22; and Immanuel Kant, *Kant: Political Writings*, trans. HB. Nisbet (Cambridge: Cambridge University Press, 1991), 54.

11. Brenkman, "Extreme Criticism," 22.

12. John Rawls, "Law of Nations," in *On Human Rights*, ed. Steven Shute and Susan Hurley (New York: BasicBooks, 1993).

13. See Jurgen Habermas, "Political Liberalism: A Debate with John Rawls," in *The Inclusion of the Other: Studies in Political Theory*, ed. Ciaran Cronin and Pablo De Greiff (Cambridge, MA: MIT Press, 1998), 49-101. Also see John Rawls, "Reply to Habermas," in *Political Liberalism* (New York: Columbia University Press, 1993), 372–434.

14. For more on the brutality of Hegelian idealism, see Enrique Dussel, "Eurocentrism and Modernity," in *The Postmodern Debate in Latin America*, ed. John Beverley, Jose Oviedo, and Michael Aronna (Durham, N.C.: Duke University Press, 1995).

15. For an intriguing discussion of how the use of "Eastern" in the designation of Africa and Asia by Europe and North America effectively Others those countries in relation to the West, see Ella Shohat and Robert Stam, *Unthinking Eurocentrism: Multiculturalism and the Media* (New York: Routledge, 1994), 2.

16. "For there is no visible viable vision of a radically egalitarian society that is of a radically egalitarian urbanized mass society. That is the squander of utopia from 1848-1949" (Brenkman, "Extreme Criticism,"14). If Brenkman means, for example, that a theory of justice is not a visible viable theory, he needs to argue why that is the case. If as it seems he is dismissing all other theories of distributive justice—such as the one, for example, offered by Amartya Sen's equality of capabilities—then he needs to say much more about why he thinks Sen's theory, which he never even mentions yet is clearly visible, is not viable. If he wants to argue that neither one is applicable to a mass, urbanized, industrial society dominated by capitalism, then he also needs to tell us why. Rawls certainly continues to defend a reasonable faith that a more egalitarian society—egalitarian enough that it would seem radical under our current form of social organization in the U.S.—is still possible. Whether one can make a definitive philosophical claim that such a faith can be theoretically foreclosed is itself a different question. The role Kant allots philosophy is defensive, and what is defended is a reasonable faith with no theoretically assured hope of actualization. For me, the complexity in our own historical situation that offers both horrifying examples of violence and national identity, combined with ethnic cleansing, and other examples of experiments in democracy and egalitarian forms of living together, such as those being attempted in South Africa, means that a faith in egalitarianism is still reasonable.

17. Kant, *Political Writings*, 74.

18. Joseph Carens, "Aliens and Citizens: The Case for Open Borders," in *Theorizing Citizenship*, ed. Ronald Beiner (Albany, N.Y.: SUNY Press, 1995), 229–255.

19. Gregory DeFreitas has given a sophisticated analysis of how one could decide to impose some limit on a nation's boundaries based on considerations of distributive justice for the members of a particular nation-state. But as he is only too well aware, the limitations mandated by an attempt to approximate a just distributional schema must still weigh in the responsibilities northern democracies have incurred to peoples of the South because of their history of imperial domination. See Gregory DeFreitas, "Immigration, Inequality, and Policy Alternatives," in *Globalization and Progressive Economic Policy,* ed. Dean Baker, Gerald Epstein, and Robert Pollin (Cambridge: Cambridge University Press, 1998).

20. Pheng Cheah makes a strong prudential defense of the nation-state as necessary for Southern countries. See "Given Culture: Rethinking Cosmopolitical Freedom in Transnationalism," in *Cosmopolitics: Thinking and Feeling Beyond the Nation*, ed. Pheng Cheah and Bruce Robbins (Minneapolis: University of Minnesota Press, 1998), 290–328.

21. For a discussion of the recent English-only movement in the U.S. and why I argue that it is indefensible against the moral mandate of Kantian dignity, see William Bratton and Drucilla Cornell's "Deadweight Costs and Intrinsic Wrongs of Nativism: Economics, Freedom, and Legal Suppression of Spanish," *Cornell Law Review* 84 (3) (March 1999).

22. "In conclusion, universality resides in this decision to recognize and accept the reciprocal relativism of different cultures, once the colonial status is irreversibly excluded." Frantz Fanon, *Toward the African Revolution,* trans. Haakon Chevalier (New York: Grove Press, 1967), 44.

23. For an argument of how this understanding of universality connects with a Kantian idea of the equal dignity of persons and how these two ideas can in turn guide us through the cultural wars, see Drucilla Cornell and Sara Murphy, "Antiracism, Multiculturalism, and The Ethics of Identification," in this collection.

24. Judith Butler, "For a Careful Reading," in *Feminist Contentions: A Philosophical Exchange* by Seyla Benhabib, Judith Butler, Drucilla Cornell, and Nancy Fraser (New York: Routledge, 1995), 130–131.

25. Brenkman, "Extreme Criticism," 29.

26. Judith Butler, *Excitable Speech: A Politics of the Performative* (New York: Routledge, 1997), 50.

27. Brenkman, "Extreme Criticism," 28.

28. Frantz Fanon, *Black Skin, White Masks* (New York: Grove Press, 1967), 232.

CHAPTER 6

This essay is dedicated to William Bratton, whose work deeply influenced my own thinking on employment at will. I am grateful to Bruce Ackerman, Richard Bernstein, William Bratton, David Carlson, and Cass Sunstein for their helpful remarks on earlier drafts. Undoubtedly, this essay profited tremendously from my ongoing correspondence with Richard Posner. A special word of thanks must go to Lawrence Sager, whose critical comments prodded me to rethink several of the crucial issues involved in the justification of rational-cause statutes. All the mistakes, of course, are my own.

1. "Symposium: The Conceptual Foundations of Labor Law," 51 *U. Chi. L. Rev.* 945 (1984).

2. 81 Tenn. 507 (1884), rev'd on other grounds sub nom. *Hutton v. Watters*, 132 Tenn. 527, 544, 179 S.W. 134, 138 (1915).

3. Id. at 518–19.

4. Richard Epstein, a militant defender of the doctrine of employment at will, does not argue that it is the *only* mechanism for ordering employee/employer relationships.

> There is thus today a widely held view that the contract at will has outlived its usefulness. But this view is mistaken. The contract at will is not ideal for every employment relation. No court or legislature should ever command its use. Nonetheless, there are two ways in which the contract at will should be respected: one deals with entitlements against regulation and the other with presumptions in the event of contractual silence.
>
> First, the parties should be permitted as of right to adopt this form of contract if they so desire. The principle behind this conclusion is that freedom of contract tends both to advance individual autonomy and to promote the efficient operation of labor markets.
>
> Second, the contract at will should be respected as a rule of construction in response to the perennial question of gaps in contract language: what term should be implied in the absence of explicit agreement on the question of duration or grounds for termination?

Epstein, "In Defense of the Contract at will," 51 *U. Chi. L. Rev.* 947, 951 (1984).

5. R. Posner, *The Economics of Justice* (1981), Cambridge, Mass.: Harvard University Press.

6. Epstein, "Common Law, Labor Law, and Reality: A Rejoinder to Professors Getman and Kohler," 92 *Yale L.J.* 1435, (1983).

7. See notes 70–74 later in this chapter and accompanying text (discussing Summers's proposal for just-cause statutes).

8. Interestingly enough, the widely shared assumption that intervention into the sphere of private right is paternalistic seems to have interfered with endeavors toward developing programs of minimum entitlements under American labor law. See Getman and Kohler, "The Common Law, Labor Law, and Reality: A Response to Professor Epstein," 92 *Yale L.J.* 1415 (1983) (relying on an appeal to community standards of fairness in responding to Epstein's argument that New Deal labor regulation should be abandoned for common law rules).

9.

> It may be that in choosing (say) an increased salary over protection from arbitrary discharges, workers make decisions that they will (or should) come to regret. Of course, such arguments threaten the foundations of classical liberal principles of contractual freedom. It is perhaps for that reason that the nature and value of paternalistic interventions into the marketplace remain one of the great unexplored areas of the law. Nevertheless, there is little doubt that the drafters of the Wagner Act were skeptical, if only implicitly, about classical liberal principles in the context of employer-employee relations.

Sunstein, "Rights, Minimal Terms, and Solidarity: A Comment," 51 *U. Chi. L. Rev.* 1041, 1047 (1984) (footnote omitted). See *Nat'l Labor Relations (Wagner) Act*, Pub. L. No. 74–198, ch. 372, 49 Stat. 449 (1935) (codified at 29 U.S.C. §§ 151–69 (1982)).

10. See, for example, R. Epstein, *Takings: Private Property and the Power of Eminent Domain* (1985), Cambridge, Mass.: Harvard University Press (discussing what is constitutionally permissible regarding state interference with individual freedom through the eminent domain clause); Epstein, "Toward a Revitalization of the Contract Clause," 51 *U. Chi. L. Rev.* 703, 705 (1984) (defending "the proposition that, properly construed, the clause extends substantial protection to economic liberties against legislative, and perhaps judicial, interference").

11. Libertarian theories, in other words, rest on an atomistic view of the self that is incompatible with an adequate account of how selves come to be persons with their individual identities. Charles Taylor provides an excellent discussion of precisely how the atomic view of the self is used to justify rights in the libertarian jurisprudence of Robert Nozick. See C. Taylor, "Atomism," in 2 *Philosophy and the Human Sciences: Philosophical Papers* 187 (1985).

12. G. Hegel, *Natural Law*, (trans. T. Knox 1975) (1802–03), Philadelphia: University of Pennsylvania Press.

13. I am adopting this very limited view of the objective to avoid entering into the disputes among Ronald Dworkin, Thomas Nagel, John Rawls, and Bernard Williams over what is or is not truly "objective" in political and ethical theory. Any of their competing positions would constitute the objective as against the subjective as I am using it here.

14. I am suggesting that it is the difference between the competing moral perspectives of the Hobbesian and the Hegelian that make different "factual" accounts relevant. Facts, such as what is efficient, do not determine the moral perspective; they are determined by it. See J. Rawls, "Political Constructivism and Public Justification" (October, 1988) (unpublished manuscript) (discussion of the relationship of "facts" and moral reasoning).

15. Posner, "Hegel and Employment at Will: A Comment," 10 *Cardozo L. Rev.* 1625 (1989).

16. Summers, "Individual Protection Against Unjust Dismissal: Time for a Statute," 62 *Va. L. Rev.* 481 (1976). For further discussion of just-cause statutes advocated by Summers, see text accompanying note 74.

17. A lawsuit designed to redress wrongful discharge may be used in tort or contract theory and, when successful, represents an exception to the common law employment-at-will doctrine. Specifically, most courts carve out exceptions to the doctrine using the general theories of public policy or implied contract. Lopatka, "The Emerging Law of Wrongful Discharge—A Quadrennial Assessment of the Labor Law Issue of the 80's," 40 *Bus. Law.* 1, 6 (1984). Most states now have some judicially made proscriptions on employment at will. See Murphy, "Employment-at-Will: Judicial Counterpoint to Labor Legislation," 15 *Stetson L. Rev.* 69 (1985); see also Bryant, "Hybrid Employees: Defining and Protecting Employees Excluded from the Coverage of the National Labor Relations Act," 41 *Vand. L. Rev.* 601 (1988) (30 states now have judicially created exception to employment at will, granting protection to a wider employee group). For another view, see Epstein "In Defense of the Contract at Will," 51 *U. Chi. L. Rev.* 951 (1984) ("No system of regulation can hope to match the benefits that the contract at will affords in employment relations").

18. I want to suggest that this is an alternative conception of equality and also diverges from Dworkin's equality of resources or the utilitarian conception he designates as equality of welfare. This alternative conception would go beyond Dworkin in insisting that some degree of "equality of capability" would be necessary for relations

of reciprocal symmetry. In doing so, it would come closer to the position advocated by Amartya Sen. For the contrast between Dworkin and Sen, compare Sen, "Rights and Agency," 11 *Phil. & Pub. Aff.* 3 (1982) (proposing "goal rights systems" approach, which incorporates rights in the evaluation of consequent states of affairs and gives these rights influence on choice of action, as an alternative approach to utilitarianism), with Dworkin, "What is Equality? Part I: Equality of Welfare," 10 *Phil. & Pub. Aff.* 185 (1981) (arguing that equality of welfare, as a way to treat people as equals, is not as attractive an ideal as it is often believed to be), and Dworkin, "What is Equality? Part 2: Equality of Resources," 10 *Phil. & Pub. Aff.* 283 (1981) (arguing for a concept of equality in which people are equal with regard to their access to privately owned resources), and Dworkin, "What is Equality? Part 3: The Place of Liberty," 73 *Iowa L. Rev.* 1 (1987) (proposing that to accept equality of resources as the optimal conception of distributional equality is to render liberty only an aspect of equality rather than a potentially conflicting political ideal), and Dworkin, "What is Equality? Part 4: Political Equality," 22 *U.S.F. L. Rev.* 1 (1987) (arguing that politics is a matter of responsibility and not a dimension of wealth, and, therefore, political impact should not be treated as a resource). The difference between my view and that of Dworkin stems from the Hegelian disavowal of the sharp divide between personality and circumstance on which Dworkin insists. See also Scanlon, "Rights, Goals, and Fairness," in *Public and Private Morality* (S. Hampshire, ed. 1978), New York: Cambridge University Press, p. 93 (proposing a two-tiered causal and consequential evaluation of rights).

19. See Epstein, "In Defense," 973–977.

20. See Hegel, *Natural Law.*

21. See T. Hobbes, *Leviathan* (C. Macpherson, ed. 1981) (1651). Harmondsworth, Middlesex: Penguin Books.

22. Hegel seeks to correct Hobbes's empiricism, but ultimately rejects it. See Hegel, *Natural Law,* 66–67.

23. Hegel reveals why it is that the internal dynamic of desire aims at recognition and not submission and mastery in his famous master/slave dialectic in the *Phenomenology.* See G. Hegel, *Phenomenology of Spirit* (trans. A. Miller, 1977) (1807), Oxford, New York: Oxford University Press [hereinafter *Phenomenology of Spirit*].

24. I am deliberately using the pronoun "he" when I refer to the master. I do so for two reasons. The first is to reflect the continuing status differential between men and women. The second is a response to Hobbes's image of the human being as a masculine subject.

25. The one who ascends to mastery does not do so simply by expressing his natural, superior strength, but by rising above his natural self through conquering the fear of death. Again, we see the contrast with Hobbes. In Hobbes, death poses a threat from without that constrains the natural individual and that ultimately prods him to resign himself to the relations with others in order to preserve himself. It is because the other can kill me and I want to survive that I accept the exterior force of political institution imposed against us both. But in Hegel, death is assumed within the self as part of the revelation of his own particularity. By facing down his fear of death, the brute singularity of being mere is overcome, as the self becomes a subject that controls his natural impulses. Even in this first battle, the other is not just an outside limit, but a necessary interlocutor for the birth of the subject. The slave who submits recognizes the achieved identity of the other as a subject, not just as a natural

being. The master's superiority lies in his achievement of at least a primitive form of subjectivity. Indeed, he has mastered himself as a form of nature.

26. G. Hegel, *Philosophy of Right*, para. 152 (trans. T. Knox 1952) (1821) [hereinafter *Philosophy of Right*], London: Oxford University Press.

27. Of course, the question arises as to why the "masters" would seek universality with everyone else if they are able to achieve it among themselves. One can think, for example, of an idealized view of the Greek city-state, in which male slave owners recognized one another. The most powerful response to this question is that they are surrounded by slaves who, like themselves, desire recognition, and that the peace among themselves will, as a result, be undisturbed. This is one way of understanding the journey of the *Phenomenology*. The *Phenomenology* unfolds the history of the slave's insistence on disturbance until she, too, achieves recognition in relations of reciprocal symmetry. Mastery, in other words, can only achieve stability through suppression. But as history demonstrates, even the most all-encompassing forms of domination do not shut out resistance completely. Second, mastery, as we have seen, is internally contradictory. We might consider the following: Once relations of mastery are the norm, it is extremely difficult for the masters to achieve satisfaction because there is the endless battle to be "on top of the heap."

To summarize: Mastery is not easy to circumscribe because it contaminates the relationship between the masters themselves. The possibility of a "peaceful" community of masters based on relations of mutual recognition is, therefore, very unlikely, if not completely implausible. Second, the masters are surrounded by those who, too, seek confirmation of their being-for-self.

28. Hegel, *Philosophy of Right*, para. 152.

29.

The right of individuals to be subjectively destined to freedom is fulfilled when they belong to an actual ethical order, because their conviction of their freedom finds its truth in such an objective order, and it is an ethical order that they are actually in possession of their own essence or their own inner universality.

Hegel, *Philosophy of Right*, para. 153.

30.

It is only because of this identity between its implicit and its posited character that positive law has obligatory force in virtue of its rightness. In being posited in positive law, the right acquires determinate existence. Into such existence there may enter the contingency of self-will and other particular circumstances and hence there may be a discrepancy between the content of the law and the principle of rightness.

Hegel, *Philosophy of Right*, para. 212.

31. Hegel explains further in his introduction to the *Philosophy of Right* (para. 33):

In correspondence with the stages in the development of the Idea of the absolutely free will, the will is

A. immediate; its concept therefore is abstract, namely personality, and its embodiment is an immediate external thing—the sphere of *Abstract or Formal Right*;

B. reflected from its external embodiment into itself—it is then characterized as subjective individuality in opposition to the universal. The universal here is characterized as something inward, the good, and also as something outward, a world presented to the will; both these sides of the Idea are here mediated only by each other. This is the Idea in its division or in its existence as particular; and here we have the right of the subjective will in relation to the right of the world and the right of the Idea, though only the Idea implicit—the sphere of *Morality;*

C. the unity and truth of both these abstract moments—the Idea of the good not only apprehended in thought but so realized both in the will reflected into itself and in the external world that freedom exists as substance, as actuality and necessity, no less than as subjective will; this is the Idea in its absolutely universal existence—*Ethical Life.*

A common mistake in interpreting Hegel's *Philosophy of Right* is to take the immediacy of abstract right as a given that can yield its own meaning. While it is true that, in Hegel, the sphere of right is not to be abstractly negated, the meaning of right can only be found "internally" in the relationship of law to the ideal, and "externally" to the larger community that embodies the shared norms of *Sittlichkeit.* The *Philosophy of Right* shows us just how and why the sphere of abstract must be controlled in the name of common good. To confuse the desire for possession, with which the *Philosophy of Right* begins, with the desire for recognition would be false consciousness in Hegel. The corrective for this mistake is to understand that the *Philosophy of Right* should be read backwards, from within the achieved vantage point of Absolute Knowledge. Each section of the *Philosophy of Right* only finds its meaning in relation to the whole. The truth of abstract right is also not to be found in abstract right but in the ideal of the relationship of reciprocal symmetry that serves as its basis and which, in turn, embodies the truth of the whole.

32. Hegel, *Phenomenology of Spirit.*

33. The danger for someone unfamiliar with Hegel's speculative philosophy is that each section of *Philosophy of Right* will be read as if it stood on its own. Such unfamiliarity may, for instance, lead a reader to mistakenly identify personhood with the possession of certain personally valued objects. Margaret Radin, for example, makes this mistake in her analysis of market inalienability. There, Radin argues that there is a bright line between subject/object in Hegel's analysis of property. See Radin, "Property and Personhood," 34 *Stan. L. Rev.* 957, 971–977 (1982) (note specifically Radin's discussion at 973 n.56). If there is a central message of Hegel's system, whether in the *Phenomenology* or the *Logic,* it is that there can be no bright line between subject and object. Radin's mistake stems from her failure to grasp Hegel's speculative philosophy. Hegel begins with the immediacy of the positive law as it has been codified. It would be a serious misunderstanding, however, to read the description of abstract right with which Hegel begins, as if it were a justification in the sense of a traditional argument. The *Philosophy of Right* is not a justification of the traditional conception of property, but must be understood as a relationship between persons. The true object of property is an "intersubjective" relationship.

34. Again to quote Hegel:

Existence as determinate being is in essence being for another . . . . One aspect of property is that it is an existent as an external thing, and in this respect property exists for other external things and is connected with their necessity and contingency. But it is also an existent as an embodiment of the will, and from this point of view the "other" for which it exists can only be the will of the another person. This relation of will to will is the true and proper ground in which freedom is existent.—The sphere of contract is made up of this mediation whereby I hold property not merely by means of a thing and my subjective will, but . . . [also] in virtue of my participation in a common will.

Philosophy of Right, para. 71.

35. In this essay, when I speak of "contractualism" I am referring primarily to Hobbes. There are new sophisticated versions of contractualism that diverge considerably from the Hobbesian understanding. See Sen, "Rights and Agency," 5. For a Hegelian, these recent attempts are interesting because of what they implicitly and explicitly suggest that the "value" of contractualism has in its interpretation of a substantive view of the person. On one understanding, then, contractualism could be understood as a necessary metaphor for how one conceives of the relationship between the state and the individual once the modern conception of personhood comes onto the stage of history.

36. Hegel effectively critiques contractualist theories of political obligation as a mistaken identification of civil society with the state.

> It is equally far from the truth to ground the nature of the state on the contractual relation, whether the state is supposed to be a contract of all with all, or of all with the monarch and the government.
>
> The intrusion of this contractual relation, and relationships concerning private property generally, into the relation between the individual and the state has been productive of the greatest confusion in both constitutional law and public life. Just as at one time political rights and duties were considered and maintained to be an unqualified private property of particular individuals, something contrasted with the right of the monarch and the state, so also in more recent times the rights of the monarch and the state have been regarded as the subjects of a contract and as grounded in contract, . . . and resulting from the arbitrariness of parties united into a state. However different these two points of view may be, they have this in common, that they have transferred the characteristics of private property into a sphere of a quite different and higher nature.

Philosophy of Right, para. 75R (footnote omitted).

37.

> Therefore those goods, or rather substantive characteristics, which constitute my own private personality and the universal essence of my self-consciousness are inalienable and my right to them is imprescriptible. Such characteristics are my personality as such, my universal freedom of will, my ethical life, my religion.

Hegel, *Philosophy of Right*, para. 66.

38. Hegel, *Philosophy of Right,* para. 57.

39.

> In contract it is the will, and therefore the substance of what is right in contract, that the stipulation enshrines. In contrast with this substance, the possession which is still being retained while the contract remains unfulfilled is in itself only something external, dependent for its character as a possession on the will alone. By making the stipulation, I have given up a property and withdrawn my particular arbitrary will from it, and it has *eo ipso* become the property of another. If then I agree to stipulated terms, I am by rights at once bound to carry them out.

Hegel, *Philosophy of Right*, para. 79.

40. Hegel, *Philosophy of Right*, para. 86.

41. Hegel, *Philosophy of Right*, para. 183.

42. "The right of individuals to their *particular* satisfaction is also contained in the ethical substantial order since particularity is the outward appearance of the ethical

order—a mode in which that order is existent." Hegel, *Philosophy of Right*, para. 154 (emphasis in original; footnote omitted).

43. As Hegel explains:

In the course of the actual attainment of selfish ends—an attainment conditioned in this way by universality—there is formed a system of complete interdependence, wherein the livelihood, happiness, and legal status of one man is interwoven with the livelihood, happiness, and rights of all. On this system, individual happiness, &c., depend, and only in this connected system are they actualized and secured. This system may be prima facie regarded as the external state, the state based on need, the state as the Understanding envisages it.

Philosophy of Right, para. 183 (footnote omitted).

44. As Hegel explains:

When the standard of living of a large mass of people falls below a certain subsistence level—a level regulated automatically as the one necessary for a member of the society— and when there is a consequent loss of the sense of right and wrong, of honesty and the self-respect which makes a man insist on maintaining himself by his own work and effort, the result is the creation of a rabble of paupers. At the same time this brings with it, at the other end of the social scale, conditions which greatly facilitate the concentration of disproportionate wealth in a few hands.

Philosophy of Right, para. 244 (footnote omitted).

45.

Poverty and, in general, the distress of every kind to which every individual is exposed from the start in the cycle of his natural life has a subjective side which demands similarly subjective aid, arising both from the special circumstances of a particular case and also from love and sympathy. This is the place where morality finds plenty to do despite all public organization.

Hegel, *Philosophy of Right*, para. 242.

46. Ernest Weinrib, "Right and Advantage in Private Law," 10 *Cardozo L. Rev.* 1283 (1989).

47. The problem of moral motivation has haunted neo-Kantian elaborations of a theory of justice. Thomas Nagel, for example, has been particularly concerned with the problem of moral motivation. See T. Nagel, T*he View from Nowhere* (1986), New York: Oxford University Press. One of the many strengths of Hegelianism is that it allows us to root the striving for a just society in desire and not in a march that must be pitted against desire.

48. See, e.g., "Comment, The Role of Federal Courts in Changing State Law: The Employment at Will Doctrine in Pennsylvania," 133 *U. Pa. L. Rev.* 227, 243–47 (1984) (tracing the change in attitude of state judiciary to the at-will doctrine).

49.

When civil society is in a state of unimpeded activity, it is engaged in expanding internally in population and industry. The amassing of wealth is intensified by generalizing *(a)* the linkage of men by their needs, and *(b)* the methods of preparing and distributing the means to satisfy these needs, because it is from this double process of generalization that the largest profits are derived. That is one side of the picture. The other side is the subdivision and restriction of particular jobs. This results in the dependence and distress of the class tied to work of that sort, and these again entail inability to feel and enjoy the broader freedoms and especially the intellectual benefits of civil society.

Hegel, *Philosophy of Right,* para. 243 (footnote omitted).

50. Summers, "The Contract of Employment and the Rights of Individual Employees. For Representation and Employment at Will," 52 *Fordham L. Rev.* 1082, 1107 (1984).

51. Hence, in Roman law,

even personality itself is only a certain standing or status contrasted with slavery. The so-called Roman law of "personal" rights, then, is concerned with family relationships, though it excludes the right over slaves (and "slaves" almost includes children too) as well as the status (called *capitis diminutio*) of having lost one's rights . . . . The Roman *jus ad personam* is therefore not the right of the person as person but at most the right of a person in his particular capacity.

Hegel, *Philosophy of Right,* para. 40R (footnote omitted).

52. To note that the doctrine of employment at will has its origins in Roman law is not intended to refute the argument that it can also be justified as well under modern contract principles. Even so, once it is recast in modern contract, it can be made more compatible with the modern idea of abstract reciprocity between legal persons than with rational-cause statutes.

53. See Alan Watson, *Legal Transplants: An Approach to Comparative Law* (1974).

54. But even if we say that the original justification of employment at will is no longer acceptable in the modern legal system, we must still respond to the economic defense of the doctrine as the favored presumption of contract construction when the parties are silent on the matter.

55. B. Ackerman, "Higher Judges and the Liberal Tradition," *Social Justice in the Liberal State* 327 (1980).

56. As I have argued elsewhere:

Understood in the context of dialogism as a regulative ideal, universality appears in a new light. It comes to mean that each of us is to be recognized as a participant in the conversation; each voice is to count and no one is to be silenced in the name of a substantive universal that denounces what is different as not being really human.

Cornell, "Toward a Modern/Post Modern Reconstruction of Ethics," 133 *U. Pa. L. Rev.* 291, 168 (1985).

57. Frank Michelman emphasizes, as I do, the significance in modernity of the normative view of the person as the basis for right. See Michelman, "Foreword: Traces of Self-Government," 100 *Harv. L. Rev.* 4 (1986).

58. The self, in other words, is not a separate reality but a part of the interlacing of relationships that gives her individuality. The interlacing is prior to the individual. Yet, she is a part of it, and by participating in it she also shapes its pattern. This reading of Hegel's understanding of our primordial interconnectedness is significant for his social philosophy not because it recognizes that the universal will of political and legal institutions is understood as an all encompassing subjectivity, *Geist,* but rather

because it is conceived of as the *Mitte*, or network of reciprocally constituted individuals, which promises individual flourishing.

We find support for this reading in Hegel's portrayal of the state in the *Philosophy of Right*.

> The state is the actuality of concrete freedom. But concrete freedom consists in this, that personal individuality and its particular interests not only achieve their complete development and gain explicit recognition for their right (as they do in the sphere of the family and civil society) but, for one thing, they also pass over of their own accord into the interest of the universal, and, for another thing, they know and will the universal; they even recognize it as their own substantive mind; they take it as their end and aim and are active in its pursuit. The result is that the universal does not prevail or achieve completion except along with particular interests and through the co-operation of particular knowing and willing; and individuals likewise do not live as private persons for their own ends alone, but in the very act of willing these they will the universal in the light of the universal, and their activity is consciously aimed at none but the universal end. The principle of modern states has prodigious strength and depth because it allows the principle of subjectivity to progress to its culmination in the extreme of self-subsistent personal particularity, and yet at the same time brings it back to the substantive unity and so maintains this unity in the principle of subjectivity itself.

Para. 260.

Spirit, Hegel's *Geist*, is thus interpreted as the primordial relativity in which the boundaries yield to our fundamental interconnectedness. This interconnection also allows for self-realization and for the possibility of transcendence because the individual is not a self-contained bounded substance.

59.

> Sovereignty, at first simply the universal *thought* of this ideality, comes into *existence* only as subjectivity sure of itself, as the will's abstract and to that extent ungrounded self-determination in which finality of decision is rooted. This is the strictly individual aspect of the state, and in virtue of this alone is the state *one*. The truth of subjectivity, however, is attained only in a subject, and the truth of personality only in a person . . . . Hence this absolutely decisive moment of the whole is not individuality in general, but a single individual, the monarch.

Hegel, *Philosophy of Right*, para. 279.

60. See Cornell, "Post-Structuralism, The Ethical Relation, and the Law," 9 *Cardozo L. Rev.* 1587 (1988).

61. Dworkin, in his earlier work, has proposed that

> government must not only treat people with concern and respect, but with equal concern and respect. It must not distribute goods or opportunities unequally on the ground that some citizens are entitled to more because they are worthy of more concern. It must not constrain liberty on the ground that one citizen's conception of the good life of one group is nobler or superior to another's. . . .
>
> Citizens governed by [this] liberal conception of equality each have a right to equal concern and respect. But there are two different rights that might be comprehended by that abstract right. The first is the right to equal treatment, that is, to the same distribution of goods or opportunities as anyone else has or is given. . . . The second is the right to treat-

ment as equal. This is the right, not to an equal distribution of some good or opportunity, but the right to equal concern and respect in the political decision about how . . . goods and opportunities are to be distributed.

R. Dworkin, *Taking Rights Seriously,* 272–273 (1978).
Dworkin has now moved away from this understanding of the central role of neutrality in liberalism. See R. Dworkin, *Law's Empire* (1986).

62. As Alan Brudner explains:

In the *Philosophy of Right*, the priority of the right is still an appearance, since it is posited within the priority of the good. The appearance, however, is now a necessary and constitutive element of the good itself, that in virtue of which alone the good is confirmed as the good *of* the agent. . . . [I]t is only through the cultivation of, and protection for, a self-affirming and intentional agent that the good can ultimately be validated in the individual's free and intelligent devotion to the whole as the the objective support of his particularity. . . . It is only through the suspension of the priority of the good so as to leave scope for the causality of the agent that the good is immanentized in the concrete individual, or that the individual can will the good as his *own*, as the rational foundation of his strictly private rights. . . . For the mature Hegel, then, the truth of private law is not something other than its appearance of independence; rather, it is just this appearance.

Brudner, "Hegel and the Crisis of Private Law," 10 *Cardozo L. Rev.* 949, 991–992 (1989).

63. I am obviously disagreeing with Jürgen Habermas's own dialogic version of Kant. See Habermas, *Theory of Communicative Action* (T. McCarthy trans. 1984).

64. R. Bernstein, "Beyond Objectivism and Relativism: Science, Hermeneutics and Praxis" (1983) (providing a critical discussion of Habermas).

65. Macneil, "Economic Analysis of Contractual Relations: Its Shortfalls and the Need for a Rich Classificatory Apparatus," n5 *Nw. U.L. Rev.* 1018, 1060 (1981).

66. Epstein, "In Defense," 955.

67. The existence and cost of training are absolutely crucial to Epstein's argument. As he explains:

The reason why these contracts at will are effective is precisely that the employer must always pay an implicit price when he exercises his right to fire. He no longer has the right to compel the employee's service, as the employee can enter the market to find another job. The costs of the employer's decision therefore are borne in large measure by the employer himself, creating an implicit system of coinsurance between employer and employee against employer abuse. Nor, it must be stressed, are the costs to the employer light. It is true that employees who work within a firm acquire specific knowledge about its operation and upon dismissal can transfer only a portion of that knowledge to the new job. Nonetheless, the problem is roughly symmetrical, as the employer must find, select, and train a replacement worker who may not turn out to be better than the first employee. Workers are no fungible, and sorting them out may be difficult: resumes can be misleading, if not fraudulent; references may be only too eager to unload an unsuitable employee; training is expensive; and the new worker may not like the job or may be forced to move out of town. In any case, firms must bear the costs of voluntary turnover by workers who quit, which gives them a frequent reminder of the need to avoid self-inflicted losses.

Epstein, "In Defense," 973–974 (footnote omitted).

68. Further, Epstein can be understood to argue that the self-interested profit-maximizer should not fire a person because of the cost involved and therefore there is no need for a just-cause rule. As Epstein argues, "the employer who decides to act for bad reason or no reason at all may not face any legal liability under the classical common law rule. But he faces very powerful adverse economic consequences." "In Defense," 968. In other words, if malice is costly because it entails a lost investment in job training, the problem of malice is solved.

69. Summers, "Individual Protection," 491 (footnote omitted) (quoting *Simmons v. Westinghouse Elec. Corp.*, 311 So. 2d 28, 31 (La. Ct. App. 1975) [quoting *Pitcher v. United Oil & Gas Syndicate, Inc.*, 174 La. 66, 70, 139 So. 760, 761 (1932)]).

70. See Alchian and Demsetz, "Production, Information Costs, and Economic Organization," 41: *Am. Econ. Rev.* 777 (1972). For an excellent discussion and critique of this paradigm, see Bratton, "The 'Nexus of Contracts' Corporation: A Critical Appraisal," 74 *Cornell L. Rev.* (1989).

71. See Jensen and Meckling, "Theory of the Firm: Managerial Behavior, Agency Costs and Ownership Structure, 3 *J. Fin Econ.* 305 (1976); see also Bratton, "Nexus" (discussing Jensen and Meckling).

72. Blades, "Employment at Will vs. Individual Freedom: On Limiting the Abusive Exercise "Employer Power," 67 *Colum. L. Rev.* 1404 (1967).

73. Summers, "Individual Protections," 521.

74. Termination of Employment Recommendation, 1963, Recommendation No. 119, in International Labour Conventions and Recommendations, 1919–1981, at 138–41, Recommendation 119 provides, in part: "Termination of employment should not take place unless there is a valid reason for such termination connected with the capacity or conduct of the worker or based on the operational requirements of the undertaking, establishment of service" (138).

Subsection III of Recommendation No. 119 addresses the work force reduction problem, encouraging the joint effort of all parties to work toward resolution of the problem while attempting to minimize the reduction of the work force without sacrificing efficiency (140).

75. See Watcher and Cohen, "The Law and Economics of Collective Bargaining: An Introduction and Application to the Problems of Subcontracting, Partial Closure, and Relocation," 136 *U. Pa. L. Rev.* 1349, 1378–79 (1988).

76. European countries distinguish between firing and layoffs and yet still recognize the need for legislation in both areas. The International Labor Organization has accepted that layoffs may be inevitable because of technological change and shifts in the economy and yet still favors protection in such situations. Recommendation 119 specifically recognizes that management and labor must participate in the efficient maintenance of the enterprise while attempting to minimize layoffs.

Indeed, real measurable efficiency can be realized with advance-warning legislation. Epstein argues that a just-cause rule is not needed because the employer/profit-maximizer would be less inclined to fire an employee due to the costs involved. See note 68 above. Epstein's argument ultimately boils down to the assertion that the greater the labor flexibility and the less the labor market regulation, the better off both employees and employers will be, because the freeing up of capital will ultimately create a bigger pie.

Yet recent studies of the regulated conditions of European labor markets have challenged the ongoing American assumption that regulation itself has acted to impede efficiency in regulated economies, suggesting that notice requirements for plant closings would actually be efficient. For those workers who lose their jobs due to plant closings, it is plausible that early notification would result in a reduction in unemployment insurance and enable workers to earn more dollars than if notification were not provided. Arguably, early notification can have the cost-saving effect because such notification would allow workers to take advantage of job retraining and would also reduce the stress on their families.

Nevertheless, fundamental differences in management-labor relations exist between American and many European countries. Worker participation in Europe is viewed as an extension of the democratic process, with less emphasis on the issues of pay, working conditions, and benefits that are of primary concern to American workers. See Levitan and Werneke. "Worker Participation and Productivity Change," *Monthly Lab. Rev.*, Sept. 1984, at 28.

CHAPTER 7

This essay was previously published by Richard A. Posner in *Overcoming Law* (Cambridge, MA.: Harvard University Press, 1995). All author's references to specific chapters are from *Overcoming Law*.

1. See, for example, her article "Institutionalization of Meaning, Recollective Imagination and the Potential for Transformative Legal Interpretation," 136 *University of Pennsylvania Law Review* 1135, 1178–1193 (1988); also Michel Rosenfeld, "Hegel and the Dialectics of Contract," 10 *Cardozo Law Review* 1199 (1989). Both Rosenfeld's article and the article by Cornell that I discuss in this chapter (see note 2) appear in the ambitious, book-length *Hegel and Legal Theory Symposium*, 10 *Cardozo Law Review* 847 (1989).

2. Cornell, "Dialogic Reciprocity and the Critique of Employment at Will," 10 *Cardozo Law Review* 1575 (1989). The best introduction to the controversy over employment at will is Paul C. Weiler, *Governing the Workplace: The Future of Labor and Employment Law* (Cambridge, MA.: Harvard University Press, 1990) ch.2; and the most thorough and rigorous economic analysis of the institution is Edward P. Lazear, "Employment-at-Will, Job Security, and Work Incentives," in *Employment, Unemployment and Labor Utilization,* Robert A. Hart, ed. (New York: Routledge, 1988) 39.

3. Richard A. Epstein, "In Defense of the Contract at Will," 51 *University of Chicago Law Review* 947 (1984). Epstein defends employment at will on both economic and ethical grounds. Other economic defenses of the institution are Lazear, "Employmentat-Will"; Mayer G. Freed, and Daniel D. Polsby, "Just Cause for Termination Rules and Economic Efficiency," 38 *Emory Law Journal* 1097 (1989); and Gail L. Heriot, "The New Feudalism: The Unintended Destination of Contemporary Trends in Employment Law," 28 *Georgia Law Review* 167 (1993).

4. Epstein, "In Defense," 951–955. I use the past tense because he has since abandoned the effort to ground his jurisprudential views on natural-rights philosophy in favor of a utilitarian-economic approach. See, for example, his articles "A Last Word on Eminent Domain," 41 *University of Miami Law Review* 253, 256–258 (1986); "The Utilitarian Foundations of Natural Law," 12 *Harvard Journal of Law and Public Pol-*

icy 713 (1989); and "Holdouts, Externalities, and the Single Owner: One More Salute to Ronald Coase," 36 *Journal of Law and Economics* 553 (1993).

5. On which, see, for example, Samuel Brittan, "How British Is the British Sickness?" in Brittan, *The Roles and Limits of Government: Essays in Political Economy* (Minneapolis: University of Minnesota Press 1983) 219: Alan Ryan, "Why Are There So Few Socialists?" in Ryan, *Property and Political Theory* (New York, N.Y.: B. Blackwell, 1984) 118; and discussion in Chapter 22.

6. Hegel's theory of property is well described in Alan Ryan's essay "Hegel and Mastering the World," in Ryan, *Property and Political Theory,* 194.

7. Radin, "Property and Personhood," 34 *Stanford Law Review* 957 (1982); see also Radin, "Time, Possession and Alienation," 64 *Washington University Law Quarterly* 739, 741 (1986) "the claim to an owned object grows stronger as, over time, the holder becomes bound up with the object". This was also Holmes's theory of property. See "The Path of the Law," 10 *Harvard Law Review* at 477.

8. Radin, "Property and Personhood," 991–996; see also Radin, "Residential Rent Control," 15 *Philosophy and Public Affairs* 350, 362–368 (1986).

9. Cornell, "Dialogic Reciprocity," 1587.

10. Donald L. Martin, "The Economics of Employment Termination Rights," 20 *Journal of Law and Economics* 187, 188–189 (1977).

11. Epstein, "In Defense," 973–976.

12. Gary S. Becker, *Human Capital: A Theoretical and Empirical Analysis, with Special Reference to Education* (Chicago: University of Chicago Press 3d. ed. 1993) 40–49.

13. Arthur S. Leonard, "A New Common Law of Employment Termination," 66 *North Carolina Law Review* 631, 677 (1988).

14. For evidence, see Robert Buchele and Jens Christiansen, "Industrial Relations and Productivity Growth: A Comparative Perspective," 2 *International Contributions to Labour Studies* 77 (1992).

15. This is an application of the Coase Theorem, discussed in chapter 20.

16. For empirical evidence that job-protection laws do increase the number of unemployed (including all able-bodied workers who do not have a job, not just jobless workers who are still searching for jobs, the narrow definition used in computing unemployment statistics), see Martin, "Economics of Termination Rights," 199–201; Richard Layard and Stephen Nickell, "Unemployment in Britain," 53 *Economica* (n.s.) S121, S165 (1986); and Layard, Nickell, and Richard Jackman, *Unemployment: Macroeconomic Performance and the Labour Market* (Oxford, London: Oxford University Press 1991) 508. The evidence, however, is weak. Organisation for Economic Co-Operation and Development, *Flexibility in the Labour Market: The Current Debate: A Technical Report* 123 (1986). (No surprise, in view of the Coase Theorem). Daniel S. Hamermesh concludes in a judicious review of the empirical literature on European job-protection laws that they "offer an industrialized economy a choice between greater employment stability (with fewer total hours worked on average) and greater employment fluctuations (with more total hours worked on average). Moreover, to the extent they cover only part of the labor market, they help create a two-tier labor market consisting of secure jobs in a declining sector and insecure jobs in an expanding sector. Hamermesh, "The Demand for Workers and Hours and the Effects of

Job Security Policies: Theory and Evidence," in Hart, *Employment, Unemployment and Labor Utilization*, 9, 29–30.

17. James E. DeFranco, "Modification of the Employee at Will Doctrine—Balancing Judicial Development of the Common Law with the Legislative Prerogative to Declare Public Policy," 30 *St. Louis University Law Journal* 65, 70–72 (1985).

18. For evidence, see W. W. Daniel and Elizabeth Stilgoe, T*he Impact of Employment Protection Laws* 78 (Policy Studies Institute, June 1978).

19. For evidence from Europe, see for example, Franco Bernabè, "The Labour Market and Unemployment," in *The European Economy: Growth and Crisis*, Andrea Boltho (New York: Oxford University Press, 1982) 159, 179, 185.

20. For evidence, see Wolfgang Franz and Heinz König, "The Nature and Causes of Unemployment in the Federal Republic of Germany since the 1970s: An Empirical Investigation," 53 *Economica* (n.s.) S219, S243 (1986).

21. For evidence, once again from Europe, see Samuel Bentolila and Guiseppe Bertola, "Firing Costs and Labour Demand: How Bad is Eurosclerosis?" 57 *Review of Economic Studies* 381, 395 (1990); Bernabè, "Labour Market," 185; and recall Hamermesh's observation on the issue, in note 16.

22. See generally David Henderson, "The Europeanization of the U.S. Labor Market," *Public Interest*, Fall 1993, 66.

CHAPTER 8

1. I refer to the norms implicit in the assimilation story as "assimilation norms."

2. See Stanley Lieberson et al., "The Course of Mother-Tongue Diversity in Nations," 81 *Am. J. Soc.* 34, 55 (1975) (asserting that the first generation's loyalty to ancestral language gives way to a preference for English among their children); Alejandro Portes and Richard Schauffler, "Language and the Second Generation: Bilingualism Yesterday and Today," 28 *Int'l Migration Rev.* 640, 643 (1994) (noting that "the first generation [learns] enough English to survive economically; the second . . . speak[s] the parental tongue at home, but English in school, at work and in public life").

3. See Portes and Schauffler, "Language and the Second Generation: Bilingualism Yesterday and Today," 643. The results of a recent generation of empirical studies of immigrant income make for an interesting comparison with this traditional three-generation acculturation story. Barry R. Chiswick, "The Effect of Americanization on the Earnings of Foreign-Born Men," 86 *J. Pol. Econ.* 897, 919 (1978), using the 1970 census, finds that foreign-born white men achieve income equality after approximately 13 years, implying that they successfully assimilate after sufficient education about the labor market and in the English language. Later studies suggest a much slower rate of convergence, partly due to lower skill levels in immigrants admitted in recent decades. See, e.g., George J. Borjas, "Assimilation, Changes in Cohort Quality, and the Earnings of Immigrants," 3 *J. Lab. Econ.* 463, 465 (1985) (arguing that declining skill levels among immigrants arriving since 1950 partly explain slow rates of earnings growth among recent immigrants); George J. Borjas, "The Economics of Immigration," 32 *J. Econ. Literature* 1667, 1713 (1994) ("The relative skills of successive

immigrant waves declined over much of the postwar period). Robert F. Schoeni et al., *The Mixed Economic Progress of Immigrants* (Santa Monica, California: Rand, 1996), 8, 24-25, studies California and segments immigrants by countries of origin using data from the 1970, 1980, and 1990 censuses. The study shows that convergence trends depend on the group—the wage gap in California was eliminated across the 20 years for Japanese, Korean, and Chinese immigrants; for Filipinos it was reduced from 64% to 74%; for Mexicans it increased from 60% to 50% (24 tbl.3.7).

4. The immigrant groups' patterns of fertility, language, residence, and socioeconomic status increasingly would resemble those of the natives. See Douglas S. Massey, "The New Immigration and Ethnicity in the United States," 21 *Population and Dev. Rev.* 631, 640–41 (1995). Intermarriage also becomes more common as the generations pass, and income and education levels incrementally rise.

5. Noting that an assimilation norm has been held out through American history, this essay should not be taken to imply that American history stands alone in this respect. Indeed, by holding out the very possibility of assimilation on the part of new arrivals, the United States has displayed a commendable and comparatively rare pluralism that contrasts with stronger strains of ethnic exclusivity, marring the records of other countries. See, e.g., F.H. Buckley, "The Political Economy of Immigration Policies," 16 *Int'l Rev. L. and Econ.* 81, 90–92, 96 (1996) (showing that Canada admits higher skilled immigrants due to more restrictive screening for skills and money to invest); "Turkish Germans?" *Economist*, Jan. 9, 1997, 17 (discussing proposed legislation changing a 1913 citizenship law that makes it difficult to become a citizen without a German bloodline).

6. The watershed events in modern immigration law were the repeal of the *Chinese Exclusion Acts* by the Act of Dec. 17, 1943, ch. 344, 57 Stat. 600, and the Act of Oct. 3, 1965, Pub. L. No. 89-236, 79 Stat. 911. These ended the ban on Asian immigration, shifted entry requirements to favor members of families of present residents, and imposed annual limits on the number of people admitted from both the Western and Eastern Hemispheres. The limits on entries from the Western Hemisphere were the first in history. See Massey, "The New Immigration," 637–638. Entries from Mexico were not previously unregulated, however (635–636). Although they were not subject to a numerical cap, entrants had to satisfy substantial visa qualification requirements. There were, as a result, hundreds of thousands of illegal Mexican entrants during the 1950s and 1960s. See Gregory DeFreitas, *Inequality at Work: Hispanics in the U.S. Labor Force* (New York: Oxford University Press, 1991).

7. Latinos/as are not identifiable by application of a generally accepted bright-line test. For the purposes of this essay, the category will include persons born in or descended from Americans born in Spanish-speaking countries in North and South America, in addition to the descendents of the Mexicans native to the southwestern states. I distinguish "Latinos/as" from "Anglos," by which I mean native-born, English-speaking, U.S. citizens. Within the category of Anglos I distinguish "white Anglos" when the context demands. In my usage, Latinos/as and Anglos are all American, whatever their citizenship or residence. Ideally, I would have a system of more particular reference to country of origin.

I use "Latinos and Latinas" and the abbreviated form "Latinos/as" to avoid the generic masculine. For use of a similar abbreviated form, see, for example, Elizabeth

M. Iglesias, "International Law, Human Rights, and LatCrit Theory," 28 *U. Miami Inter-Am. L. Rev.* 177 (1996–1997). I note that most of the Latino/a writers I rely on throughout this essay still use the generic "Latinos." But anyone who is a feminist must analyze that usage. Luce Irigaray has been one of the most eloquent critics of the designation of human beings (as well as objects) through the differentiation of the masculine and the feminine in Romance languages. See Luce Irigaray, *I Love to You* (Alison Martin trans., New York: Routledge, 1996), 79–95. The language, she tells us, differentiates in such a way as to perpetuate fantasies of the masculine and the feminine and thereby has the masculine stand in for the universal human.

8. See, e.g., "Economic and Demographic Consequences of Immigration: Hearings Before the Subcommon Econ. Resources, Competitiveness, and Sec. Econ. of the Joint Econ. Comm.," 99th Cong. 359 (1986) (statement of Gov. Richard Lamm) ("English [is] one of the common threads that hold us together. We should be color blind, but we can't be linguistically deaf").

9. One advocated remedy is revision of the immigration laws. See, e.g., Juan F. Perea, "Demography and Distrust: An Essay on American Languages, Cultural Pluralism, and Official English," 77 *Minn. L. Rev.* 269, 332–47 (1992) (discussing the history of and advocating reforms for the current literacy requirement of immigration laws).

10. The use of the term "nativism" implies a normative repudiation of the point of view denoted thereby. See Linda S. Bosniak, "'Nativism' the Concept: Some Reflections," in *Immigrants Out!: The New Nativism and the Anti-immigrant Impulse in the United States*, (Juan F. Perea. ed., New York: New York University Press, 1997), 279, 290–291.

11. The notion that common language defined the nation and its people, substituting for a common culture and history, gained currency during the Colonial and Early Independence eras. See Dennis Baron*, The English-Only Question: An Official Language forAmericans?* (New Haven: Yale University Press, 1990), 28–46. Benjamin Franklin provides an example, expressing concern in 1751 about the number of German immigrants in Pennsylvania and their failure to adopt "our Language or Customs." 4 Benjamin Franklin, "Observations Concerning the Increase of Mankind," in *The Papers of Benjamin Franklin* (Leonard W. Labaree ed., New Haven: Yale University Press, 1961), 234.

12. The mid-1990s have seen a resurgence of nativist sentiment. Thomas Muller, "Nativism in the Mid-1990s: Why Now?" in Perea, *Immigrants Out!*, 105, 106-114, attributes this resurgence to economic and job insecurity among natives, cultural and social disparities, and continued inflows of immigrants. For a well-known text that expresses contemporary nativist sentiment and quite explicitly focuses on race and ethnicity, see Peter Brimelow*, Alien Nation: Common Sense About America's Immigration Disaster* (New York: Random House, 1995), xvii, 10, 57, 117, 129. Daniel Kanstroom, "Dangerous Undertones of the New Nativism: Peter Brimelow and the Decline of the West," in Perea, *Immigrants Out!*, provides a useful discussion of Brimelow's work, reviewing the dangerous history of racist discourse.

13. For a recounting of the history of nativist animus, see Joe R. Feagin, "Old Poison in New Bottles: The Deep Roots of Modern Nativism," in Perea, *Immigrants Out!*, 13–34.

14. John Rawls has clarified the relationship between the operation of wrong- and right-making characteristics—the facts "cited in giving reasons why an . . . institution

is . . . just or unjust"—in Kantian constructivism. John Rawls, *Political Liberalism* (New York: Columbia University Press, 1993), 121–25. Although it is beyond the scope of this essay fully to explore this issue, I agree with Rawls that some form of Kantian constructivism is the most philosophically justified path to take in the justification of political and, I would add, moral ideals of right.

15. I write of "treatment as an equal" rather than "equal treatment," borrowing this distinction from Ronald Dworkin, *Taking Rights Seriously* (Cambridge, MA: Harvard University Press, 1977), 227. Treatment as an equal is fundamental, consisting of the right to be treated with respect and concern equal to anyone else. Equal treatment, in contrast, is the equal right to an opportunity, resource, or burden.

16. I accept this result without joining the discussants in debating the truth about the constitution of the modern or postmodern subject. My argument does not require us to answer the question of who we really are as subjects. Its central point is that such basic decisions about the meaning of identification must remain with individuals themselves. Indeed, in my view, the focus of legal debates about minority rights and multiculturalism should shift away from the question of the truth of the subject and, instead, ask how and why state recognition of the person demands the right of personhood—the right I call the imaginary domain. This need to change the question is not solely of philosophical interest. It allows us to rethink the ethical stakes in political debates about identity without attaching ourselves to a simplistic or, worse yet, naturalized conception of identity.

17. Some thinkers that psychoanalysis has influenced have redefined autonomy to make it consistent with the recognition that we are constructed through and by a symbolic Other with which we inevitably engage in defining a self. Cornelius Castoriadis, for example, defines autonomy as follows:

> Autonomy then appears as: my discourse must take the place of the discourse of the Other, of a foreign discourse that is in me, ruling over me: speaking through myself. This clarification immediately indicates the *social* dimension of the problem (little matter that the Other in question at the start is the 'narrow' parental other; through a series of obvious connections, the parental couple finally refers to society as a whole and to its history).

Cornelius Castoriadis, *The Imaginary Institution of Society* (Kathleen Blamey trans., Cambridge, MA: MIT Press, 1987)(1975) 102.

18. See generally Martin Heidegger, *Kant and the Problem of Metaphysics* (Richard Taft trans., Bloomington: Indiana University Press, 5th ed., 1990)(1973) (examining Kantian idealism in light of existentialism and hermeneutic phenomenology).

19. See George Fletcher, "The Case for Linguistic Self-Defense," in *The Morality of Nationalism* (Robert McKim and Jeff McMahan eds., New York: Oxford University Press, 1997), 324, 333–335.

20. For a discussion of the difference between a metaphysical conception of the subject and our political and moral interpretation of the free person, see Drucilla Cornell, *At the Heart of Freedom: Feminism, Sex, and Equality* (Princeton, N.J.: Princeton University Press, 1998), 3–65 [hereinafter Cornell, *At the Heart*]; Drucilla Cornell, *The Imaginary Domain* (New York: Routledge, 1995), 3–27 [hereinafter Cornell, *Domain*].

21. According to Hegel, the hallmark of modernity is the historical and normative construction of the legal and moral person through a concept of right, which in turn

legitimates the State on the basis of whether or not the State allows for the actualization of this construct. See Hegel's *Philosophy of Right* (T.M. Knox trans., London: Oxford University Press, 1967)(1821), 15–24.

22. Almost all of the important debates in western liberal jurisprudence and political philosophy have been over what it means to treat people as free and equal persons. For an excellent discussion of how widely this ideal is held, see Ronald Dworkin, "Why We Are All Liberals,"(Oct. 19 and 27, 1995) (paper presented at the Program for the Study of Law, Philosophy, and Social Theory) (on file with author).

23. The most searing critique of the liberal ideal of the person remains that of Karl Marx. See Karl Marx, *Critique of Hegel's "Philosophy of Right"* (Annette Jolin and Joseph O'Malley trans., Joseph O'Malley ed., Cambridge, England: Cambridge University Press, 1970) (1964). The last hundred years have generated fierce dispute about what Marx's critique of the legal, moral, and political critique of the person actually means: Was Marx arguing against this category altogether? Was he instead arguing that it was "undialectical," hence one-sided? I cannot explore the voluminous literature, let alone examine the history of the sweat and blood that has been spilt because of the state enforcement of the position that there is no moral nor political validity to the ideal of the person. I stand behind the interpretation that a Marxist should believe in right and thus, the persons who have them. See Drucilla Cornell, "Should a Marxist Believe in Rights?,"*Praxis International*, 1984.

24. Since the Kantian person is an idea that, by definition, must be in the abstract, it often has been thought to be inconsistent with any recognition of our phenomenological existence. I have tried to show, however, that we can use a philosophical anthropology that can recognize certain aspects of our phenomenological existence, such as our sexuate being, but recognize it in such a way that it does not controvert the freedom that is maintained in the abstract definition of the idea of the person. Of course, in this essay, I am trying to make a similar argument about how we should grapple with another crucial aspect of our phenomenological existence, i.e., language. See Cornell, *At the Heart*, 37–39; Cornell, *Domain*, 3–27.

25. See *The Moral Law: Kant's Groundwork of the Metaphysic of Morals*, (H.J. Paton ed. and trans., London, New York: Hutchinson & Co. Ltd., 1961), 61–64 [hereinafter *Kant's Groundwork*]. For an excellent discussion of Kant's Formula of Humanity, see Christine M. Korsgaard, *Creating the Kingdom of Ends* (Cambridge, New York: Cambridge University Press, 1996), 106–132.

26. The Formula of Humanity is Kant's second formulation of the universal law. The first is the Categorical Imperative. For readers unfamiliar with Kant, he states the Categorical Imperative as follows: "Act only on that maxim which you can at the same time will that it should become a universal law." *Kant's Groundwork*, 88 (footnote omitted and typeface altered). The Formula of Humanity is stated as follows: "Act in such a way that you always treat humanity, whether in your own person or in the person of any other, never simply as a means but at the same time as an end."(86).

27. One could term Kant's elaboration of our equal worth as persons as "metaphysical" and thus philosophically outdated because it relies on ontological dualism. See *Kant's Groundwork*, 104–108. To defend free will, which is our capacity to set our end by reason, Kant understood dualism as the division of the "human being" into the "noumenal" world of moral freedom and the "phenomenal" world of causal determination by the laws of nature. See also Korsgaard, *Creating the Kingdom*,

159–160 (providing a summary of the relationship between Kant's noumenal world and the phenomenal world). For Kant, we are free if we make ourselves a law unto ourselves; if we, in other words, are self-legislating. We can only become self-legislating if we act solely in accordance with the idea of law and not with any particular aspect of its substantiation. The preeminent good, which Kant calls moral, is the idea of law itself and only that. Since the must of the moral law is the idea of law that only a rational being can apprehend, when we act in accordance with this law, we also are acting solely in accordance with our free will or with our rational nature. We know that our maxims are rational and therefore freely chosen by subjecting them to the test of universalizability—the test of the moral law. My maxim is rationally chosen and thus freely chosen if it can be understood as a maxim of all other rational beings who subject themselves to the moral law. Because the must of the moral law is the idea of law that only a rational being can approach, as free beings we become self-legislating and act solely in accordance with free will by following the Categorical Imperative. See *Kant's Groundwork*, 95–104. One may note the ethical irony of a theory of moral freedom that appears to incorporate an act of subjection to the moral law. Kant's need to understand moral freedom in this way stems from his acceptance of the proposition that all human action must be understood through laws of causality (110–113). By making ourselves subject to the Categorical Imperative it is our free will, our capacity to set our ends by reason, that makes us the cause of the value we give to those ends. Thus, by subjecting ourselves to the idea of law, we can be self-legislating rather than legislated-to. See, for example, Theodor Adorno and Max Horkheimer, *Dialectic of Enlightenment* (John Cummings trans., New York: Continuum Pub. Co., 1944)(1972), for an excellent discussion of the ethical difficulty of a theory of moral freedom that seeks to render itself fully consistent with a Newtonian conception of causality. For an excellent critique of the Kantian notion of causality, with which Kant starts in his definition of the free will as causality, see Charles Sanders Peirce, "Causation and Force," in *Reasoning and the Logic of Things* (Kenneth Laine Ketner ed., Cambridge, Mass.: Harvard University Press, 1992), 197.

28. See *Kant's Groundwork*, 61–66.

29. See *Kant's Groundwork*, 61–66.

30. See Immanuel Kant, "On the Relationship of Theory to Practice in Morality in General," in *Kant: Political Writings* (Hans Reiss, ed. and H.B. Nisbet, trans., Cambridge, England; New York: Cambridge University Press, 2d.ed. 1991), 64, 67, ("The maxim of absolute obedience to a categorically binding law of the free will . . . is good in itself, but [happiness] is not. [It] may, if it conflicts with duty, be thoroughly evil").

31. See Immanuel Kant, "Introduction to the Theory of Right," in *Kant: Political Writings*, 132; *Kant's Groundwork*, 96–98.

32. For an excellent discussion of why Kant's two standpoints need not rely on ontological dualism, see Korsgaard, *Creating the Kingdom*, 159–187.

33. See Peirce, *Causation and Force*, 197–217.

34. See Heidegger, *Kant and the Problem*, 89–142.

35. See Heidegger, *Kant and the Problem*, 89–142. I am well aware that one can read Heidegger to have dropped all lingering aspects of his "humanism" in his later writings. See Reiner Schürmann, *Heidegger on Being and Acting* (Christine-Marie Gros trans., Bloomington: Indiana University Press, 1987). My intent is not to enter into the debate about the meaning of Heidegger's "turn" for his understanding of ac-

tion and more specifically of self-assertion. I only argue that it is possible to maintain something close to Kant's understanding of our equal worth because we are value-bestowing creatures who turn our actions into ends that we justify through reasons by giving moral or ethical narrations of our lives. The process of narrating a moral or ethical story is how we bring forth the moral self, which then takes responsibility for her actions, valuations, and judgments as if they had been her ends all along. This process we call the practice of self-responsibility. Both Herbert Marcuse and Hannah Arendt took up the Heidegger-Kant dialogue and made it central to their own thinking. See Hannah Arendt, *On Revolution* (New York: Viking Press, 1963), 47–50 (elaborating on the Kantian ideal of freedom and the role it has played in inspiring revolutions). For an important discussion of Marcuse's appropriation of the ideal of moral freedom as a practice of responsibility, see Martin J. Beck Matuštík, *Specters of Liberation* (Albany: State University of New York Press,1998), 25–47. For an excellent discussion of the Kant-Heidegger dialogue as Heidegger conceived it, see Ian Ward, *Kantianism, Postmodernism and Critical Legal Thought,* (Dordrecht, Boston, London: Kluwer Academic Publishers, Law and Philosophy Library, Vol. 31, 1997), 36–56.

36. See, e.g., Jürgen Habermas, *Between Facts and Norms: Contributions to a Discourse Theory of Law and Democracy* (William Rehg trans., Cambridge, Mass.: MIT Press, 1996).

37. John Rawls's work, which profoundly has shaped the last two generations of liberal political, ethical, and legal thought, develops his entire theory from the initial recognition of equal dignity in the sense that human beings must be politically recognizable as having both of these capacities or capabilities; that is, they are both reasonable and rational. See Rawls, *Political Liberalism*, 48–54. For the purposes of this essay, we will use capacity and capability interchangeably.

38. I endorse John Rawls's definition of the reasonable:

> If we ask how the reasonable is understood, we say: for our purposes here, the content of the reasonable is specified by the content of a reasonable political conception. The idea of the reasonable itself is given in part, again for our purposes, by the two aspects of persons' being reasonable: their willingness to propose and abide by fair terms of social cooperation among equals and their recognition of and willingness to accept the consequences of the burdens of judgment.

Rawls, *Political Liberalism*, 94. We can highlight the moral and political significance of the reasonable by contrasting it to the unreasonable:

> By contrast, people are unreasonable in the same basic aspect when they plan to engage in cooperative schemes but are unwilling to honor, or even to propose, except as a necessary public pretense, any general principles or standards for specifying fair terms of cooperation. They are ready to violate such terms as suits their interests when circumstances allow. (50)

39. See, e.g., Sara Ruddick, *Maternal Thinking: Toward a Politics of Peace* (Boston: Beacon Press, 1989) (arguing that mothering gives rise to a distinct mode of thinking and exploring the implications of this thought).

40. For an example of a "thicker" conception of self, see Robin West, *Narrative, Authority and Law* (Annarbor: University of Michigan Press,1993), 251–263 (comparing her "literary woman" with Richard Posner's "economic man").

41. See Cornell, *Domain* 3–27; and Cornell, *At the Heart*, 3–32, for a more elaborate defense of why scholars should maintain the ideal of the person in political philosophy. For an example of a feminist who criticizes the abstract ideal of the person, see Ruddick, *Maternal Thinking*.

42. Later I will defend the degradation prohibition as it is a limit on the equal protection of each person's imaginary domain implied by the way we define the ideal.

43. Ronald Dworkin uses a similar concept of the relationship between freedom and responsibility to base the legal authorization of ourselves as the only legitimate source of value for the evaluative design of our lives. To quote Dworkin's understanding of his own second principle of ethical individualism:

> The second principle is not just a general principle assigning each person major responsibility for what happens to him. It is more specific. It assigns people for the evaluative design of their life; it assigns each person the responsibility to shape his life to a conception of ethical value that is chosen or endorsed by him rather than by any other person or group. We must take considerable care not to misunderstand that assignment. It assumes and demands a kind of freedom but it is not metaphysical freedom—it is not, that is, people's power by an act of free will to alter the chain of events predetermined by physical or mental causation. The second principle is not offended or undermined in any way by a commitment to determinism, because it neither demands nor presupposes what we may call relational freedom: it insists that so far as your life is guided by convictions, assumptions, or instincts about ethical value, that they must be your convictions, assumptions, or instincts. You rather than anyone else have the right and responsibility to choose the ethical values that you will try to embody in your life.

Ronald Dworkin, *The Roots of Justice* 29 (Aug. 28, 1997) (unpublished manuscript, on file with authors).

44. In particular, aesthetic ideas can draw out the moral dimension of experience. Although Kant never directly would have connected aesthetic ideas with his conceptualization of the morally free person, I have argued that we can use such ideas to try to give body to what would otherwise remain abstract. So, for example, when Rawls argues that the veil of ignorance is a representative devise, I would argue that it is more precisely thought of as an aesthetic idea. For Rawls's most recent discussion of his understanding of the original position or the veil of ignorance as a representational devise, see Rawls, *Political Liberalism*, 27–28. For a more elaborate discussion of my own use of the aesthetic idea of the imaginary domain, see Cornell, *At the Heart*, 295.

45. See Cornell, *At the Heart*, 295.

46. Rawls, *Political Liberalism*, 304–309.

47. Critics of Rawls wrongly have attacked the idealized representations behind the veil of ignorance as if they were supposed to be real human beings. Thus, these critics argue that Rawls gives us a hopelessly abstract ideal of the person that cannot guide our moral reflection in real life. Real life, of course, is infused with the hierarchies that corrupt our thinking about equality. These critics neglect the purpose of a hypothetical experiment in the imagination, which demands that we try to represent the conditions for moral reflection of free and equal persons. Such an experience does not start with reality, particularly a social reality that hierarchies bind together, because the point of the representative device is to imagine a basis for moral reflec-

tion on the moral legitimacy of the hierarchies. How would we think about justice if we did not know how those hierarchies would treat us?

48. For a more extensive discussion of the imaginary domain and Rawls's hypothetical experiment in the imagination, see Cornell, *At the Heart*, 14–19.

49. Cornell, *At the Heart*, 17–18.

50. For an excellent summation of the communitarian critique of the liberal person, particularly as it has been elaborated in the work of John Rawls, see Michael J. Sandel, *Liberalism and the Limits of Justice* (Cambridge, UK, New York: Cambridge University Press, 2d. ed., 1998). For a rich analysis of the relationship between race-critical theory and the liberal ideal of the person, see Patricia Williams, *The Alchemy of Race and Rights* (Cambridge, Mass.: Harvard University Press, 1991).

51. See, e.g., Sandel, *Liberalism and the Limits*, 1 ("This is an essay about liberalism. . . . Against the primacy of justice, I shall argue for the limits of justice and, by implication, for the limits of liberalism as well").

52. It is important to remember that long before the "new" communitarians, Hegel made the same point about the constitution of human identity. See Hegel's *Philosophy of Right*, 38–40. But Hegel also understood that people could draw different moral and ethical lessons from the recognition of how human identity is rooted in history, language, and culture. Indeed Hegel argues that the modern person is distinguishable from other legal and moral forms given to our humanity (39–40). The person of modernity is no longer reducible to her social role in established hierarchy. Nor is she identical with any of the final ends of her community or even with the state. Given the complexity of the modern state, the individual herself no longer can have a simple identity. She must subjectively identify with the ends of her community—the nation state in which she is a citizen (155–159). This insistence on the split and complex nature of modern individuality separates Hegel from modern communitarians such as Michael Sandel who argues that, because our communities' ends are constitutive of who we are, it is legitimate for the state to impose restrictions on people's ability to revise those ends. See Sandel, *Liberalism and the Limits*, 183 (examining deontological liberalism and concluding that it neglects the power of politics to achieve a level of common good that individuals alone cannot achieve).

53. For a more extended articulation of what I mean by an "ethics of identification," see "Antiracism, Multiculturalism, and the Ethics of Identification," co-authored with Sara Murphy in this volume.

54. For an excellent response to the communitarian argument that we can revise our own ideals, Ronald Dworkin, "Foundations of Liberal Equality," in 11 *The Tanner Lectures on Human Values* 1, 66–71 (Grethe B. Peterson ed., Salt Lake City: University of Utah Press, 1990).

55. See Sandel, *Liberalism and the Limits*, 59–65.

56. See Sandel, *Liberalism and the Limits*, 59–65.

57. See Sandel, *Liberalism and the Limits*, 59–65.

58. For an excellent discussion of the political demarcations that either create or reinforce identities, see Iris Marion Young, "Together in Difference: Transforming the Logic of Group Political Conflict," in *The Rights of Minority Cultures*, 155 (Will Kymlicka ed., Oxford, New York: Oxford University Press, 1995).

59. Anzaldúa, *Borderlands=La Frontera: The New Mestiza* (San Francisco: Aunt Lute, 1987), 63.

60. See Dworkin, *Foundations of Liberal Equality*, 67.

61. I borrow the distinction between parameters and limits from Ronald Dworkin. See *Foundations of Liberal Equality*, 68.

62. As Dworkin explains:

The ideal life is always the same: it is a life creating as much independent value—as powerful a pleasing of God or as much human happiness—as it is conceivable for a human being to create. Circumstances act as limits on the degree to which the ideal can be achieved. Mortality, for example, is a very important limit: most people could create more pleasure if they lived longer. Talent, wealth, personality, language, technology, and culture provide other limits, and their force as limits will be much greater for some people, and in some times and places, than others. If we take an indexed challenge view of ethics, however, and treat living well as responding in the right way to one's situation, then we must treat some of the circumstances in which a particular person lives differently, as parameters that help define what a good performance of living would be for him.

Dworkin, *Foundations of Liberal Equality*, 66–67.

63. When a commentator argues that bilingualism in Spanish and English is a disability in the United States, he is setting out Spanish as a limit on people's lives that must be addressed in the name of equality. See Mirandé, "En La Tierra del Ciego, El Tuerto es Rey ('In the Land of the Blind, the One Eyed Person is King'): Biligualism as a Disability," 26 *N.M. L. Rev.*, 103. For this commentator, it is only by addressing bilingualism as a disability that we can hope legally to interpret statutes that forbid the speaking of Spanish in workplaces as discrimination (102-103). How an ability to speak two languages at home sensibly could be rendered as a disability demands more discussion. Clearly, this conception of bilingualism in Spanish and English as a disability is inseparable from the treatment of Latinos/as in the United States.

64. As Dworkin articulates this point:

Anyone who reflects seriously on the question which of the various lives he might lead is right for him will consciously or unconsciously discriminate among these, treating some as limits and others as parameters. I might treat the fact that I am an American, for example, as just a fact that in some cases might help and in others hinder my leading the life I think best. Or I must treat my nationality as a parameter and assume, whether or not self-consciously, that being an American is part of what makes a particular life the right one for me.

Dworkin, *Foundations of Liberal Equality*, 67.

65. Interview by Sonia Moria with Jorge Luis Borges, Buenos Aires, Argentina (May 1985).

66. By using the term "Latin American culture," we isolate the culture of South America from that of Spain.

67. See Dworkin, *Foundations of Liberal Equality*, 70. Dworkin elaborates:

We must distinguish between what I shall call hard and soft parameters. Parameters, as I said, enter into the description of any challenge or assignment: they describe the conditions of successful performance. Hard parameters state essential conditions: if they are violated the performance is a total failure, no matter how successful in other respects. The formal structure of a sonnet imposes hard parameters: we cannot make a sonnet better by adding an extra line, no matter how beautiful it is. Soft parameters are those aspects of assignment that, when violated, reduce the value of the performance but do not annihilate it: they act as standards of good performance that permit defects to be compensated by high success against other standards. Compulsory figures in competitive iceskating are treated as soft parameters. It is part of the assignment that the performance execute a particular figure, and any deviations, no matter how beautifully executed, count as faults. But deviations are not absolutely fatal to winning any points at all, and a performance that includes a brilliant deviation may win more overall than a lackluster but perfectly faithful one.

68. Toni Morrison, "Unspeakable Things Unspoken: The Afro-American Presence in American Literature," in 11 Peterson, *The Tanner Lectures on Human Values*, 121, 146.

69. Morrison, "Unspeakable Things Unspoken," 121,146.

70. Morrison, "Unspeakable Things Unspoken," 162.

71. Morrison, "Unspeakable Things Unspoken," 121.

72. Toni Morrison, *The Bluest Eye* 5 (New York: Alfred A. Knopf, 1994)(1970).

73. Morrison, "Unspeakable Things Unspoken," 147.

74. Morrison, "Unspeakable Things Unspoken," 150.

75. Steven Pinker, *The Language Instinct* (New York: W. Morrow and Co., 1994), 55–82.

76. Pinker, *The Language Instinct*, 82.

77. See generally James Joyce, *Finnegans Wake* (London: Faber & Faber, 3d. ed., 1964)(1939). Toni Morrison evokes this "paradise" as she ends her new novel by the same name:

> There is nothing to beat this solace which is what Piedade's song is about, although the words evoke memories neither one has ever had: of reaching age in the company of the other; of speech shared and divided bread smoking from the fire; the unambivalent bliss of going home to be at home—the ease of coming back to love begun.

Toni Morrison, *Paradise* (New York: A.A. Knopf, 1998), 318.

78. See generally Benjamin Lee Whorf, *Language, Thought, and Reality* (Cambridge: Technology Press of Massachusetts Institute of Technology, 1964)(illustrating the principle of linguistic relativity, which states that the structure of a human being's language influences her understanding of reality and her behavior).

79. As the anthropologist Gananath Obeyeskere has observed:

> There are people who are thoroughly fluent in an alien language but are quite incapable of understanding the alien culture. This is simply because culture is not coterminous with language. The variety of normative behavior governed by implicit meanings, nonverbal communication, and nonlinguistic symbolic forms shows that language provides at best access to the culture.

Gananth Obeyesekere, *The Work of Culture* (Chicago: University of Chicago Press, 1990), 230.

80. See DeFreitas, *Inequality at Work*, 26–36 (describing Puerto Rico's historic and current status).

81. See Fletcher, "The Case for Linguistic Self-Defense," 329.

82. See Fletcher, "The Case for Linguistic Self-Defense," 329–331.

83. See Fletcher, "The Case for Linguistic Self-Defense," 330.

84. See Fletcher, "The Case for Linguistic Self-Defense," 330–332.

85. See Fletcher, "The Case for Linguistic Self-Defense," 331.

86. See Fletcher, "The Case for Linguistic Self-Defense," 331.

87. See Jeremy Waldron, "Minority Cultures and the Cosmopolitan Alternative," in Kymlicka, *The Rights of Minority Cultures*, 95.

88. Waldron, "Minority Cultures," 95.

89. See Waldron, "Minority Cultures," 105–108.

90. See Will Kymlicka, "From Enlightenment Cosmopolitanism to Liberal Nationalism," 10–11 (Sept. 11, 1997) (paper presented at the Program for the Study of Law, Philosophy, and Social Theory) (on file with authors).

91. See Kymlicka, "From Enlightenment Cosmopolitanism," 101.

92. Cosmopolitanism as a special, overarching, constructed identification has faced criticism as a mask for the more particular white, male, middle-class identification of a handful of academics. See Bruce Robbins, "Comparative Cosmopolitanisms," in *Cosmopolitics* 246 (1998) (discussing some of the pitfalls of cosmopolitanism either as a reality achieved by globalization of an elite or as an ethical or political identification that recognizes the value of freedom and the equality of all human beings); see also Pheng Cheah, "Given Culture: Rethinking Cosmopolitical Freedom in Transnationalism," in *Cosmopolitics* 290 (criticizing northern academics who critique nationalism as a weapon for southern nations resisting re-colonization and control by multinational corporations).

93. We must note here, that economic discrimination remains central to the lives of large numbers of Latinos/as in this country. This discrimination against immigrants, particularly immigrants who are racialized, is not limited to Latinos/as. But because of the discrimination, there is a sense in which cosmopolitanism may not be a rational alternative for many Latinos/as. We must distinguish the decision to stay within a *barrio* to reduce the risk of exposure to a brutally discriminatory "outside" culture from the affirmance of loyalty to a group identification made by a person whose means give rise to alternative choices.

94. Anzaldúa, *Borderlands*, 79.

95. See Waldron, "Minority Cultures," 111–112.

96. Anzaldúa, *Borderlands*, 16.

97. See Will Kymlicka, *Multicultural Citizenship: A Liberal Theory of Minority Rights*. (Oxford; New York: Oxford University Press, 1995), 83.

98. Strictly from the standpoint of practical reason, autonomy demands that our phenomenal relationships or ties do not define us. If we were to treat ourselves as constituted by these ties then we would be treating ourselves as objects of study, controlled or constructed by forces that theoretical reason could grasp. For an excellent explanation of why Kant need not defend dualisms in order to defend the self because it is a practical standpoint and a theoretically demonstrable conception, see Korsgaard, *Creating the Kingdom*, 159–187.

99. See Waldron, "Minority Cultures," 110–112.

100. See Waldron, "Minority Cultures," 110–112.

101. Kymlicka, *Multicultural Citizenship*, 89 (quoting Avishai Margalit and Joseph Raz, "National Self-Determination," 87 *J. Phil.* 439, 449 (1990).

102. See Morrison, "Unspeakable Things Unspoken," 146.

103. See Dworkin, "Foundations of Liberal Equality," 69–70.

104. Dworkin, "Foundations of Liberal Equality," 70. ("Soft parameters are those

aspects of assignment that, when violated, reduce the value of the performance but do not annihilate it: they act as standards of good performance that permit defects to be compensated by high success against other standards.")

105. Dworkin, "Foundations of Liberal Equality," 70. ("Hard parameters state essential conditions: if they are violated the performance is a total failure, no matter how successful in other respects.")

106. Anzaldúa, *Borderlands*, 55.

107. Therefore, I disagree with Chandran Kukathas's argument that we do not need to have cultural rights because the right to exit is sufficient. See Chandran Kukathas, "Are There Any Cultural Rights?," in *The Rights of Minority Cultures*, 251–252.

108. Cornell, *At the Heart*, 60.

109. This means, for example, that no one can treat someone as less than worthy of her personhood because of her lived sexuality. See Cornell, *At the Heart*, 3–32 (discussing sexual freedom). To treat someone in such a manner is first and foremost to deny them their freedom by making their sex or sexuality an imposed limit on how they can live their lives (33–65).

110. Anzaldúa, *Borderlands*, 151-152 (describing the brutal punishment of school children in parts of the United States for speaking their native languages).

111. Anzaldúa, *Borderlands*, 59.

112. One commentator has attempted to subvert the courts' volition reading in Workplace English cases by arguing that bilingualism is a "disability," making it an immutable characteristic. See Mirandé, "En La Tierra del Ciego,"103. Mirandé relies on studies showing that "code switching" takes place automatically for many bilingual speakers (94). Code switching means at least two things. First, bilingual speakers semiconsciously incorporate words from both languages when they speak. Second, they unconsciously respond in the language in which they are addressed. That is, if a worker addresses a coworker in Spanish on the job, she will answer in Spanish before she has a chance to catch herself. Under this analysis, those bilingual in Spanish and English cannot help themselves from code switching; therefore the argument goes, bilingualism is both something like an immutable characteristic and a disability (94–98).

I sympathize with Mirandé's goal of reforming the law to protect bilingual Spanish speakers from losing their jobs for their "aberrant" speech. But I would find it sad indeed if we had to interpret bilingualism in Spanish in this way in order to make Workplace English legally redressable. I offer a more direct approach to the same end.

113. See Avishai Margalit and Joseph Raz, "National Self-Determination," 87 *J. Phil.* 439, 449 (1990). They write:

> It may be no more than a brute fact that people's sense of their own identity is bound up with their sense of belonging to encompassing groups and that their self-respect is affected by the esteem in which these groups are held. But these facts, too, have important consequences. They mean that individual dignity and self-respect require that the groups, membership of which contributes to one's sense of identity, be generally respected and not be made a subject of ridicule, hatred, discrimination, or persecution. (449).

114. One, of course, can judge this imposition as a form of denial because one just as easily can perceive the Spanish language, particularly in the Southwest, as crucial to what it means to be an "American" who lives in that part of the country.

115. See David J. Richards, *Women, Gays, and the Constitution: The Grounds for Feminism and Gay Rights in Culture and Law* (Chicago: University of Chicago Press, 1998), 355.

116. See Richards, *Women, Gays and the Constitution*, 355

117. Not all claims of polyethnic right are this strong. The demand, for example, for bilingual education for Spanish-speaking children in New York City does not include forbidding a language minority to have its language in the schools. The opposite is the case. The demand is, instead, that the Spanish language be allowed to have a presence in the schools, a presence needed because of the large numbers of Spanish-speaking children in New York City.

118. See Fletcher, "The Case for Linguistic Self-Defense," 337.

119. See Fletcher, "The Case for Linguistic Self-Defense," 337.

120. See Fletcher, "The Case for Linguistic Self-Defense," 337.

121. See Fletcher, "The Case for Linguistic Self-Defense," 337–338. I note that although Fletcher takes linguistic patriotism very seriously, he still questions whether it ever would be necessary to impose the majority language in all public offices and services.

122. I see this right as a group-differentiated right in Kymlicka's sense, but one that still adheres to individuals.

123. This loss occurred despite a reservation of equal rights in Article IX of the Treaty of Guadalupe Hidalgo, Feb. 2, 1848, U.S.-Mex., 9 Stat. 922. For an account of the disappearance of official bilingualism in the Southwestern states, see Perea, "Demography and Distrust," 316–323.

Index

Acknowledgments

The author gratefully acknowledges permission to reprint previously published material in this collection.

"Enlightening the Enlightenment," in *Critical Inquiry* 26:1 (1999). "*Las Greñudas*: Recollections on Consciousness Raising," forthcoming from *SIGNS*. "Diverging Differences," from *SIGNS* 26:1 (1997). All reprinted with permission from The University of Chicago Press.

"Antiracism, Muticulturalism, and the Ethics of Identification," written with Sara Murphy, forthcoming in *Philosophy and Social Criticism*. Reprinted with permission from Sage Publications Ltd.

"Freedom's Conscience," in 24 *N.Y.U. Rev. L. & Soc. Change* 149 (1998). Reprinted with permission from *New York University Review of Law & Social Change*.

"Spanish Language Rights: Identification, Freedom, and the Imaginary Domain," in *Cornell Law Review* 84:3, 1999. Reprinted with permission from *Cornell Law Review*.

About the Author

Drucilla Cornell is a professor of law, women's studies, and political science at Rutgers University. Prior to beginning her academic life, Professor Cornell was a union organizer for a number of years, working for the UAW, the UE, and the IUE in California, New Jersey, and New York. She played a key role in organizing the conferences on Deconstruction and Justice with Jacques Derrida, held at the Benjamin N. Cardozo School of Law in 1989, 1990, and 1993. In addition, she has worked to coordinate the Law and Humantities Speakers Series with the Jacob Burns Institute for Advanced Legal Studies and the Committee on Liberal Studies at the New School for Social Research. Professor Cornell was professor at the Cardozo School of Law from 1989 to 1994 and spent the 1991–92 academic year at the institute for Advanced Study at Princeton. She has authored numerous articles on critical theory, feminism and "postmodern" theories of ethics. She is the co-editor, with Seyla Benhabib, of *Feminism as Critique: On the Politics of Gender;* with Michel Rosenfeld and David Gray Carlson, of *Deconstruction and the Possibility of Justice;* and has published five books: *At the Heart of Freedom: Feminism, Sex, and Equality; The Imaginary Domain: Abortion, Pornography and Sexual Harassment; Beyond Accommodation: Ethical Feminism, Deconstruction and the Law; The Philosophy of the Limit;* and *Transformations: Recollective Imagination and Sexual Difference.* She is part of a published philosophical exchange with Seyla Benhabib, Judith Butler, and Nancy Fraser entitled *Feminist Contentions.* She is also a produced playwright—productions of her plays *The Dream Cure* and *Background Interference* have been performed in New York and Los Angeles.